MW01194847

BASEBALL'S FIRST SUPERSTAR

Alan D. Gaff

BASEBALL'S FIRST SUPERSTAR

The Lost Life Story of Christy Mathewson

UNIVERSITY OF NEBRASKA PRESS / LINCOLN

Acknowledgments for the use of copyrighted material appear on page xi, which constitutes an extension of the copyright page.

Manufactured in the United States of America

The University of Nebraska Press is part of a land-grant institution with campuses and programs on the past, present, and future homelands of the Pawnee, Ponca, Otoe-Missouria, Omaha, Dakota, Lakota, Kaw, Cheyenne, and Arapaho Peoples, as well as those of the relocated Ho-Chunk, Sac and Fox, and Iowa Peoples.

Library of Congress Cataloging-in-Publication Data
Names: Gaff, Alan D., author.
Title: Baseball's first superstar: the lost life story of Christy Mathewson / Alan D. Gaff, University of Nebraska Press.
Description: Lincoln: University of Nebraska Press, [2025] | Includes bibliographical references.
Identifiers: LCCN 2024051356
ISBN 9781496243270 (hardback)
ISBN 9781496243683 (epub)
ISBN 9781496243690 (pdf)
Subjects: LCSH: Mathewson, Christy, 1880–1925. | Pitchers (Baseball)—United States—Biography. | Baseball players—United States—Biography. | Christian athletes—United States—Biography. | Mass media and sports—United States—History—20th century. | Baseball—Social aspects—United States—History—20th century.
Classification: LCC GV865.M327 G32 2025 | DDC 796.357092 [B]—dc23/eng/20241231
LC record available at https://lccn.loc.gov/2024051356

Set in Miller Text by A. Shahan.

Dedicated to Donald Lee Gaff, our family's baseball superstar

CONTENTS

ILLUSTRATIONS *Following page 66*

ACKNOWLEDGMENTS

It has been a pleasure to work with Rob Taylor at the University of Nebraska Press. The process between author and editor could not have been more seamless. Thanks should also go to Taylor Martin, Rob's assistant, who led me through the production process. John Horne, Rights and Reproduction Coordinator at the National Baseball Hall of Fame and Museum, was able to provide over a dozen illustrations to enhance Christy Mathewson's story. My family, who are too shy to be named, have provided wonderful assistance and technical support. They are, in essence, my ghost editors.

BASEBALL'S FIRST SUPERSTAR

PRELUDE

New York's Polo Grounds were awash in avid spectators who had come to see their Giants baseball team clinch the World Series on October 14, 1905. Many fans had left home by 9 a.m., carrying carefully wrapped lunches. Traffic was crazy. The L trains dropped passengers off at 135th Street where thousands had to wait for connections with Harlem trains to finish their journey. Fistfights between impatient riders broke out on the platforms. Many people gave up waiting and either took cabs or hitched rides with strangers in automobiles.

At the Polo Grounds, paid attendance was 24,187, but thousands more actually saw the game. It was a perfect day for baseball, so those who could not get tickets became creative in finding ways to view the action. Men balanced on fences that filled gaps between the stands and clubhouse. Others sat atop the grandstand roof, clung to utility poles, or stared through binoculars from adjacent rooftops. Hundreds watched from Coogan's Bluff, which overshadowed the stadium.

Inside, men and women sat on chairs in the covered grandstand where there was a modicum of space. In the cheaper, uncovered stands extending along the foul lines, two people were crammed into a space that normally held one. More spectators, ten deep, stood behind ropes in right and left field, although center field was left clear. They were all there to support their idols: New York Giants' John McGraw, and

Christy Mathewson, the famous pitcher who had won 31 games and lost 9 during the regular season.

Mathewson had shut out the Philadelphia Athletics in the first game of the World Series, 3–0. After the Athletics came back to win game two, Mathewson then pitched another shutout, 9–0. When Joe McGinnity threw another shutout for New York, 1–0, the Giants were poised to become world champions. This final game proved to be another pitcher's battle. Mathewson spread six hits over nine innings in a game that lasted an hour and twenty-eight minutes. It was his third shutout in the space of six days, a record that still stands. A *New York Times* reporter wrote of how Mathewson, while chewing gum on the mound, "bestrode the field like a mighty Colossus and the Athletics peeped about the diamond like pigmies who struggled gallantly for their lives, but in vain."[1] In the stands, "rooters rooted until they couldn't root another root."[2]

When Lave Cross hit a grounder to Bill Dahlen at shortstop, who easily whipped the ball to first baseman Dan McGann for the last out, spectators went crazy. One Brooklyn reporter described the tumult: "Insane with joy, they jumped, climbed and tumbled from the stands, swept aside a weak-looking string of bluecoats and rushed as if mad upon the diamond, to surround the New York players."[3] Throngs of deranged men and women raced to cut off the Giants as they ran for safety, but the victors were swamped in a tidal wave of fans who mauled them, especially Christy Mathewson, in attempts to gain souvenirs or shreds of uniforms. Several players were raised up on men's shoulders and borne to the clubhouse entrance. Blue-coated cops were overwhelmed as they sought to restore some semblance of order.

Nobody wanted to leave the stadium. Enthusiastic fans remaining in the upper and lower levels of the grandstand tossed cushions, pop bottles, and remnants of picnic lunches into the crowd surging in front of the dugouts. These missiles were immediately hurled back, starting an impromptu cushion fight. Soon the ball field looked as though a huge picnic had been held there. Thousands gathered in front of the clubhouse, screaming for their heroes to make an appearance. In between these masses of humanity, the Catholic Protectory Band blasted out tunes as it marched around the field followed by several thousand New Yorkers dancing, prancing, singing, waving blue pennants, and tossing their hats. This rollicking parade finally halted at the clubhouse to reinforce that crowd while the band continued to crash out more tunes.

The Athletics quickly changed into street clothes and headed for the railway station with demands for the Giants to show themselves ringing in their ears. Several of the new World Champions emerged on the clubhouse balcony to wave and toss their ball caps and gloves into the mob below, where each souvenir brought about a mad scramble. Cries for John McGraw were rewarded when the Giants manager appeared, prompting the band to pump out "When Johnny Comes Marching Home." After the din subsided somewhat, McGraw made a brief statement: "Ladies and Gentlemen, I appreciate the great victory as well as you. I thank you for your patronage, and hope to see you all next Spring."[4] Then a wave and McGraw ducked back inside.

Cries now went up for the incomparable Mathewson. Within minutes, two men emerged—Christy, the tall, solidly built winning pitcher, and Roger Bresnahan, his squattier catcher. Neatly dressed after their brief showers and grinning from ear to ear, the pair walked back and forth, waving to the cheering multitude. Stopping at the center point, they produced a long sheet of paper, which proved to be a hastily improvised banner that they unrolled in the slight breeze. Thousands shoved and pushed forward to read the inscription: "THE GIANTS. WORLD'S CHAMPIONS, 1905." The roar that followed was compared to the eruption of a volcano in Manhattan. Mathewson could not leave until he, like McGraw, said a few words. Holding his hands up for quiet, Mathewson made a brief comment heard only by those directly in front of him: "Gentlemen, I want to thank you for this kindness, but you must remember that there were eight other members of the team who worked for our success just as much as I did."[5] With a final wave, the battery mates stepped inside to join teammates in celebrating their victory.

NEWSPAPERS CREATED THE FIRST BASEBALL SUPERSTAR

Newspapers spurred the growth of America. They began as small operations, usually an editor with a few typesetters, that reported on current events and local political affairs, with most income generated by advertising rather than subscriptions. As the country began to expand, editors started to fill pages from exchanges, simply arrangements for different newspapers to share information. This allowed editors to include more regional and national coverage for their readers. Another step forward came during the Mexican War when correspondents went out to gather news rather than wait for information to trickle back home. This use of paid correspondents would cover such topics as the California Gold Rush, the Civil War, Reconstruction, westward expansion, immigration, and the Spanish-American War. By the dawn of the twentieth century, newspapers were poised to report on another major topic that would profoundly affect American life—the rise of professional baseball.

Journalism in New York City was a cutthroat business. Joseph Pulitzer purchased the *New York World* in 1883 and, capitalizing on his business acumen gained with the *St. Louis Post-Dispatch*, within four years it became the most successful newspaper in the city. Pulitzer's success hinged on his emphasis of reporting sensational stories about lurid criminal acts, disasters of all sorts, and scandals involving prominent politicians and society's elite. The *World*'s most aggressive competitor was another morning paper, the *New York Sun*, owned by Charles A. Dana, a former assistant secretary of war.

Competition between Pulitzer and Dana increased in 1887 when the latter began to publish the *Evening Sun*, a move countered by the former launching the *Evening World*. Employees of the original *World* derisively referred to this new upstart as *World Junior*. As if to emphasize his importance in journalism, Pulitzer built the New York World Building, then the tallest structure in the metropolis, which stood across from City Hall on Park Avenue and stretched from Frankfort Street to the Brooklyn Bridge. Dana's *Evening Sun* soon began to lose traction and William Randolph Hearst brought forward a new competitor in 1896, the *Evening Journal*. This new rivalry became even more intense than the previous Pulitzer-Dana clash. Rather than presenting a background on New York City newspapers in general, this narrative will focus on how the *Evening World* organized its staff to cover its two Major League baseball teams.

To counter the popularity of Hearst's paper, Joseph Pulitzer hired Foster Coates as managing editor of the *Evening World*. Coates set out to immediately increase circulation by using shocking headlines and huge typefaces to attract readers. He compared his front page to the window of a department store: "One must display his wares attractively," he argued, "or the other fellow would reap the largest sales."[1] When exceptional news stories came, there was no way to promote them beyond a typical front page other than to resort to red ink to catch attention. This step soon failed when women complained that red ink ruined their white gloves. Women were critical to any newspaper since they read the advertisements that brought in the bulk of its profits. For example, the *Evening World* for years sold at just one penny an issue.

Hearst stole Foster Coates in 1900, but his front-page layout remained. In the very middle were baseball scores for the New York Giants and Brooklyn Superbas. Coates had discovered that baseball scores were just as important to circulation as horrific murders and natural disasters. But he had a target audience in mind. Wall Street shut down at three in the afternoon, so the Giants and Superbas accommodated this elite crowd by throwing out the first ball at four, giving these well-dressed sports fans time to get to the stadiums. Editions of the *Evening World* were printed early, then held for baseball scores to be inserted as games concluded. Extra-inning games played hell with distribution as newsboys had to wait for late deliveries. Interestingly, these ball scores appeared in a fainter type than all other stories on the front page.

Sports scores intruded on the bailiwick of Charles E. Chapin, the city editor. Bugs Baer recalled that Chapin "was crazier than a bedbug in a burning boardinghouse."[2] At one time he had sent a reporter to report on whether penguins had knees (they do). O. O. McIntyre wrote that he was "the fabled ogre of the *Evening World*—a reputed monster with a tittupy manner and high thin voice, but who swallowed seasoned reporters raw and heckled cubs until they rushed in panic to other vocations."[3] One day when he heard that Chapin had stayed home sick, Irvin S. Cobb retorted, "Hope it's nothing trivial."[4] Chapin loved to torment his employees. One time a man called in because he had injured his foot by falling in a bathtub. After he returned to work, Chapin sent him marching back and forth to a telephone to transcribe copy. After three days, Chapin fired him with the remark, "I would have fired you earlier, but I wanted to see how long you could fake that limp."[5] As he aged and mellowed somewhat, underlings claimed their editor suffered from "a fatty degeneration of the hate gland."[6] One of the few times Chapin's attitude changed was when his wife, a rabid Giants fan, nagged him incessantly about adding more sports coverage to the point where he finally gave in. During 1918, broke by bad investments on Wall Street and gambling debts, Charles Chapin killed his wife and spent the rest of his days in Sing Sing Prison.

To rein in Chapin, Pulitzer moved John Tennant from the *World* to the *Evening World* as managing editor. When asked by a visitor to the newsroom, "How many men work here?" he quickly responded, "About half of them."[7] Tennant always stuck up for his reporters. When one man repeated some stories that had appeared years earlier, Tennant simply smiled and said, "A good article is not hurt by being repeated."[8] Charles Chapin would occasionally fire Bugs Baer, but, understanding his value to the paper, Tennant would rehire him immediately. Some reporters became so addicted to alcohol that Tennant changed payday from Saturday to Tuesday to save marriages of men "who would sell you his underwear on top of a Fifth Avenue bus"[9] to buy booze. Frank I. Cobb, chief editorial writer for the *World*, said of Tennant, "The thing that makes him a really good managing editor is his quality to know news the moment he sees it, and get it into the paper without a minute's delay."[10]

A sportswriter and cartoonist, Bob Edgren got his start in San Francisco but his talent soon led him to New York where he was employed by Hearst. Sent as a reporter to Cuba during the Spanish-American War, he was captured by Spanish troops and held for trial but escaped to Key West while carrying drawings of Spanish atrocities that won nationwide acclaim when published as *Sketches from Death*. In 1904 Pulitzer lured Edgren away from the Hearst organization and made him head of the *Evening World* sports department. His specialty was boxing and he knew the ins and outs of that sport to a degree that made him a national expert. His columns were illustrated with boxing cartoons, but he also furnished sketches for other writers on subjects like horse racing, track, golf, tennis, football, and baseball.

Edgren's assistant in the sporting department was Vincent Treanor, another veteran of the original *World*. While technically an assistant, Treanor found most of the department's work shifted to his shoulders by his boss. Treanor's beats were the horse track and boxing ring, but he never hesitated to advise younger writers as they circulated in and out of the newsroom. His loyalty was to the *Evening World* and he stayed there until that paper went out of business. Readers were impressed with his selections at New York racetracks, once picking the entire card at Belmont Park, although he would personally ignore his own picks and talk himself into other choices.

Bob Edgren and Vincent Treanor assembled a collection of reporters, writers, and rewrite men in their sports department. The *Evening World* shared the services of telegraphers at ballparks to save money. Albert Lattin was one of those premier key tappers, sending out millions of words in his career. Telegraphed baseball reports from other cities were generally assigned to stringers, rather than to more established authorities with bylines who would write up the Giants and Superbas of the National League. When New York's Highlanders joined the newly formed American League in 1903, Edgren and Treanor began to search for first-class correspondents who could juggle coverage of three metropolitan teams. Their hunt ended in spring of 1905 when two new men—Allen Sangree and Bozeman Bulger—were hired to add their talents to the *Evening World*, which could now proclaim its final (pink) edition as "the most complete sporting paper published in New York."[11] Bob Edgren would boast, "With the best baseball men in the country, Allen Sangree and Bozeman Bulger, sticking closer to the Giants and the Highlanders than the lamb ever stuck to Mary, there will be little of straight baseball or the humorous incident characteristic of the game that readers of the *Evening World* will miss."[12] Edgren concluded by promising that "Mr. Sangree and Mr. Bulger are sure to knock out a home run every day."[13]

A graduate of Franklin and Marshall College, Sangree was employed on the *Evening World* staff when tapped by *Ainslee's Magazine* to head for South Africa and report on tensions between Britain and Boer settlers. When smaller conflicts erupted into the Boer War, Sangree sent reports back to *Collier's Weekly*, *Munsey's Magazine*, and *Cosmopolitan* in which he espoused the South African side, going so far as to enlist in one of the Boer commandos. Upon returning to America, he worked for the *New York Globe and Commercial Advertiser*. Damon Runyon thought highly of his contemporary, saying, "Sangree was a good writer, adventurous. He thrived on excitement."[14] Runyon added that he "had a vein of keen humor" and "brought a new literary style to sports writing."[15] Sangree also "was the first writer to weave real baseball into fiction."[16] As the most experienced writer of the new pair, he would be assigned to cover the Giants.

Largely forgotten today, Allen Sangree is best known for coining the word "jinx." He would later recall a conversation with Arthur Devlin of the Giants who had committed three errors in a single game: "By jinksy," he said, "there was a cross-eyed girl sitting back of third and she must have had it on me. By jinksy, she had my goat and I'm not so superstitious as most players at that."[17] After he wrote up the incident, Sangree told his readers, "Devlin claims he was jinksed by a cross-eyed girl."[18] When the foreman of the *Evening World's* composing room asked for clarification on spelling between "j-i-n-k-s" or "j-i-n-x," the reporter, ever conscious of space considerations, replied, "Spell it with an x. It's shorter."[19]

March 14, 1904, was the day that would impact sports coverage by the *Evening World*. John McGraw's New York Giants arrived in Birmingham, Alabama, for a two-week stint of spring training and exhibition games. Bozeman Bulger, nicknamed the "Poet Laureate of the Slag-Pile,"[20] a reference to the minor league ballpark, acted as host to the northern reporters. These included Sangree, Sam Crane of the *Journal*, and James Hammond of the *Evening World*. When the Giants clobbered the local Barons 13–0 in an exhibition game, Bulger, then sports editor of the local *Age-Herald*, wryly noted that the contest was "as exciting as a closely contested game of croquet."[21] After another Barons loss, Bozeman wrote "they fought their big opponents to a standstill and whacked the ball into the daisies at all stages of the game."[22] Sam Crane noticed Bulger's wit and insight while reading his baseball columns, so when they met again at the Democratic National Convention later that year, Crane urged him to bring those skills to New York.

While covering the Giants 1904 exhibition season for the *Globe and Commercial Advertiser*, Sangree stirred up a hornet's nest by his characterization of southern society. He paid special attention to Birmingham, Alabama, which had rolled out the red carpet for the New York team. A local paper immediately shot back, writing that "he plays the Judas by writing, purely from imagination, the most incredible drivel about the people here attending lynchings and local hangings with the greatest gusto, carrying huge pistols around all the time, wearing sombrero hats, and conducting themselves in a manner close akin to savagery."[23] Worse than that, "this ass from Gotham" cast aspersions on southern women, going so far as to mention how a young girl "set fire to a negro."[24] Allen Sangree would no longer be welcome in Birmingham.

Sangree was back in Alabama for the 1905 exhibition season and he brought his prejudices with him. He was among a crowd of baseball reporters who were feted on March 10 in Montgomery, the local press noting, "An elegant menu was served and good fellowship reigned."[25] While Sangree may have been welcome in the state capital, he had not been forgotten in Birmingham, "For the good of the game and the fair name of the South, and McGraw and his players, it is hoped that the willful distorter of the truth is not with the New York club on this visit South. Birmingham or any other Southern city is not the place for men of that character."[26]

McGraw's Giants arrived in Birmingham with nearly a full roster, the one exception being Archie Graham, a new utility outfielder, who was still taking his exams at Baltimore Medical College where he would soon become a full-fledged physician. To the delight of everyone in town, that notorious New York ass, Allen Sangree, was nowhere to be seen. Bozeman Bulger, despite having no national or international experience, had been reassigned to send reports on the Giants to the *Evening World.*

Meanwhile, Sangree would continue to insult southerners while reporting on an American League team. One of his first columns on the New York Highlanders in Montgomery began with a canard. He repeated a rumor that the team "was going to follow the bloodhounds who were to follow a convict, the idea being to show Northerners how surely a negro could be run down and masticated."[27] Manager Clark Griffith immediately denied this scurrilous story, but Sangree wrote that a citizens committee would be happy to throw together a coon hunt for their visitors. Griffith denied this offer. Not satisfied with insulting southern society and southern belles in particular, Sangree even took a swipe at the hounds, noting they ate nothing but "chitterlings, corn pone and rice."[28]

From Montgomery Sangree followed the Highlanders to New Orleans, but nearly lost half the team when their sleeper car derailed near a high trestle about twenty miles south of Vicksburg. Upon reaching the Crescent City, news of the team's arrival "spread like small-pox in a negro village,"[29] according to Sangree. Living conditions were abysmal. For several days ten men slept in a room measuring ten by twelve feet, and the night before they left, six men were still on cots. To make matters worse, the local team consistently beat the professionals, leading Sangree to complain about "minor league hirelings who eat hard tack, hoe cake and rice."[30] He agreed with Griffith when the coach remarked that "the quicker I can get out of New Orleans the better."[31]

While his colleague was filing stories with offensive comments as he followed the Highlanders, Bozeman Bulger began to forge a lasting relationship with the New York Giants. Born on November 22, 1877, in Dadeville, Alabama, Bulger was a true son of the South with a family pedigree of military service. After graduating with a law degree from the University of Alabama, he started writing for the *Birmingham Age-Herald* and working in his father's law office. From politics, Bulger soon turned his attention to writing sports columns and became a big booster of the Birmingham Barons. He used to reminisce about "when Birmingham fired its manager, who promptly stole home plate and sold it for $5."[32] Following six years on the staff of the *Age-Herald*, Bulger finally became managing editor where he did everything except "set the type and sweep the office,"[33] all for $22.50 per week.

After considering his options, Bozeman and his wife, whom he always called Miss Louie, boarded a train for a new life in New York City in the winter of 1905. Within weeks he had been given a job reading copy and in a month was writing sports columns. Bozeman's charming manners and musical southern drawl won friends instantly. This newcomer from the wilds of Alabama quickly became a favorite among those sportswriters who smoked incessantly and moved from one watering hole to another. His first byline appeared in the *Evening World* in March 1905 after being assigned to follow the Highlanders that spring. Because Sangree would be lynched in Birmingham, the writers switched coverage with Bulger then following the Giants everywhere. It was a cushy job, as contemporary Fred Lieb described: "It was customary then for the ball clubs to pay the full expenses of writers—railroad and Pullman fares, hotel and dining room bills. As far as I can recall, all New York newspapers accepted this courtesy. They were, after all, giving the ball clubs free advertising."[34]

Although Bozeman Bulger did a fine job of reporting on the Giants, southern editors were not about to forgive the ballplayers. By the time McGraw's team got to Louisville, it had proved itself to be unpopular below the Mason-Dixon Line: "Rowdy tactics, horse play that threw ridicule upon the opposing team, and the careless remarks of New York reporters have queered the team with the touchy Southerners."[35] Birmingham residents were still irate over Sangree's statements and even more mad at McGraw who had allowed him to travel with the team, but never apologized for the vile lies spewed about the city. This lack of an apology meant tacit approval of the falsehoods in the eyes of the locals. Anger increased even more when the Giants left for Memphis after staying in Alabama only five days rather than two weeks. Although the team would return for a few more days, the city had turned against it because of Sangree's newest article about Montgomery's citizens chasing convicts for "amusement and recreation."[36] While Alabamans said good riddance to the New Yorkers, ballplayers left with an odd recollection of the city. On March 25, at the invitation of the country sheriff, Giants players trooped to the county jail where they watched the hanging of a Negro convicted of murder.

Back in New York, it did not take long for a new problem to erupt for Allen Sangree. John McGraw confronted him in a Philadelphia hotel lobby, swore at him, and offered to smash in his face, screaming, "Don't you write any more articles about me getting Frank Bowerman to fight my battles. My name is J. J. McGraw and I can do all the scrapping that is to be done on this team. Now get out and don't speak to me anymore!"[37] Bowerman, who stood nearby, put up his fists, but bystanders restrained him. Sangree, who had created chaos during spring training, would never cover the Giants again. These new kids would soon learn one of the world's most important lessons—newspapers can make or break anything or anybody.

Not everyone could become a sportswriter in the early 1900s. Journalism professor Lawrence W. Murphy delineated what was basically necessary to become an accomplished newspaper reporter: "In all reporting it is important that there be shown a knowledge of the subject, a knowledge of good English, adequate imagination, planful initiative, ability to observe and record accurately, specially trained judgment, and facility in the use of journalistic technique."[38] A writer of sports columns should have a general knowledge of which he writes, in addition to current information about teams and players. Murphy noted that newspapers were printed for a general circulation and should be directed to the average reader: "Sport writing is seldom used as a vehicle for a reporter to display his wisdom; it is used chiefly to tell stories in such a way that the casual reader can understand what has happened or may happen."[39]

Experience in playing or writing about a particular sport allowed a writer to give context to a story. Memories of past events could place a current event into perspective, but individuals could be stimulated by different encounters. According to Murphy, "A game may recall a dozen experiences to one man and nothing to another."[40] An active imagination might also link a baseball story to other stories readily available to the general public. But no matter how imaginative a story, it had to be accurate. All sportswriters needed a good command of the English language, not just to avoid embarrassment but to stand out among his peers who often indulged too freely in slang.

In Murphy's opinion, "It is one thing to recognize good writing; it is another thing to be able to do good writing."[41] His advice was to practice, practice, and practice even more until a personal style could be achieved with grammar, spelling, sentence and paragraph structure, and transitions flowing naturally. The best writers never wasted words and became masters of condensation without omitting important details or observations. But a good reporter had to do more than write. Under high pressure from time constraints, he also had to show initiative in getting information into print before rival newspapers, cover stories that were unique, and obtain the most complete, timely, and accurate information while arranging prompt transmission of stories to copyeditors and typesetters. Often the lead for an article could not be composed until after a game had concluded due to ninth-inning heroics, sometimes by a second author back at the office.

Baseball writers were the direct connection between the game and its fans. According to Frederic J. Haskin, prominent writer for the *St.*

Louis Globe-Democrat in the first decade of the twentieth century, "writing baseball has developed into a highly specialized branch of newspaper work."[42] While thousands of fans could see a game every day, millions would have to read about those contests. According to Haskin, "The baseball writer is the medium through which the vast majority of the fans see and enjoy the game."[43] Sports columns led to a mutual upsurge in attendance at ball games and subscriptions for newspapers. For half the year, baseball provided papers with daily news, updates on game outcomes, box scores, and individual statistics. Telegraphers sent copy across the country so that individuals all over the United States could awaken every morning to learn how their favorite teams had performed. For fans unable to attend contests in person, sportswriters, according to Whitney Martin, "glamorized the game, surrounded it with an aura of romance, personalized and humanized the players, built reputations."[44]

Baseball scribes, including those on the *Evening World*, by positive coverage of local teams in the National and American Leagues, could increase attendance and make national figures of outstanding athletes. By making players available for interviews, a team could expect favorable treatment in a journalist's columns. This back-and-forth was made easier by writers traveling on trains and even sharing rooms with the athletes on away games. This intertwined relationship meant that both players and writers ate together, played cards and dice with one another, and hung out in hotel lobbies with the same crowds. Ballplayers hoped to score favorable notice in a future column, while writers kept their ears open for snippets of conversation that could be turned into a scoop.

Journalist Elmo Scott Watson noted that a sportswriter generally shared the same interests as his readers: "He should remember that in covering an athletic contest he is acting as the eye and ear for thousands who cannot be present at that contest, see all the color and action of it, sense the atmosphere of competition and feel the thrill of the stirring situations. But, through him and his ability to reproduce all these elements in his writing, they can catch some idea of what they missed seeing and experiencing."[45] Out in the Pacific Coast League, one observer said simply, "The apparent improvement in the game is due to the fact that baseball writing has advanced, and that the papers tell things about the games they never saw for themselves, or, if they did see them, forgot immediately. The papers are telling about the games in a more entertaining manner than ever."[46] In 1911 Thomas S. Rice, writing in the *Brooklyn Daily Eagle*, said simply that "newspapers nurtured baseball from a waif into a husky giant."[47]

This change in baseball reporting was due primarily to the association between players and those writers who became almost as close as teammates. One result of this interaction was that slang terms began to appear in newspaper columns. Sportswriter W. B. Hanna explained the phenomenon: "The professional baseball player recognizes two classes of slang. First, what he calls natural slang, meaning phrases and expressions coined by himself and nearly all pithy and picturesque. Second, what he calls invented slang, little of which comes from players, but mostly from writers and other onlookers and which as a rule doesn't hit the bull's-eye of aptness nearly as well as the players' coined vocabulary."[48] One example would be the words used to describe a ballplayer's head. Professional athletes almost universally used the word "bean" (hence "beanball") while professional writers preferred to jazz up their columns with words like "dome," "cupola," "knob," and "sconce." A player always spent nine innings in a game, whereas the writers would write of frames, stanzas, and cantos. The game was played with a baseball, or simply a ball, to players, but scribes outdid themselves in referring to a pill, pellet, globule, missile, sphere, orb, apple, onion, marble, or the horsehide.

The use of slang was more prevalent in the larger metropolitan cities as dueling reporters sought to outdo each other. Newspapers nationwide carried an article describing Cleveland pitchers variously as "hurlers, flingers, mound artists, spit-ballers, side-winders, southpaws, kink-projectors, knob-decorators, human catapults and pill-heavers."[49] On the other side of the ball, a bat could be referred to as a club, war stick, bludgeon, crutch, shillelagh, a willow, the ash, or the hickory. Spectators even had their own distinctive names—fans, rooters, and bugs. The fan comes to see the game, enjoying a good contest while hoping for a home team victory, but accepting a loss graciously. The rooter watches only to see his favorite team win, no matter under what circumstances. A bug is a rabid, enthusiastic, usually outspoken super-rooter who suffers from a condition often called baseballitis. Whether fans, rooters, or bugs, they all understood baseball slang as a true joy that "changes overnight and varies with the ingenuity of the reporter."[50]

Editors often included longer descriptions of fans, players, and umpires. Consider the fan: "An animal that is almost human in some respects. Runs wild from April through to September, when species flock together in bunches between the hours of 3 and 5 p.m. Go out of business in the winter season. The chief attribute of a Fan is dexterity in wielding the hammer, lungs like a rhinoceros, and a remarkably keen eyesight, which enables him to see a play better from bleachers or grandstand than the umpire, whose nose is dangled over the contestants. The Fan subsists chiefly upon peanuts and pop. Ever and anon, he chews tobacco or smokes a stogie."[51]

Then there is the definition of a generic umpire: "A bandit and a pirate—a buccaneer and an octopus. Few umpires have any eyesight and those who have see but dimly. One of the few animals that has no friends—to this extent being classed as one of the lucky specimens of the race."[52] A game would not be complete without a ballplayer definition: "A slave doomed to complete captivity at a rate between $20 and $100 per day. A hero one day and a hobo the next. A nectarine one week and a lemon the next. The whole show when he makes a hit and a large hunk of cheese when he strikes out. There are only two existent types—those that are and those that are not."[53]

Not surprisingly, many of these baseball slang terms jumped into common conversation prior to World War I. Billy Sunday, the famous evangelist, incorporated baseball into his revivals. Throwing off his dress coat, opening his collar, and pretending to be at bat, Sunday began his sermon, "From then on his forceful remarks were punctuated with motions suggesting a catcher's throw to second, picking up a hot liner at short, throwing from third base to first, mitting a fly and other gestures familiar to all baseball enthusiasts."[54] Sunday's sermon was also punctuated with baseball references, such as, "Believe what I tell you and you will be able to strike out the Devil with three straight ones over the pan" or "Accept Christ and you can knock a home run every time the Devil winds up."[55]

Billy Sunday's allusions to baseball came from his undistinguished career in the National League, but the language permeated every level of society. When John J. McGraw, then manager of the Baltimore Orioles, married May Blanche Sindall in May 1902, Reverend C. P. Thomas loaded on the vernacular: "The game will not be lost as long as you work together. Bunch your hits and the victory is yours. This young lady will fulfill the fondest hopes reposed in her. She will cheer you, aid you, support you and share your triumphs and participate in your defeats. . . . Lead her around the hard bases of life. Make her steal her way under the watchful eye of the enemy, until she reaches the home of happiness. Make her score many bright and joyous days, that the pennant of prosperity may continuously wave over your heads."[56]

Baseball jargon even was picked up by children. Alexander Bascom, six years old, became the object of a court case between his divorced parents in St. Louis. He worshipped Rogers Hornsby, then with the Cardinals, who was noted for being prolific at both hitting and cursing. The disgruntled wife testified that Alexander's attitude became outrageous under his father's care and that the child "talks baseball incessantly, uses slang to excess, is occasionally profane, and disrespects his mother."[57] Mom told the judge that, after being spanked, the youngster blurted out, "You'll get hell for this. He also said I was full of bunk."[58] If little Alexander could absorb slang and profanity from a few trips to a ballfield with his dad, it is staggering to even imagine how teenagers and young men would talk.

Baseball introduced more than slang into New Yorkers' vocabulary. It also "lifted the once despised hot dog out of its plebian reputation and garish environment at Coney Island into a succulent fame synonymous with baseball itself."[59] Harry Stevens began a career selling nickel scorecards outside the Polo Grounds, added bags of peanuts, and eventually won the concession rights at the Giants stadium where he introduced the now-traditional hot dog. He eventually made millions off an original investment of eight dollars, his empire including concessions at five ballparks and ten racetracks. Stevens explained the different tastes exhibited by fans: "Well, the New York customer has his likes and dislikes. We have tried, without success, to make him buy popcorn, lemonade and cake. Western fans like those things. Here your fan wants his hot dog, his sack of peanuts, his coffee or pop, and an occasional sandwich."[60] Harry, like Christy Mathewson, could see that baseball was changing and correctly predicted the future: "The game will go on and on. Crowds which are now considered phenomenal will be rated only ordinary ten years from today. Our ballparks will have to be enlarged."[61]

This was the baseball world into which Bozeman Bulger entered in New York City, the center of America's information during the baseball season of 1905. He wanted to chronicle baseball as it was and baseball how it would be. After Allen Sangree had offended nearly every newspaper editor in the South, Bulger gracefully moved into the plum assignment of covering the Giants. He was lucky enough to room on road trips with Christy Mathewson, an acknowledged star who had won 63 games in the past two years. After several years writing his own baseball columns, Christy had found that being a sportswriter had some downsides: "Whenever I lost a game, everybody said it was because I sat up late writing my articles, and could not give proper attention either to baseball training or my sleep. Then it was said that I was making enemies of all the New York players by criticizing them, and, altogether, I had an awful time."[62] Christy shared these experiences with Bozeman in their hotel room and the writer reciprocated with details about the publishing process: "At the end of three days, he knew every detail of the newspaper business from the reporter right on through the telegraph desk, the editing, the headlines and even the system of mark-up. His questions were direct and piercing."[63] During these private conversations, Bulger received valuable tips on what information to include in his columns to satisfy New York readers.

Mathewson's advice gave Bulger additional insights beyond what Sam Crane, sportswriter for the competitive *Journal*, would impart. Both these writers would cover the Giants for decades and they became personal friends with manager John McGraw. Crane was McGraw's closest buddy, "skylarking, arguing, wrestling with each other."[64] One day at a party in Pittsburgh, McGraw confounded Sam by placing glass cubes into his whiskey in place of ice. After waiting expectantly for his drink to chill, Crane finally declared there was something wrong with his booze as McGraw laughed himself silly. Every Saturday during spring training McGraw would rent a room, hire a piano player, lock the doors, and let the team blow off steam. During one of these sprees in Marlin, Texas, Bulger, probably having had a few too many drinks, thought he could teach McGraw how to properly perform a hook slide on the waxed floor. He broke his leg.

Bozeman and his unofficial mentor shared numerous adventures. Once when Hughie Jennings, then a coach for the Giants, got sick and was confined to his room, a friend sent him a bottle of bourbon. Taking along a loquacious colleague, they went to console Hughie. While the friend kept up a conversation, Sam and Bozeman continued to pour drinks until the bottle was empty. As the last drop disappeared, all three got up, in the middle of one of Hughie's sentences, and walked out of his room. Weeks later, Jennings confronted Crane and Bulger: "You know, I've just about come to the conclusion that you fellows didn't care whether I lived or died. You just wanted my bourbon."[65] On another occasion the nearly inseparable pair were in Chicago, a hotbed of hate when the Giants were in town. As they tried to reach their hotel by an open carriage, Cub fans pelted them with a salvo of rotten cabbages.

Sam Crane and Bozeman Bulger were part of the cadre of New York writers that controlled the destinies of players or teams. According to Abe Yager, this bunch of arrogant men thought they owned the press box in every stadium: "They grabbed the front seats in the Press Box at old Washington Park by right and might whenever they came to Brooklyn."[66] Their importance to the game could not be overstated: "Those boys up there out of sight are like the god from the machine. Their criticisms of the games are telegraphed to the home town papers and mold the opinions of the thousands of fans in every city."[67] Within a few years Bulger would demonstrate his exceptional talent in popular columns, emerging as one of the best New York had to offer after the publication in 1908 of a series of fictional yarns about Swat Milligan, baseball's greatest slugger. At that time, Bulger's Milligan columns were considered a standard production that put no additional money in his pocket. But Damon Runyon claimed these Milligan stories boosted the *Evening World*'s circulation by at least a hundred fifty thousand subscribers.

Being a sportswriter prior to the world war meant joining a unique fraternity that assembled at the various watering holes in New York City. Doyle's billiard parlor and bar, at the outskirts of Manhattan's business district on Forty-Second Street near Sixth Avenue, was one of the most popular. Owned by John McGraw, Jack Doyle from the old Orioles, and jockey Tod Sloan, the billiard hall opened in February 1910. According to Doyle, if you were looking for a journalist who drank, you followed a trail that ended at his establishment: "We were the furthest spot North. Up past 42nd St. was dark, in those days. If you wanted to find a friend of yours in those days, you'd start at the Café Martin, downtown; drop in at the Victoria, the Hoffman House, Bartholdi's, the Fifth Avenue, St. James, Gilsey House, the Gedney, Jim Corbett's. Then Sturdevant's, the Marlborough, the Normandy, Criterion, St. Cloud, Metropole, and Doyle's."[68] Shortly after the opening, McGraw fought with a minority investor, left Doyle's, and started McGraw's Billiard Academy seven blocks closer to downtown. His big draw was the veteran Cap Anson who would give billiard exhibitions. Both businesses served as gambling centers for professionals, locals, and out-of-town visitors.

When not swilling booze, caroming billiard balls, or wagering on horses, baseball, boxing matches, and other sporting events, baseball's journalists tended to congregate at various New York restaurants and nightspots. Among the most popular were Churchill's, Rector's, Lipton's, Beekman's, Considine's, Wallick's, Shanley's or the Majestic Hotel. Two more upscale meeting places were the four-sided bar at the Hotel Astor and the grill room at the Lambs Club.

If the Giants were to play at the Polo Grounds in the afternoon, writers abandoned the billiard parlors, bars, and hotel lobbies to hop a ride on the Third Avenue L toward the ballpark. Over time scribes from various papers would take over the last car where you could bump into Bill McGeehan, Walter St. Denis, Bill Slocum, Sid Mercer, Irvin Cobb, Bill Farnsworth, and cartoonist Tad Dorgan. Occasionally the novelist O. Henry would make an appearance. Bozeman Bulger, called "the Cervantes of the profession,"[69] would be aboard dressed in a fancy suit and carrying his walking stick while telling tales of the Alabama swamps. After Damon Runyon arrived from Colorado in 1910, Bozeman became his unofficial mentor in New York City. A snappy dresser himself, Runyon could often be seen sporting a porkpie hat wherever he traveled. He stood out in the writing crowd as a recovered alcoholic who drank nothing stronger than coffee. Bulger could make it best, his recipe being to "take a quart of coffee and a pint of water and with a little stewing produce an elixir that will grow hair on a billiard ball."[70] John Wheeler, one of the heavier drinkers, remembered how Runyon "could sit up all night with the biggest rumpots in town and down a cup of coffee for every round. Some nights the total reached 12 to 15 cups."[71] Fred Lieb agreed with that observation, claiming "he would drink quarts and maybe gallons of coffee while the others were putting away beer, rye highballs, and sloe gin."[72]

Once the writers reached the Polo Grounds (or any other stadium for that matter), they passed through turnstiles toward the press section located at ground level behind home plate. Elder statesmen of the profession, "luminaries in the firmament of king-pin typewriter-ticklers,"[73] filled the lowest seats where they could interact with managers, coaches, players, and umpires as the teams warmed up. During the game, "they chatted freely and good naturedly among their ranks, now and then declaring recess in order to tear off a few lines and hand them to the operators to shoot the latest from the ringside to their respective sheets all over the country."[74] In 1918 a new press box appeared at the Polo Grounds, this one built under the second deck. Reporters and telegraphers hated the new arrangement since it was cramped, unsafe, protected only by chicken wire, and had no restroom facilities.

One problem encountered in ballparks during the early days was overcrowding of those prime seats, reserved for the press, by fans who were not journalists. Politicians, actors, and others who felt entitled ignored press section signs so that out-of-state writers could never find seats. This situation came to a head during the National League playoff game between the Giants and Cubs in 1908. So many trespassers felt entitled to seats in the press box and refused to give them up that Hugh Fullerton, one of the country's premier writers, "was forced to sit on the edge of the box with his feet dangling outside while he dashed off copy for his operator."[75] On October 14, 1908, sportswriters from the national newspapers met in Detroit to form Baseball Writers Association of America, an organization devoted to bringing respect to their craft. Its primary object was "to abate the press box nuisances at league games and at world's series games, by barring butters-in who interfere with, when they do not actually crowd out, men who have work to do."[76]

While baseball writers won the fight to keep interlopers out of their press boxes at games, their close association with players would lead to a unique situation. After reading accounts of their favorite players, fans wanted to hear from them personally. This interest would result in journalists and athletes pairing off, the concept being that the latter, most of whom at the time were not particularly literate, would dictate their thoughts to the former who would then type them into acceptable newspaper copy. These arrangements were considered continuations of historical agreements. Aulus Hirtius completed Julius Caesar's *Commentaries on the Gallic War*. Seneca wrote for the emperor Nero. Auguste Maquet partnered with Alexandre Dumas on historical novels. George Washington consulted with Alexander Hamilton and James Madison on his famous Farewell Address. Some authors even claimed that Moses gave God a helping hand with the Ten Commandments.

Why not do the same in baseball? It seemed like a great idea to boost circulation and satisfy readers while putting money in the pockets of woefully underpaid athletes. Every athlete with name recognition did this for years. Although there were murmurings, this dirty secret came out in the open over the 1912 and 1913 seasons. The *Washington Post* was one of the first to break this story during the 1912 World Series when players from the Giants and Red Sox claimed to have written personal thoughts for syndication: "This 'expert' stuff is the bunk, anyway. There is only one baseball player in the country who writes his own stuff and only two who actually dictate it. The articles written by all others are written by newspaper men. And in a majority of the cases are not even seen by its alleged author until he reads it in the newspaper. One of the humorous phases of the series is the dash of the player critics to the newsstand each morning to learn what they said the night before. No one grudges the players the soft money they pick up. But they are making a farce of baseball reporting."[77] Readers had been duped, according to writer William Peet: "The dear old public fell for this stuff and swallowed hook, bait and sinker."[78]

While Christy Walsh is generally credited with establishing the practice now derogatorily referred to as ghostwriting, he was a latecomer, signing Babe Ruth as his first client in 1921. John (Jack) Wheeler had him beat by a decade, signing Christy Mathewson to a contract to publish in 1911. Up to this time, Mathewson had written his own columns "unhaunted,"[79] as Ring Lardner put it. A year later, Wheeler and Mathewson produced the popular *Pitching in a Pinch*, a classic baseball title still available from the University of Nebraska Press. William Peet listed *just some* of those sports writing combos who covered the 1912 World Series: Christy Mathewson (Jack Wheeler); Walter Johnson (Ralph McMillan); Jeff Tesreau (Jack Wheeler); John McGraw (Walter Trumbull); Chief Meyers (Jim MacBeth); Rube Marquard (Bill Farnsworth); Cy Young (Sam Carrick); Heinie Wagner (Paul Shannon); Bill Carrigan (A. H. C. Mitchell); Tris Speaker (Tim Murnane); Joe Wood (Jack O'Leary); Hughie Jennings (Roger Tidden); and Ty Cobb (Stoney McGlynn). Players received from $250 to $1,000 for columns they did not write. Larry Doyle, second baseman for the Giants and the National League MVP in 1912, was the individual who blew the lid off this literary scam: "It was the hardest I ever tackled. I did not write a line, but it was awful hard on the nerves to listen to what some reporter wrote for me and then sign my name to stuff that looked to me like inklings from the pen of King Solomon. But, you know, I got $600 in coin for the work, and that's pretty good for a reporter who is no reporter at all."[80] Peet laid the blame on newspaper owners, who wanted to pump up circulation, rather than the athletes, writing, "No one can blame a baseball star for pulling down a little soft money."[81]

Attempts were made by the National Commission, but this "serio-comic conspiracy"[82] could not be stopped. In fact, this literary make-believe or authorship by proxy continued to grow, especially under the oversight of the Christy Walsh Syndicate. Called the literary godfather of this famous athlete/behind-the-scenes writer tandem, Walsh convinced the country that "a vast amount of remarkable literary talent in the field of professional athletics was going to waste,"[83] and he assured the reading public that only he could deliver "the best thoughts of the best athletic mind in the best manner."[84] By the time he wrote his memoir *Adios to Ghosts*, Walsh had faked stories by twenty-six of the biggest baseball stars in the early twentieth century. Among the ghosts was Bozeman Bulger who, in addition to his *Evening World* columns, had secretly written for Ty Cobb, Rogers Hornsby, Miller Huggins, and John McGraw. Westbrook Pegler would comment that Bozeman Bulger "had ghosted for McGraw so long that he had become McGraw's other self."[85] Bulger literally did become McGraw, ghostwriting his entire autobiography *My Thirty Years in Baseball*, which appeared in 1923.

As sportswriters filled newspaper columns by hook or by crook, there was another important aspect in the contemporary press. Readers wanted desperately to see their heroes as well as read about them. A significant percentage of the American baseball fans was still illiterate, so they clamored for illustrations of their stars. Bob Edgren's sketches could help explain certain events, but only in caricature form. The *Evening World*, like other competitors, began publishing sketches of stars like Christy Mathewson and Hans Wagner. As technology developed, these early sketches changed to studio photographs, often incorporating fake backgrounds with players in uniform, appearing in either head shots or full-length images holding a glove or a bat. Neither the player drawings or early photographs showed any action. Readers demanded more.

The next step in the evolution of baseball photography was the posed shot. Normally made during practice, the subject is more important than the setting and, while they have illustrative value, do not show real action. Posed photos were as fake as ghostwritten articles and true fans were not fooled. Leonard C. Lee Jr., an expert on baseball photography, had tips for the cameramen. Pitchers should be depicted in the actual pitching motion: "The best time to photograph a pitcher is either when his hands are above his head in the 'wind-up' or the moment after he releases the ball in his forward motion."[86] The latter is generally better since the man's face is visible. For a catcher, the camera should catch the action as his mitt reaches for the ball at the same instant the batter swings a bat.

A typical image for an outfielder was to show him as if catching a high, hard liner. This could be accomplished two ways, according to Lee: "It is better to have the ball actually thrown to the fielder, and caught by him, than to have him stand, stork-fashion, on one leg, with a ball gripped in his glove."[87] This first shot is better, even if it has to be taken repeatedly, since the second would look unnatural no matter how unstork-like the cameraman could make the outfielder look. A first baseman could be shot with his foot on the bag while stretching for a ground ball thrown wide to his right. Other infielders could be photographed throwing a ball, catching a fly or fielding a grounder.

Staged photos soon gave way to action shots taken during actual games. The least successful of these were taken from the stands where the finished product showed a wide-angle view of the field from the grandstand. From these distances, players looked like ants. The best action photographs were taken by photographers stationed directly on the field. Plays at first base were generally ignored since there was nothing but repetitive motion as the runner is either safe or out while the baseman catches the ball. Second base was too far for the ordinary camera to catch anything close up.

Sliding was the action most desirable to photograph. Third base offered the most activity since several plays could be caught on film in nearly every game. Photographers were advised to set up past third base since the baseman would not block the shot as the runner slides. Small quantities of dust would always enhance the reality of a photo. Photographs of plays at home plate were always in demand since they could often illustrate a turning point in the game. But action at the plate was rare, compounded by the confluence of runner, umpire, and catcher. Being on the field to obtain these illustrations for newspaper columns proved to be risky, as Leonard Lee explained: "The writer once had his head buried in the hood of a Press Graflex, ready to snap the batter, when he heard—or rather felt—two crashes in quick succession. The first was when the bat hit the ball, the second when the ball hit the Graflex."[88] After numerous broken cameras and human ribs, photographers were banned from the playing field and began to experiment more with telephoto lens.

Editors quickly realized that illustrations added value to unadorned text. According to Elmo Scott Watson, "A picture invariably attracts the attention of the reader and pictorial news can be grasped instantly by all who can see even if they cannot read."[89] This combination of photography with talented writers who could tell of the newest phenom at spring training as well as the fading veteran whose career was ending, was syndicated from New York City all across the nation. Star players in what used to be inconsequential baseball games became heroes to total strangers. Clayton Hamilton explained how Christy Mathewson became so exalted:

> It was beautiful to see him as he strolled serenely to the center of the diamond, apparently unconscious of the plaudits of the crowd. He was a great man in his own profession, and he had the dignity of greatness. He excelled all other pitchers, and this excellence was testified immediately to the eye by the unusual simplicity and ease of his bodily movements. His two arms swept superbly upward in an absolute curve that reminded the spectator of Græco-Roman statues of athletes in the Vatican, and that was all. He had perfect personal poise, he was never nervous, never flustered, never angry. Mathewson made himself a hero not merely by his prowess, but also by his personality. The multitude adored him. And, by awakening this admiration, he bestowed a benefit upon uncounted crowds, for nothing more effectually emanates the average man from his dreary prison-cell of self than a wished-for opportunity to worship some big person who does something—it does not really matter what it

> is—much better than that same thing could be done by himself or by anybody else.[90]

In Hamilton's opinion, the need for heroes elevated outstanding baseball players to a new level.

Citizens of New York went bonkers over the National League playoff game between the heroic hometown Giants and the despised Cubs in 1908: "Broadway talked of nothing else. In all the cafes, hotel lobbies and restaurants people kept track of the score. Waiters whispered the latest returns; they were given out mixed with orange bitters and the carbonic; barbers poured them out between strokes of the razor."[91] Manicure girls knew that the Giants had been beaten long before thousands of disappointed fans streamed back into the city from the Polo Grounds. Their sainted Christy Mathewson had been beaten, but the masses forgave him and he would return again to that sacred ballfield to win again and again.

Edwin Greenlaw and Dudley Miles described this level of baseball enthusiasm as a religious experience: "An ideal faith, this religion of baseball, the more you examine it. See, for instance, how it satisfies the prime requirement of a true faith that it shall ever be present in the hearts of the faithful; practiced not once a week on Sunday, but six times a week—and in the West seven times a week; professed not only in the proper place of worship, but in the Subway before the game, and in the Subway after the game, and in the offices and shops and factories on rainy days."[92] Instead of a church, New York baseball fans assembled at the Polo Grounds where they worshipped in a temple of "iron girders, green wooden benches, and back fence frescoed with safety-razors and ready-made clothing."[93] This pair of authors bolstered their premise with the following question: "If religion has its origin in primitive man's worship of the eternal rebirth of earth's fructifying powers with the advent of spring, how can we neglect the vivid stirring in the hearts of millions that marks the departure of the teams for spring training in Texas?"[94]

Mathewson, often referred to as a Christian gentleman in the press, had been raised to know that the Sabbath was a day of "restful observance." His mother would remember, "When my children were little, I used to read to them on Sundays. When they grew older, I made them read to me." After Christy left home, she added, "He has held to the old rule. He has never played in any of the Sunday games." Immensely proud of her famous son, Mrs. Mathewson boasted, "I was always particular about regular hours of sleep and plenty of plain, wholesome food, good milk, fresh air—and *The Golden Rule*."[95]

This religion of baseball spread countrywide, from the manicured Polo Grounds in New York City to those rocky and weed-strewn ballfields in the smallest country villages. There was a spiritual fervor "from mid-April to mid-October, growing in ardor with the procession of the months, until it attains a climax of orgiastic frenzy in the World's Series."[96] It would be a near-religious experience for "when Mathewson winds himself up for delivering the ball, he is not far removed from the sacred warrior dancer of Polynesia."[97] The daily newspaper had changed baseball: "The sporting page has long ceased to be a mere chronicle of sport and has become an encyclopedia, an anthology, a five-foot book-shelf, a little university in itself."[98] The sports page had become baseball's bible.

In this new religion, Christy Mathewson, called Matty by friends and writers, became baseball's greatest idol. Depictions of him in the press gave off the same magnetism that still inspired millions to attend revivals to hear preachers such as Billy Sunday. Bob Edgren, who oversaw hundreds of columns on Mathewson while sports editor of the *Evening World*, put him into perspective: "Matty is more famous than any of our presidents . . . His strike-out records have filled columns in every newspaper in the country when the sinking of a battleship has been reported in one small paragraph."[99] Although professional baseball was a team game, very few players had the ability to stand out personally as a drawing card. Mathewson had it all—intelligence, skill, drawing power, color, showmanship, and sex appeal for the ladies. Often if there was a dearth of sporting news, the *Evening World* would simply insert large photos of Christy to fill space. As he neared the end of his career, Matty had been overwhelmingly chosen by the New York media as baseball's superstar of the prewar era.

In 1929, Damon Runyon, who had covered sports for nearly two decades, summed up what the majority of the country's fans had felt when he wrote that Christy Mathewson "is one of the three greatest ball players that ever lived, and surely the greatest pitcher."[100] Years after his death, the thought of Christy Mathewson walking from the bull pen into a tight situation would stir memories for Runyon. He recalled, "How I loved that old megaphonic mumble of the announcer when the Giants were in a tough spot—'Mathewson now pitching for New York!' Man, that was MAGIC!"[101]

CANDIDATES FOR THE FIRST BASEBALL SUPERSTAR

When asked today who baseball's first superstar was, nearly everyone, whether casual fan or avid rooter, would say that, of course, it was Babe Ruth. By the middle of the second decade of the twentieth century, "superstar" was a term already in general use to describe actors on stage, in movies, and on the vaudeville circuit. Grantland Rice, sportswriter for the *New York Tribune,* seems to be first to apply that term to athletics, commencing with football stars in 1914 and then applying it to prominent baseball players in 1915. A year later Christy Mathewson, the actual first superstar, was ending his distinguished seventeen-year career with the New York Giants while Ruth was pitching in just his second year with the Boston Red Sox. Babe was a latecomer to that distinctive title, as evidenced by the first stanza of Grantland Rice's poem titled "Mathewson to Ruth."

Or ever the lost years went their rounds
From Gotham to the Hub,
I was a star at the Polo Grounds
And you were a Bush League Dub.[1]

The Baseball Writers' Association of America gave an assist in selecting the sport's first superstar by its voting for entry into the Baseball Hall of Fame in 1936. Veterans, whose careers were mainly before

1900, would be included later, but the first five inductees—Ty Cobb (222); Babe Ruth (215); Hans Wagner (215); Christy Mathewson (205); and Walter Johnson (189)—easily passed the magic number of 170 votes for inclusion. All five men—two pitchers, one infielder, and two outfielders—were active in 1915 when Grantland Rice began to use the word "superstar." So, it remained my task to sift through five records to determine who was the toast of American baseball. Statistics verified the Baseball Writers Association in its selections to the Baseball Hall of Fame, but there were other issues that pushed Christy Mathewson to the forefront as the reigning superstar.

The question remains, how does a person evaluate players who played different positions on different teams over different spans of time? Connie Mack, elder statesman of baseball, confronted this very issue in a conversation with sportswriter Grantland Rice: "Grantland, you can't judge or measure the ball players of one era by those of another. From 1900 to 1920, baseball was an entirely different game from the game we now know. Until 1920, it was Ty Cobb's type of game—belonging more to speed, skill and agility than to power. They played with a dead ball, so it was a day of base running. Came the Golden Twenties and we had Ruth, the livelier ball and we watched speed give way to power."[2] Baseball's popularity increased prior to World War I because it was a game governed by rules, which were supposed to even the playing field for all participants so that athleticism, not deceit or fraud, would win out.

Twelve years before this first enshrinement at Cooperstown, *Vanity Fair* persuaded twenty sportswriters to decide the greatest athletes in American sports. Players were divided into categories and Grantland Rice wrote up the results when it came to baseball. Hans Wagner was a shoo-in as the best infielder, "being not only a hustling, sensational short-stop, but, in addition, one of the greatest batsmen in the game." There was a serious debate over the best hitter. A compromise was reached by agreeing that Babe Ruth was "supreme among the sluggers, the range finders, the extra baseleaders." Ty Cobb led "the parade for straightaway hitting, for establishing figures that may never be challenged." A decision on the best pitcher boiled down to Christy

Mathewson or Walter Johnson. Rice explained why Christy came out ahead: "Mathewson, one of the greatest figures baseball has ever known, still had the advantage over Walter Johnson of being most of the time with a winning team, while his rival was serving with second division outfits which often forced him to pitch shut-outs in order to win."[3]

One important component of being a superstar is to have ability beyond his rivals. Babe was five years old when Mathewson began his National League career in 1900. Opposing players soon claimed that Matty had such precise control that he could clip the buttons off their jerseys if he wished. By the time Babe was ten, Christy had established a record that has never been nor ever will be broken—over the space of six days in the 1905 World Series he pitched three complete-game shutouts against the Philadelphia Athletics. In 1908 he won thirty-seven games, still a National League record since 1901, back when a pitcher was expected to go nine innings each game without the modern benefit of middle-relief pitchers or closers. Christy finished his career with 373 wins, even now tied for first place in National League records and third in the Major Leagues during the twentieth and twenty-first centuries.

But it was not statistics alone that won Christy Mathewson the admiration of America. Any superstar needs to connect with and be embraced by the public as well. Christy gave baseball a touch of class that it badly required in the early twentieth century, one visitor describing his impression of players from that era: "Alongside Matty they looked vulgar and coarse. Their language was vile. They were rude. Their eating habits were crude. Many of them were coal miners or common laborers. No polish. No breeding. The poor fellows just had no education. They drank, caroused, and played professional ball."[4] On the other hand, Christy, who had been educated at Bucknell College, exhibited a character that set him apart from other ballplayers of his time.

America embraced its new baseball idol with open arms. President William Taft insisted that his private rail car be attached to the Giants' train so that he would not miss a pitching duel between Matty and Mordecai "Three Finger" Brown in Chicago. President Warren Harding would declare, "Mathewson typified all that is best in the national pastime."[5] Every baseball fan knew his name. Nicknamed "Big Six" by the press, a postal clerk discovered a letter addressed simply with a large numeral 6 and correctly dispatched it to Mathewson. After Matty had been confined to a sanatorium at Saranac Lake, New York, for treatment of tuberculosis, other fans addressed letters simply "Christy Mathewson, Adirondack Mountains" and they were also correctly delivered. As a former postal employee, I can guarantee this would never happen today.

Despite his natural reticence, Christy Mathewson really was a superstar. The *New York Herald* wrote, "What J. P. Morgan is to finance, what the pianola is to the Harlem flat, what Caruso is to the opera, Mathewson is to baseball."[6] Even out in far-off Montana an editor would assert, "If Washington had never been born, they would probably have named the monument for Christy Mathewson or Theodore Roosevelt."[7] Sportswriter Cullen Cain admitted, "I never saw Matty pitch a ball game, but nevertheless, he was my idol."[8] Millions felt the same way. Not only did men and boys worship him; ladies adored him as well. When a female reporter for the *New York Tribune* attended a Giants game, she became an instant fan, writing, "There was Matty, looking like a sun god, standing square in the full limelight, as it were . . . Girls, your Aunt Kate joined the worshippers at Matty's shrine in those few seconds. Oh, the subtlety of the pitcher's art!"[9]

Beside uncommon ability and public adoration, a superstar needs to receive top dollar in his contracts. By 1911 Matty was making $10,000 a year, as was Hans Wagner of the Pirates. Ty Cobb received $9,000 from the Tigers and Walter Johnson got $7,000 from the Senators. Babe Ruth did not receive his first major league salary until 1914 and did not reach the $10,000 plateau until traded by the Red Sox to the Yankees in 1919. Wise investments and product endorsements allowed Christy to capitalize on his celebrity. He pitched cars, batteries, and pipe tobacco; cowrote books and newspaper columns; appeared in vaudeville skits and silent movies; and even invented a board game playable by children and adults. It was rumored that the Giants hurler was eventually worth a staggering $200,000, more than $3 million today.

Finally, a superstar needs to bring change to his chosen profession. Prior to Mathewson's arrival with the Giants, Americans generally thought of baseball payers as knuckle-dragging Neandertals whose only attribute was raw talent. In addition to his skill as a pitcher, Christy brought a style and class from his years at Bucknell University that gave baseball a new image. His emergence coincided with the nation's newspapers devoting more coverage to baseball. Playing in New York City, center of the country's media, propelled him into the spotlight which, in turn, saw newspaper sales skyrocket. Christy's incredible talent, college background, self-effacing personality, and movie-star good looks made him more popular than politicians, military officers, or literary figures. Parents secretly hoped that their children would grow up to emulate this blond god from rural Pennsylvania.

Many baseball players are like shooting stars, sparkling in the heavens for several seasons before flaming out and being quickly replaced and forgotten. For well over a decade, Christy's star was the brightest in baseball's sky and his light burned brightly in the hearts and minds of baseball fans. Talent is common but marvelous talent is quite rare. When combined with the character of a true sportsman and gentlemanly behavior, this country takes notice, as it did with Christy Mathewson, who was upheld as a symbol of American sportsmanship. But there is more to his story than the public image and statistics—the narrative of a quiet, reserved family man who would rather have played football or checkers than pitch in a World Series. This book will explore the private side of baseball's first superstar, the gentleman behind the facade of fame, as well as the four men who challenged him for that title.

John Peter "Hans" Wagner

Some may argue that John Peter Wagner, known more commonly as Honus but preferring the moniker "Hans," should be acknowledged as the first superstar. He did join the National League Louisville Colonels in 1897, three years prior to Christy Mathewson's major league appearance, but Hans had some downsides. He was definitely not photogenic. Standing about six feet tall and weighing near two hundred pounds,

Hans looked like he had been put together by God out of mismatched spare parts. His legs were short and extremely bowlegged, shaped much like barrel staves. Some observers said a pig could run between his legs without touching his pants or stockings. His feet were also pigeon-toed, making his fielding look like a clumsy, lumbering wannabe. In a profile of the famous shortstop, Harry Daniel, sports editor of the *Chicago Inter-Ocean*, observed, "He shuffles around on the base line between second and third with a strange, gorilla-like movement, reaching down a pair of long, swinging arms and scooping up the ball with hands that seem far too large for the rest of him."[10] To complete his physical profile, Wagner's shoulders humped forward and he had the largest nose, combined with a huge chin, in the National League.

Bozeman Bulger, writer for the *Evening World*, noted that despite his appearance Hans was a natural infielder: "He would skim over the ground like a giant crab. His huge hands, like a crab's claw, grabbed everything in reach. Once he took hold, those hands never turned loose."[11] Wagner, who palmed a baseball like an average man could hold a golf ball, called his hands "Cincinnati hams."[12] Keeping with the food analogy, Hans won the nickname of "the human omelet"[13] because of his ability to spread out to cover so much ground. He fielded hot grounders and blazing line drives with his bare hands. When breaking in a new glove, he first cut a large circle of leather out of the pocket so he could feel the ball. His glove was like a steam shovel that would field the ball before it suddenly appeared streaking to first base amid a shower of sand and pebbles. In addition to his fielding, Wagner had a rocket arm. Back in 1898 he threw a baseball over 134 yards, a feat not even outfielders could match.

Harry Daniel continued his description of Hans who always appeared "so strangely out of place on a baseball diamond." As Daniel watched, "When it is his time to bat he comes across the field with long, measured strides, putting his feet down heavily, heels first, and carrying his bat as if he had never seen such a thing before in all his life." Wagner still looked clumsy in the batter's box: "He stands there, facing the pitcher with a peculiar stooping crouch and his legs twisted into such an odd tangle that they cease to look like legs at all."[14] Like his fielding,

Wagner's hitting was extraordinary. From 1900 through 1911, Hans won six National League batting titles. He missed that title in 1901 and 1905, despite batting .353 and .363 in those years. Calling attention to Wagner's batting skill would be like saying Christmas comes on December 25. Veteran writer Hugh Fullerton succinctly summed up his career in a single sentence, "He is the nearest approach to a baseball machine ever constructed."[15]

Wagner was discovered in 1896 when Ed Barrow, then manager of the Paterson, New Jersey, Silk Weavers, found Hans outside a saloon in Pittsburgh. Barrow soon learned the background of this twenty-two-year-old phenom. Born in 1874 in a Pittsburgh suburb, John Peter Wagner went to school until the age of fifteen when he left to work in a brother's barber shop. Although he cut hair for three years, barbering did not suit his character since he was "a very poor talker"[16] who hated to carry on a conversation. A town lot player up to this time, Hans now began to play on a series of semi-pro teams in Pennsylvania, Ohio, and Michigan prior to signing with Barrow's Paterson team. Barrow was looking for talent, not book learning, and Hans did not disappoint, hitting .313 in 1896 and .375 in 1897. Wagner became a real ballplayer under the loose tutelage of Ed Barrow, as he later recalled, "You can't manufacture a ball player. It must be in him naturally. He must be a natural batter and a natural fielder and a natural base runner or he never will amount to anything. And he must be allowed to get along naturally and do just as he pleases."[17] While this method does not work for most athletes, a free rein to develop at his own pace won Hans a contract for $2,000 with the Louisville Colonels of the National League.

Harry Pulliam, secretary of the Colonels, wired Barney Dreyfuss, then the team owner: "Have found and signed a wonder. Am bringing him back with me."[18] When they reached the team's office, Pulliam introduced his new signee. Owner Dreyfuss bellowed out, "Who got you to buy that big, clumsy looking piece of baseball furniture?"[19] However, one look at Wagner's performance on the diamond convinced him that Pulliam was a genius. After the National League consolidated from twelve teams to eight following the 1899 season, Barney Dreyfuss assumed control of the Pittsburgh Pirates and took the best players from Louisville along with him. Wagner was shifted from position to position until he became the team shortstop in 1903.

Newspaper writers called him the Flying Dutchman, but his teammates simply referred to him as Dutch. They were both misnomers since he could neither read nor write German. During his playing days, Hans remained unmarried for years and lived with his father in the house where he was born. Wagner wished to be left alone, had few friends, and refused to give interviews in his early days. He enjoyed long walks or driving his automobile over country roads. When approached by fans and admirers, Hans would slink in back doors and use freight elevators to avoid giving autographs or indulging in conversations.

One constant companion was Jason Weatherbee, his dependable dog. This mongrel had been with Wagner since 1903, sitting on the bench for home games and even traveling occasionally on road trips. According to his owner, "There's many a big-league player who doesn't know as much about the game as Jason did. He'd bark when the club began to rally and sulk in the corner of the dugout when we were behind."[20] Hans strenuously objected to a call by umpire Brick Owens on May 30, 1912, and was tossed out of the game. Like an irate manager, Jason Weatherbee jumped down from the bench and raced onto the field, yapping the whole way. Jason tried to bite Owens, but the ump had avoided plenty of encounters with real managers and kept his legs from being treated as beefsteaks. Sadly, Jason died just six weeks later and Wager was greatly depressed. It was a long time before he could joke about the incident, finally saying "You know something? Jason never seemed well after he went up against Owens that day in Pittsburgh. I shouldn't wonder if he got hold of that umpire's leg and it poisoned him."[21]

Wagner never tried to hide his character weaknesses. Like many players of his era, a cheek always bulged with a huge cud of chewing tobacco and he spit successive streams of spittle. Former pitcher Al Demaree explained one reason for this widespread use of chewing tobacco in baseball: "After the first inning [the baseball] was as black as an undertaker's derby. The pitcher and infielders had changed its color by a mixture of tobacco juice, resin, licorice and dirt. On a dark day it was almost impossible to see."[22] While chewing tobacco may have given the pitcher a little edge, it deeply offended women who considered it a gross and filthy habit that should be condemned in public. Hans was also guilty of chain-smoking cigars and eating lots of his favorite food—limburger cheese. Despite smelling of chewing tobacco, stogies, and stinky cheese, he did eventually find a wife, marrying Bessie Smith on December 30, 1916.

Another bad habit condemned by women was the excessive consumption of alcohol in any form. Hans got an early introduction to the mixture of beer and baseball, as he recalled, "My first job at Louisville was to carry in beer for the other players at lunch time. And how they could drink it! Fred Clarke ordered morning practice and the boys usually remained in the park and sent out for lunch. The rookies were always dispatched for large buckets of beer."[23] In off-hours, players frequented Louisville beer gardens where, according to Wagner, "with a 5-cent glass of beer you could help yourself to a beef sandwich, cheese, pickles, pickled eel and sour rabbit."[24] It is no wonder that the thirsty Pirate developed a taste for draft beer. After each game, no matter where it was played, he would head for a saloon and order six glasses of beer. If the bartender would happen to inquire where his friends were, Hans would snap, "There ain't no other fellows." According to sportswriter Bill Corum, "Whereupon he would knock over the six seidels and sidle out the door. I hasten to add that this was in the days when beer was beer."[25]

Playing in the dead ball era, Hans Wagner would reminisce about how tough Louisville was when he joined the Colonels, "I remember when the bleachers didn't like a decision, men would get out their guns and shoot up into the air."[26] Women refused to attend ball games then because shocking profanity from coaches, players, and umpires could be heard throughout the grandstand. Veterans of these early teams, when men had mustaches and muscles, and writers who covered them would look with disgust upon players in the 1940s and '50s: "The elite of the modern game go in for men's perfume, monogrammed silk lounging robes, and thrice-a-week manicures and facials. Compared to the old boys, they are luxurious pretenders to the thrones of the immortals." Sportswriter Vincent X. Flaherty continued, "Therefore, good, honest, calloused hands are no longer a part of baseball. No longer are gnarled fingers, resembling a wayward bunch of bananas, a badge of the profession."[27] The days of giving oneself a manicure with a pocket knife were over.

But there were always memories, as he remembered in 1947: "They played tougher baseball in those days. The runners didn't just try to take you out to break up double plays. They tried to do it on every play. . . . I never had a fight, but had a lot of arguments. The clubs were always yelling at each from the benches before the game started, and kept it up afterward. By the seventh or eighth inning everybody wanted to fight."[28] As his career drew to a close in 1916, Hans admitted, "My flare-ups with umpires, though none has been serious, would run into a high figure during my career."[29]

Upon entering the National League, Hans quicky realized that baseball had some not-so-subtle overtones of football. He would always remember one particular game against the Orioles: "I hit one that should have been a home run, but when I got to first base Jack Doyle gave me the hip, Heinie Reitz almost killed me rounding second, Hughey Jennings tripped me at short and John McGraw was waiting for me with everything but a shotgun at third, and I was held to a triple."[30] Life on the basepaths was a war. Every team's mantra was "Get there at any cost,"[31] even if that meant spiking an infielder or two while rounding the bases. Hans paid a price for his years on the basepaths and at shortstop, "I have been ripped and torn from my waist down, and I bear spike marks numbering a hundred at least."[32] His lower limbs looked like legs of lamb that had been gnawed on, but not all wounds were inflicted by opponents. In one game, he slid into second, tore loose the bag, and gashed his leg so badly that it required twenty-six stitches.

Wagner kept his baseball success in perspective as that storied career began to wind down, "Praise that came from diamond achievements was nothing, for when your playing days are over it does not allow you much."[33] Retiring following the 1917 season, Hans ran a sporting goods store in Pittsburgh until he lost it during the Depression, but his greatest joy was to rejoin the Pirates as a coach for almost forty years. Hans never lost his sense of humor. When Bing Crosby once asked him why he only batted .354 one year, Wagner quipped, "We had prohibition that year."[34] (He had retired by the time Prohibition would be enacted.) His last visit to the Pirates' clubhouse was late in 1951. Al Abrams, a local sportswriter, and player Ralph Kiner watched before his final game as Hans stood moving only his head as he took one long look around his baseball home, noting "his watery eyes and the shaking of a hand gripped with palsy." Kiner quietly whispered, "What memories this place must hold for Honus." As Wagner began to dress for his last appearance in a Pirates uniform, Abrams asked what he had been thinking. Hans answered he had been thinking of the men he had played with and all the changes that he had seen in baseball over the years. He concluded, "We had fun in those days. That's all I've got left now in baseball, my memories, but they're worth a million bucks to me."[35] Hans lived with those memories, sharing them now and then for a beer or two, until his death on December 6, 1955. John Peter Wagner's odd appearance, propensity to fight in his early years, addiction to alcohol and tobacco, and playing on a small-market team in Pittsburgh kept him from being the first national superstar.

Tyrus Raymond "The Georgia Peach" Cobb

Tyrus Raymond Cobb was also in the running for first superstar. Born at Narrows, Georgia, a small village nestled in the red clay hills of that state, on December 18, 1886, Cobb took the world by storm. He had blue eyes, blond hair, and a slender physique that would bloom into a playing weight of a hundred seventy-five pounds on a six-foot frame. Following his high school graduation, he spent a few days playing baseball for the Augusta Tourists before being sent to the Anniston, Alabama, Steelers. Ty recalled his first days with the Steelers: "My main trouble at the start was that I didn't take my job on the Augusta team seriously. I will never forget the first time I was benched. I used to like my peanut taffy and one day I went out to center fields chewing on a big chunk of this candy. A fly ball was hit out to me, but I forgot to throw away the candy and everything got so mixed up that I lost the ball and, incidentally, the game. For that I was benched and I should have been."[36] By 1905 he was back in Augusta, but "he wasn't much of a whirlwind, so folks down there thought, and nobody paid any attention to him at all."[37]

Nap Rucker, Clyde Engle, and Eddie Cicotte were future Major Leaguers on that team. So was Louis Staub, who had been banned from baseball after a bar brawl but changed his name to Bull Durham after the country's most popular tobacco brand. Rucker would one day reminisce about Cobb's days in 1905: "He wasn't a real good hitter at the start of the season and he had trouble catching the ball in the outfield. But he had that burning desire, and he had the greatest legs. My, how he punished them. They should have made a model of those legs. No one could start quicker and stop quicker."[38] When asked if Cobb ever got into fights, Rucker laughed before responding, "He was easy to get along with unless you tried to get ahead of him. He never backed away from a fight. But he couldn't fight. I never heard of him licking anybody, but he'd try 'em all."[39]

Detroit's Tigers spent their spring training in Augusta that year and had hoped to sign Clyde Engle, but he was in a bad batting slump so they settled on signing Ty Cobb for a pittance. Ken Smith wrote that Cobb's arrival from the South was like "an eagle swooping upon the baseball scene with spikes for talons."[40] That eagle image would be delayed. The 1905 season being pretty advanced, Cobb only played in forty-one games after replacing the regular center fielder, batted only .238, and stole two bases.

His new teammates were not impressed. They were infuriated that this new kid had immediately broken into the lineup without sitting on the bench like they had done. Cobb would later accept part of the blame: "The reason I had so many fights at the start was because I did not understand what was meant by 'kidding.' I took it as an insult until I learned better. The ballplayers in the big league also use a lot of bad language that I had not heard spoken in jest before and it took me a long time to understand it that way. When a man called me a foul name, I did not take time to consider that it was just a jest, but wanted to fight right on the spot."[41] Ty would later understand, confessing that "I didn't understand human nature and my success came too quickly."[42]

Achievement came in 1906, but not respect from Tiger players. Cobb would bat .316 with twenty-three stolen bases. When rookie Ed Willett moved in to share a room with Ty, other players cornered him and convinced Ed to move out. Grantland Rice observed, "From the first, Cobb's life was a constant war, and Ty lived in a hostile camp."[43] Early in the season after a good day at the plate, using two black bats he had brought from Augusta, he arrived at the stadium to find them missing. Someone pointed outside the fence where he discovered that some teammates had chopped them up with a hatchet, leaving his lucky bats in splinters. Writer H. G. Salsinger said that Cobb obviously "found it difficult to get into the ways and habit of his team-mates. He did not like them and they detested him. He was pretty much alone."[44]

This loneliness allowed Ty to concentrate on baseball full time. Results were unheard of—twenty-three consecutive years batting over .300, three over .400, 895 stolen bases over that period, and a Most Valuable Player title in 1911. Cobb's hitting secret lay in his eyes. To protect them, managers would shift him from one fielding position to the other to protect his eyes from the glaring sun. Ty held some pseudoscientific beliefs that helped his eyesight. He thought coffee enhanced his vision and would always drink some before each game. Milk seemed to blur his gaze and he avoided it before game time. Chewing gum was to be avoided because it caused muscles around the eyes to be overworked, hence interfering with clarity. Cobb tried to sleep from ten to twelve hours at night to rest those precious eyes.

In an extensive feature on Cobb in 1910, Harry Daniel commented on his extraordinary speed on the basepaths by the left-handed batter, writing that "he is so fast that he can get to first many times with a hit that almost any other player would fail on. He starts for first the very instant the bat touches the ball and he can get down to the initial bag on the puniest of bunts." Daniel concluded, "It is safe to say that he is the fleetest and most daring baserunner that ever dashed around the game."[45] Ty's reputation as a daring runner was well known throughout the American League. In a game against the St. Louis Browns, he bunted, reached first safely, and headed for second on a wild throw. Catcher Hank Severeid had run to back up the first baseman, but when he saw Cobb racing toward second, he screamed, "Somebody guard home plate!"[46]

Harry Tuttle, trainer for the Tigers, had the unenviable task of keeping Ty healthy and in top shape to steal bases and cover his part of the outfield. Tuttle explained the effect of sliding so often: "From his ankles to his waist Cobb is simply covered with bruises and scratches. None of them is bad enough to interfere with his playing and they are not very painful, but he is sliding and tearing around so much that his legs are always covered with scratches and scars."[47] Tuttle said that he used more medical plaster and adhesive tape on Ty than the rest of the Tiger roster combined. There was more to worry about than sliding into bases. During the 1909 World Series against the Pirates, Cobb reached first and yelled to shortstop Hans Wagner to get ready. He was. Ty slid into second, Hans took a perfect throw, and slammed his glove into Ty's mouth for the put out. Ty went for stitches.

An encounter in the early hours of September 4, 1909, received national attention. Cobb was out late after the Tigers lost a double-header in Cleveland. He got into an argument with the elevator boy and hit him, leading to a confrontation from the night watchman, George Stanfield. Cobb cursed, Stanfield struck him, and a struggle ensued. Cobb pulled a knife and drove it through Stanfield's hand. The watchman regained his feet, backed up, and pulled a pistol. That was enough for Cobb and he went to his room. Within days, Cobb had been charged with intent to kill in criminal court and faced a suit in civil court demanding $5,000 for Stanfield's injuries. To stem the unfavorable publicity and make the civil case go away, Tigers president Frank Navin called long distance and agreed to pay Stanfield's expenses with an additional lump settlement. In criminal court, the charge was reduced to assault and battery with a fine of $100.

An even bigger media explosion burst on May 15, 1912. In a game against the New York Highlanders, Cobb was ruthlessly heckled by hometown fans. According to him, one loudmouth yelled at Donie Bush and Davy Jones "that they ought to be ashamed to be playing with a 'half n——.' He said that the center fielder of the Detroit team was 'part coon,' and added a few more curse words."[48] Amid a cacophony of yells and boos, Ty picked out the man he thought responsible—Claude Lueker, who worked in the office of Sheriff Tom Foley after having lost one hand and some fingers off the other. Cobb jumped the fence and waded into the crowd until he could strike Lueker, knock him down, and begin kicking him. When one of Lueker's friends screamed, "Don't kick him, he has no hands," Cobb yelled back, "I don't care if he has no feet!"[49] Ty was quickly pried off Lueker, who was bleeding from multiple cuts to his head, side, and shins, most of which were caused by his spikes. Cobb was ejected, received a $50 fine, and was suspended. It remains one of the ugliest incidents in Major League baseball.

When this suspension was announced, the remainder of the Tigers held a secret meeting, voted to support Cobb, and notified Ban Johnson, league president, that they would not play another game until their star was reinstated. Their reason was simple, "He was fully justified in his action, as no one could stand such personal abuse from anyone."[50] Eighteen Tigers refused to play on May 18 and the manager was forced to cobble together a team to keep management from forfeiting at a cost of $5,000. Two Tigers took the field against Philadelphia, reinforced by seven players from St. Joseph College, who each received $10 for a game they lost 24 to 2. Cobb broke the strike by telling his teammates to go back on the diamond where he finally joined them on May 26.

The Tigers had gone to the 1907, 1908, and 1909 World Series, but would not go to another until years after Ty Cobb had retired. In spring of 1913 President Navin got to the heart of the situation: "Mr. Cobb did not make baseball; baseball made him. A player cannot be bigger than the game which creates him."[51] Navin continued to vent his frustrations: "If Mr. Cobb does not like a room a hotel clerk gives him, he quits the club for a week. If he doesn't like what a silly man in the grandstand yells at him, he punches his face and is again out of the game. He quits the game when we are fighting for a pennant and publicly stated that he would not play with his comrade D. Jones on account of some misunderstanding with that player. If he doesn't feel like practicing, he stays away from the park. He has grown to believe that his greatness precludes his being a subject to club discipline."[52] Suspended by the team, Ty was reinstated by the National Commission after paying a $50 fine.

As his statistics soared to unimaginable heights, Ty Cobb "exuded so much personal magnetism that fans could not keep their eyes off him."[53] Clashes with authority, whether in the form of rules, regulations, laws or persons assigned to enforce them, continued for the remainder of his career. In June 1914 Cobb's wife was not satisfied with a purchase of some fish. She returned them to the market but complained to Ty that she had been rudely treated. Several hours later he appeared in the market brandishing a .32 pistol. Cobb forced the butcher to telephone his wife and apologize. Whisked away in a patrol wagon, Cobb pled his charge down to disturbing the peace, paid a $50 fine, and hurried away from reporters.

For someone who had been christened The Georgia Peach, Ty Cobb never acted like a sweet Elberta. His remaining years in baseball were checkered by suspensions and fines. Tiger management finally got rid of Cobb after 1926, sending him to the Philadelphia Athletics where his body began to fail although his batting average clocked in at .357 in 1927 and .323 in 1928, his last season. A misanthrope nearly all his playing days, sound investments had made him a millionaire and he became somewhat philanthropic in his retirement. He built a hospital in Royston, Georgia, where he had lived. Ty also endowed a college scholarship fund, the only requirements being for a student be a resident of Georgia and desire a university education.

Ty spent his life after baseball hunting, fishing, and playing golf. He eventually moved to California, but wherever he lived, Cobb had his memories: "His home is a picture gallery and the walls are covered with pictures of himself, other baseball stars, United States Presidents, celebrities of all kinds. His scrapbooks are filled with action pictures. The walls of his den are covered with animals he has killed, bear skins, tanned deer hides."[54] Writer Jim Murray summed up Cobb's life: "Ty Cobb died as he had lived—lonely, defiant, cantankerous, shunned and feared. He went to his grave as he had come to every other home plate in his life—spikes up, a snarl on his lips."[55]

Ty Cobb and the citizens of Royston may have remembered his baseball career, but baseball had forgotten him by the time he died on July 17, 1961. His last words were "Nobody gives a damn."[56] As evidence of his observation, baseball was represented at his funeral by just three old players—Mickey Cochrane, Ray Schalk, and Nap Rucker—and Sid Keener of the Baseball Hall of Fame. Yet fans all over the country were devastated, as if Cobb had invented Christmas. Newspapers, radio, and television would broadcast news of Ty's death but it was personal at Royston. As the hearse moved along the road, farmers stopped plowing to stand silently, families in front of brick houses and shanties stood without saying a word, boys took off their ball caps to show respect. Royston had sent Tyrus Raymond Cobb off to conquer the baseball world and now he was coming home. Although beloved by Royston residents, Ty Cobb's fiery temper and constant scuffles kept him from being the first baseball superstar.

Walter Perry "Big Train" Johnson

Walter Perry Johnson was another candidate for first baseball superstar. The beginning of Johnson's rise to baseball immortality can be best expressed in his own words, from an interview given in 1923:

I was born November 6, 1887, on a farm four miles out of Humbolt, Kansas. We had no near neighbors; there weren't any kids to play with, so up to the time I was fourteen years old I had never heard of baseball.

Then my family moved to Fullerton, California, in the oil fields, and I started to high school. All the boys played baseball there, so I took it up and I liked it—I always have.

I started my first game of baseball as catcher. Halfway through the game the kids thought I could throw pretty good so I was put in as pitcher—and I've pitched ever since.

I'll never forget the first game I pitched for the high school. I got beat 21 to 0.

The next Saturday our club imported a catcher who could corral the balls and we played the opposing team on its home grounds. In fifteen innings the score stood 0 to 0. I was sixteen then, and I guess that's the greatest game I ever played.

After leaving high school I went to work in the oil fields and attended business college in Santa Ana. One day I was a spectator at a semi-professional game. The manager of one team asked me to pitch for him. I pitched about a dozen games during that year and won a good part of them. I received about ten dollars for the whole series—and that was big money to me then, I tell you.

In 1906 a friend of mine who was in Tacoma, Washington, persuaded me to join that team in the Northwestern League. But the San Francisco earthquake broke up the Pacific Coast League so the Northwestern could get all the seasoned players it wanted, and all us young fellows were let out without being given a chance to do much.

Following that I went to a little town in Idaho called Weiser. I dropped off the train and asked the way to baseball headquarters. At that instant I saw my friend from Tacoma on the street—he had said he would be in Weiser—and he took me over and got me on one of the clubs. I played two months in 1906. I went back home that autumn and played a little here and there. The New York Giants were training in California that next spring and they were willing to take me on. But I didn't know anything about the Giants and I was afraid they might drop me off in the sticks somewhere without money enough to get back home, so I wouldn't go with them.[57]

Thus, the Giants missed a once-in-a-lifetime opportunity to have two future Hall of Famers—Christy Mathewson and Walter Johnson—pitching in the same rotation.

If the Giants did not want Johnson, the Washington Senators did. But the phenom from Weiser was no fool. Before signing a contract, he made sure that his travel expenses included a roundtrip ticket. Umpire Billy Evans happened to be chatting with a couple friends outside the old Regent House when Walter Johnson arrived in the nation's capital. Evans would always remember his first introduction to this new kid from Idaho: "I could see he was well over six feet, despite the fact that there was a bit of a stoop at the shoulders. His features were clean cut as if chiseled. He was good to look at. His arms were tremendously long. He was in perfect condition. There wasn't an ounce of fat on his giant physique."[58] Johnson had spent nearly a week on his journey from Idaho, sticking his head out the train window to watch America's countryside pass by. He appeared to be just another country bumpkin, six feet tall with wavy brown hair, stars in his light blue eyes, and hope in his heart.

Johnson pitched his first game for the Senators on August 2, 1907, but soon learned that Washington, DC, was no Weiser, Idaho. During his first three seasons he compiled a record of 32 and 48, rather a good showing for the Senators of that era. Walter would later tell how he managed to stay away from the night life in Washington and on the road:

> In Weiser about every other business place was a saloon, but the sports of the town always told me to take care of myself and leave cards and liquor alone. Then, after I came to Washington, I noticed that the fellows who played the liquor and bright lights were "dopey" on the diamond next day, had slumps and all that, and yet they were fine fellows. They seemed to want to see me make good and they always advised me to "lay off the rough stuff." I followed their advice—some of the very chaps who ruined their game by their habits.
>
> Reputation has a lot to do with a man's success, I figure. I had a friend who liked to visit summer gardens, listen to the music and drink beer. I went out with him a few times, but I drank ginger ale. I had not been out with him more than half a dozen times until word reached the manager of the club that "young Johnson is playing the night life." So, I saw I couldn't even keep the company of visiting the beer gardens without getting a bad reputation. I took to staying in my hotel and reading a lot.[59]

According to information published in the *Congressional Record* on the fiftieth anniversary of Walter Johnson's first game with the Senators, all of the following were true: "Among the virtues of Walter Johnson were his modesty and his decency. He never smoked or drank. He never beefed at an umpire or argued with a teammate. He did not swear, and he never had the semblance of a swelled head."[60]

Johnson explained how he seemed to be so calm during games, it being a matter of self-control to avoid clashes with the umpires: "Throughout my entire career I have tried, and largely succeeded, in keeping my temper down. It isn't that I haven't a temper. I have, and I showed it when I lost [my] second game of the [1924] World's Series. But the fact of the matter is I have tried to be master of myself, realizing that I had to do it in order to pitch the right kind of ball for my club."[61] On rare occasions Walter lost his composure and would burst out with a stream of obscenities, such as "Goodness gracious, sakes alive."[62]

One day Billy Evans asked Johnson what his secret to success had been over his career, he answered simply, "Play fair and work hard."[63] He elaborated on this question in another interview: "To be a successful baseball player a man must have great endurance, indomitable will and that baseball instinct which enables him to do the right thing at the right time. If a pitcher, he must have speed, control, curves, change of pace and the ability to size up the batsman. And it goes without saying he must possess a 'pitching arm.'"[64]

Everyone agreed that Walter Johnson's greatest attribute was speed. This was aided by wide, bony shoulders and unusually long arms that gave him leverage for his fast ones. His fingers were so long they could touch his thumb while holding a baseball. Bill Dinneen, former pitcher and umpire, claimed, "Nobody could ever throw a baseball as fast as Johnson."[65] When putting a little extra velocity on the ball, Walter had a habit of snorting like a locomotive. This may have been the reason that Grantland Rice nicknamed him Big Train. According to Ring Lardner, one opposing manager was supposed to have said, "I always know when it's Johnson's turn to pitch because that's the day half my ball club comes up sick and can't play."[66]

Gabby Street, his catcher for several years, remembered those fast balls: "His control and his fast one was straight," boasting, "I could have caught him in a rocking chair."[67] Over twenty-one years of pitching, Johnson compiled a record of 417–279 for a winning percentage of .599. He was honored with two Most Valuable Player awards and strung together ten seasons of at least twenty wins. Johnson struck out 3,509 batters in his career and compiled a 2.17 earned run average. He was the fourth pitcher in baseball history to strike out four batters in a single inning. In a game with the Indians, Walter torched two fast balls past Ray Chapman who saw only a pair of blurs. He turned in disgust and started for the bench, yelling to the umpire, "You can have the third one."[68] Grantland Rice would sum up Johnson's strength: "Bullet speed, too fast for the eye to follow—for the hands to match. The only pitcher who never needed a curve."[69] Rice could describe Walter's speed with two lines from a poem:

> How do they know what Johnson's got?
> Nobody's seen it yet.[70]

Ray Schalk, catcher for the White Sox, remembered that by 1912, "Johnson's straight ball was whipping in there like sleet in Labrador."[71] Baseball reporter Bugs Baer disagreed with these claims, explaining, "Centrifugal force, rotary attraction, gravity, air currents and concentrated essence of muzzle velocity all combined to make every throw bend like a snake swallowing a sofa spring."[72]

News of Walter Johnson's prowess reached around the world, from Japan to Europe, and all across America. Guy Butler, Miami sports editor, explained his conundrum about picking the greatest Major League pitcher: "Walter Johnson was one of my idols. As a teen-aged youngster I became a great admirer of the Washington pitching ace and albeit I held Christy Mathewson, contemporary mound standout with the Giants, as my idol of idols, I always conceded that the Humbolt Thunderbolt from Kansas was a bang-up No. 2. And in later years, after Matty was through, when the speedball king continued to burn 'em over and crack record after record, I finally had to admit that Johnson, with a far weaker club than Matty had behind him down the years, probably had a thin shade on Big Six."[73] Christy Mathewson thought the world of Johnson, saying in December 1910, "I never fully appreciated what wonderful natural ability Walter Johnson had until I saw him in action in the closing weeks of last season. He is unquestionably one of the grandest twirlers baseball has ever known," then added, "It was from these observations that I reached the conclusion that Johnson will go down in history as one of the best ever."[74] To reinforce Mathewson's opinion, Walter threw a no-hitter against the Red Sox on July 1, 1920.

When Johnson won the World Series title for the Senators in 1924 as a relief pitcher, his speed had begun to fade. Support from his team had faded long before that. Writer Joe Williams was only half-joking when he wrote, "At that time the Washington club consisted of Walter Johnson, fifteen baseball suits filled indiscriminately with strange and curious specimens of mankind, a dugout that leaked and a water bottle in which two vagabond pollywogs basked discontentedly."[75] But by the time of his retirement after the 1927 season, he was a celebrity in the nation's capital. He had even married Hazel Roberts, daughter of Congressman Edwin Roberts of Nevada. Humorist Will Rogers said of Johnson, "He will return home with as much Glory as a Congressman who has succeeded in swindling the Government Taxpayers out of money for a new Post Office Building for a town where 4 picture Post Cards in one mail constitute a rush."[76] Johnson managed the Senators from 1929 to 1932 and the Indians from 1933 to 1935, ending with a record of 529–432.

Walter bought a 460-acre farm outside Germantown, Maryland, where he raised cattle and would admit, "I'm happy out here. I was raised on a farm and never have gotten the dirt out of my shoes. I guess I'll always be a country boy."[77] A visitor was overwhelmed by Johnson menagerie: "In addition to his cattle, Walter has many horses, including some thoroughbred racing animals. He has about a dozen dogs, some excellent fox hounds and some valuable Irish terriers. Ducks and chickens, turkeys, pheasants and peacocks roam over the land around his barn."[78] His wife died suddenly in 1930, leaving her husband with a brood of young children to raise. Johnson failed in an attempt to run for Congress, and enjoyed teaching young boys how to play baseball, but he was happiest when strolling his farm in denim overalls and knee-length boots. Stricken with a brain tumor in April, Walter Johnson lapsed into a coma and died on December 10, 1946.

Speaking through his press secretary, President Harry Truman sent his sympathies: "He was one of his athletic heroes. He admired him both as an athlete and as a man, as did millions of other persons."[79] Although notice by a president is nice, it was left to Ken Smith, former sports reporter and later director of the National Baseball Hall of Fame and Museum, to craft the most deeply moving eulogy: "It seems that Walter Johnson will remain forever the perfect baseball player in the memories and words of people who knew him. He held a unique and enviable place in the hearts of all fans, a symbol of Christ-like patience, fortitude and hope in the face of more tragedy than it seems right for one mortal to bear."[80] Although Walter Johnson shared many personal characteristics with Christy Mathewson, as well as extraordinary skills, he never developed a nationwide following among baseball fans. There were three important reasons for this. First, Mathewson got there ahead of Johnson and had gained national attention following the 1905 World Series, two years prior to Johnson joining the Senators. Second, Washington's team was so atrocious that for years it aspired only to reaching a fourth-place finish in the American League. Third, Johnson, like Hans Wagner in Pittsburgh, played in a Washington market with only a few newspapers that concentrated on politics.

George Herman "Babe" Ruth

A last candidate to challenge Christy Mathewson for the title of baseball's first superstar was George Herman "Babe" Ruth, who began his American League career as a pitcher for the Red Sox in 1914 and ended as a slugging outfielder for the Yankees. Ken Smith would rightly assert, "He was the biggest, the most glamorous and the best copy that sports writers ever enjoyed. He was good copy even after he retired, always worth a story."[81] Ruth was acknowledged as the biggest attraction in baseball. The reason was obvious: "There was an appeal in Ruth because of the Americanism of his story: the start from an orphanage in Baltimore and a rise to headline fame possible only in this country where a lusty bat can earn far more than a skilled trade."[82]

Born in Baltimore on February 6, 1895, by the age of seven Ruth had become recalcitrant to the point that his parents placed him in St. Mary's Industrial School for Boys. Babe would explain the purpose of this reform school: "In thinking of St. Mary's, people unjustly lost sight of the fact that the boys were there to be trained, not to be punished. They forgot that many of the boys were homeless, friendless little orphans being befriended, taught trades and kept out of mischief.

Many of the lads had never done a wrong thing. Others had played hookey."[83] Spanking by his father had no effect, so St. Mary's would be George's home for twelve years under the oversight of Brother Matthias Boutlier. Days at St. Mary's were filled with church services, classrooms, learning to be a shirtmaker, playing baseball, and repeated punishments for chewing tobacco, smoking, and drinking beer.

In 1914 Ruth signed with the minor league Baltimore Orioles, was purchased by the Red Sox, who promptly sent him down to play with the minor league Providence Grays, then came back to pitch a couple of games for Boston. His record in the minors was 23–8 and 2–1 with the Sox. Early in 1915 he persuaded Cleveland's Shoeless Joe Jackson to share his stance at the plate, where to place his feet, and how to hold the bat at its very end. As his popularity grew, other players, as well as boys across the country, began to emulate his style so that baseball quickly changed from a game of bunts, stolen bases, and sacrifice flies to wham-bam hit it with all your might.

Babe Ruth was not an attractive man. He had brown eyes and black hair with a face that was called anything from moon-faced to dog-butt ugly. Ruth also developed what would now be called a beer gut and supported himself on spindly legs atop what seemed to be a woman's ankles. George's nickname at St. Mary's was "n—— lips,"[84] which became over time shortened to n—— because of his wide nose and big lips. There is no indication that Babe had any Black ancestors and Black ballplayers thought him merely unattractive. According to Buck O'Neil, star of the Negro Leagues, he said simply, "To us, Ruth was a white man. He wasn't the only white man with a flat nose and full lips."[85]

One woman who was not offended by Babe's appearance was Helen Woodford, who worked as a waitress at a lunchroom around the corner from Putnam's Hotel where he then resided. They double-dated with a friend of Helen's and moved in together in a Back Bay apartment, went to Providence, and returned to Boston late in 1915 when they married. As Ruth got bigger contracts, they moved to more upscale apartments and in 1919 the couple bought a sixteen-room house on a large farm near Sudbury, Massachusetts. This is where Babe found a sanctuary: "He fished through the ice of the nearby ponds, hunted, trapped, cut down trees and split his own kindling. It was a common sight for passersby to see the famous ball player trundling a wheelbarrow full of wood or swinging an axe. The healthful outdoor exercise and the early hours of the country worked wonders on him. Some of his neighbors were surprised at his versatility, as he seemed able to paint a house, do carpenter work, build a stone wall or fill an ice house, with equal ease."[86] For a diversion, Babe and Helen would play poker with their chauffeur and maid for burned matches. In the off-season he was as happy as a puppy at Sudbury Farm.

Fellow ballplayers were appalled by Ruth's crude behavior while with the Red Sox. Ernie Shore announced to management that he could no longer room with Babe, explaining, "I told him he was using my toothbrush, and he said, 'That's all right. I'm not particular.'" Ernie also complained, "A man wants some privacy in the bathroom."[87] Larry Gardner would queasily recall, "One of the first times I saw Ruth, the guy was lying on the floor, being screwed by a prostitute. He was smoking a cigar and eating peanuts, and this woman was working on him."[88] Babe's attitude on sex never changed. Later in his career he would assert, "I'll promise to go easier on drinking, and get to bed earlier, but not for you, fifty thousand dollars, or two hundred and fifty thousand dollars, will I give up women. They're too much fun."[89]

Babe Ruth's career with Boston began as a pitcher, but the organization came to realize that he would be more valuable as a batter in every game rather than during a pitching rotation. That is not to downgrade his pitching ability which, from 1914 to 1919, resulted in a record of 89–46. But Ruth became a magnet for fans in Boston and respect for the game diminished as his reputation grew. In a home game against the Senators on June 23, 1917, Babe began by pitching four balls to the first batter. An argument ensued with umpire Brick Owens, who tossed Babe from the game. Ruth responded, "You run me out and I will come in and bust you on the nose."[90] When Owens again told him to get out, Babe came running in and punched him in the head. It took several policemen to finally pull him off the umpire. For this grievous infraction, Ruth was suspended for ten days and fined $100. There would be many more fines and suspensions to follow. Ruth's year ended badly when his touring car slammed into an electric trolley car that November. This accident occurred at 6:05 a.m. when Babe, with a woman not his wife as companion and apparently driving too fast, derailed the trolley, broke several windows, and destroyed the vestibule.

Breaking rules and regulations would become common practice for Babe as he also began a descent into decadence that would rival that of Roman emperors. On June 17, 1915, he was done in by his appetite for lobster in a game against the St. Louis Browns. To celebrate an imagined rain day, Babe began "eating a flock of broiled live lobsters . . . and went at the crustaceans in a fashion that would indicate that he suspected no more of them were to be trapped."[91] Leading 9–1 when the Browns came to bat in the eighth inning, the lobsters suddenly became St. Louis fans and started cheering in his stomach. Ruth virtually collapsed and gave up seven runs before being yanked in favor of a relief pitcher. Stories like this began to multiply over his career, such as the following from Chicago, dated June 5, 1924: "Babe Ruth is the possessor of another crown, baseball writers here agree. The King of Swat challenged 12 hot-dog sandwiches and five bottles of soft drinks during a stop at Steubenville, O., en route here from New York, and later reported a side-ache to the club trainer."[92] Babe blamed his discomfort as coming from a bruise sustained in a recent game.

From 1914 to 1919, Babe Ruth hit forty-nine home runs and drove in 224 runs. But he wanted to stop pitching and play the outfield. Manager Ed Barrow decided that Ruth would pitch first and pinch hit and play outfield second. A reporter commented on the ensuing confrontation: "Reports of an imminent clash between Barrow and Ruth had been circulating for a week. The star batsman had formed his own idea of training rules and what they were for and, we are told, flaunted his disregard for the rules before the other players. Naturally Barrow could not keep up discipline and condone Ruth's action, so he had to suspend Ruth, for which action he must be commended."[93] Babe was suspended for the game on June 30, costing him about sixty dollars. In essence, "Barrow did not like the punctuality, or rather the lack of punctuality, of Babe as regards the hour he should tuck his massive form between the sheets o' nights, and the big fellow did not like the way Manager Ed verbally chastised him."[94] The last straw had come when Barrow entered Babe's room at 6:00 a.m. only to find him tucked in and smoking a pipe. Barrow ripped off the covers and found Babe fully dressed, including his shoes.

Ruth had a great year in 1919, batting .322 and leading the Major Leagues in home runs (29), runs (103), and runs batted in (113). Red Sox rooters hoped for better things in 1920, but were stunned when Harry Frazee, team president, announced on January 6 that Ruth had been sold to the Yankees. Frazee explained his decision: "The other players have little incentive or encouragement for great effort when the spectators can see only one man in the game, and so the one man has an upsetting influence on the others. It rarely does, and never should, win a championship."[95] Fans had placed Ruth on a pedestal after the 1919 season, but management considered him selfish, disobedient, and greedy. Frazee thought him unmanageable and a detriment to the team despite his individual statistics: "Ruth has been insubordinate on occasions and has insisted upon having his own way to such an extent that he endangered the discipline of the whole squad."[96]

Concerns about Ruth's behavior became apparent in an exhibition game on March 20, 1920. As the Yankees left the field after the ninth inning, a loud-mouthed spectator who had been heckling Babe all game yelled that he was a "piece of cheese."[97] Apparently that phrase was more derogatory then than it is currently, so Babe, supported by coach Charley O'Leary, headed into the stands. There they were confronted by a Florida cracker who pulled out a knife. Ruth claimed it was a Bowie knife, but witnesses said it was simply a pen knife. Pitcher Ernie Shore stepped between the antagonists and pulled Ruth away. Determined not to lose the encounter, Babe yelled to "lay off ball players in the future."[98] Umpires completely ignored the ruckus.

Bill McGeehan stunned the nation with news that Babe Ruth had come close to being killed on July 7 when his touring car crashed near Wawa, Pennsylvania. En route from Baltimore to Philadelphia on what is now US 1, he was driving fast early in the morning and pulled to the right to avoid an oncoming car, went into a ditch, and overturned. Owners Jacob Ruppert and Tillinghast Huston were greatly relieved, although they had insured Ruth for more than his purchase price.

Babe continued to have difficulties with autos. During the 1920s he had a series of run-ins with the law over his constant speeding. He was caught driving fifty miles an hour on the Harlem Speedway, sixty on his way from Boston to Sudbury, and "driving along Commonwealth Av at a fast rate, cutting in and out of traffic."[99] In 1921 Ruth was sentenced to a day in jail for speeding on Riverside Drive, but the day only consisted of six hours so he was released in time for the afternoon game against Cleveland. This Yankee jailbird was followed by an inquisitive reporter who watched as "Babe violated the self-same speed law before he had been out ten minutes. He covered the nine miles to the Polo Grounds in about 19 minutes."[100] Nabbed again for speeding in 1924, it was discovered that Babe's Massachusetts driving license had been suspended since 1914 after he had struck a man in Cambridge. Ruth also admitted that he had failed to register his vehicle since 1920.

This disregard for the law carried over to his Yankee career. In violation of the National Commission's rule that pennant-winning teams were not allowed to barnstorm after a World Series, Ruth and a few of his teammates were suspended for the first six weeks of the 1922 season. On the sixth day after his return, in a game at Chicago, Babe was called out at second while trying to stretch a single into a double. He protested violently, then threw a handful of dirt into the face and hair of umpire George Hildebrand who immediately tossed him from the game. As Babe headed for the bench amid a roar of jeers, "he stopped and invited the entire right field section of the grandstand to come onto the field and have it out with no holds barred."[101] One foghorned rooter became particularly obnoxious (and probably vulgar), so Babe jumped over the dugout and went for the man who wisely fled. Ban Johnson, president of the American League, fined Ruth $200 and removed him from his position as captain of the Yankees.

While Babe Ruth continued on his well-known path to baseball fame and fortune, his arrogance, drinking, smoking, gambling, and excessive womanizing spiraled out of control. Columnist Earl Wilson told how Babe "could destroy a maximum of liquor with a minimum of effect."[102] This led one reporter to comment, "The baseball writers have helped to construct Ruth as the ideal baseball player, in so far as his work on the field alone has been concerned, merely by reporting his baseball feats." He then compared Babe to Christy Mathewson: "When Big Six was in his prime with the Giants he was the beau ideal as a baseball star and as a man as well. Never the breath of scandal about Matty. Never any stories of late parties, insinuation about loose conduct and suits by alleged outraged womanhood."[103] Writers who covered the Yankees could keep quiet about Babe's off-field antics, but when news reporters got hold of a Ruth story and put it on page one, it all blew up in 1925.

In almost a perfect storm, two stories, one professional and one personal, emerged in the waning days of summer that year. The first to break came on August 29 when manager Miller Huggins suspended Babe indefinitely and fined him $5,000 for "misconduct off the field."[104] While New York went berserk over this news, coverage was flashed across the country. The *Baltimore Sun* carried the story on page one and recounted how the slugger had been on a sort of double-secret probation since June. Babe's violation of team restrictions on the last road trip to St. Louis had left Huggins with no choice. When a reporter asked the manager if that meant drinking, Huggins responded, "Of course it means drinking and it means a lot of other things besides. There are various kinds of misconduct."[105] Babe would plead his case with the baseball commissioner and owner Jacob Ruppert, but both rebuffed him. He found no friendly face in the office of President Ban Johnson who stated publicly, "Ruth has the mind of a 15-year-old boy and must be made to understand where he belongs. The American league is no place for a player who dissipates and misbehaves."[106]

A second story dropped just after his suspension began, this one alluding to Huggins's reference to various kinds of misconduct. Rumors circulated in the press that Helen Ruth planned to divorce Babe and receive a $100,000 settlement. She immediately called her husband to tell him that these tales were not true, but did say "she wanted to discuss with Babe several matters, including his friendship with Mrs. Claire Hodgson, beautiful young widow, of which Mrs. Ruth said she 'knew absolutely nothing.'"[107] A veteran of Ziegfeld Follies and Vaudeville, Claire went into hiding as soon as her photograph began to appear in newspapers coast to coast. When her photo popped up in Oakland, California, the caption read: "Introducing MRS. CLAIRE HODGSON, a rich widow, who is alleged to have been in company with Babe Ruth, slugging outfielder of the New York Yankees. When Ruth was suspended by the Yankees and the name of the rich widow mentioned, the Bambino had to do a lot of explaining to his wife."[108] To prove that bad luck comes in threes, on September 6 Babe's English bull terrier Dot got loose and killed a neighbor's prize cow.

Helen Ruth died in a fire under suspicious circumstances on January 11, 1929. Babe and Helen were both Catholics and had spent several years living apart. Following her death and subsequent unpleasant newspaper coverage, Helen's mother exclaimed, "If they continue to blacken her, I will have something to say about that fat slob and everything I say we can prove."[109] A sister had gone with Helen to a Yankees game months prior to her death where the aggrieved wife pointed to a blonde in a first-row box seat and whispered, "That's Claire Hodgson, who broke up my home."[110] After Helen's death, Babe waited a respectful length of time and wed Claire three months later.

Little attention has been paid here to Babe Ruth's statistics and later life since they are either well known or readily available. His face had been seen so often in America that Babe almost seemed liked a member of the family: "Babe Ruth could have lived to be 150 and tottered into Yankee Stadium or down a street in any city or hamlet in the country on age-tortured legs and there would have been a grand welcome for him. Picturesque in his misshapen bulk and vast expanse of swarthy countenance, he was utterly unforgettable."[111] There is no doubt that he spent a good share of his income and time on philanthropic causes, especially those involving young children, often being called just a big, overgrown kid. One writer would correct that assertion in 1925 during the uproar over Babe's suspension, Claire Hodgson, and his

English bull terrier: "That's pure and unadulterated gush. Ruth isn't an overgrown boy any longer. He has been a voter for nine years. He has knocked about the country a lot, seeing and hearing things—and doing things. He no longer can be defended with that 'big, overgrown boy' mush."[112]

Paul Gallico was one man who confessed that the newspaper industry was responsible for Ruth's actions: "The sport writers who have known of Ruth's shortcomings for many years and have deliberately withheld the truth, are as much to blame as the Babe for his troubles, because Master Ruth has been nursed along to the belief that he could get away with it; that because he was Ruth the newspapers would keep quiet about his behavior, and that because he was needed by the Yankees, Miller Huggins would condone his actions."[113] Gallico continued, "Thus we all carry a share of Mr. Ruth's disgrace, although I am not inclined to lose any sleep over it."[114]

Frank G. Menke also admitted that the true Babe Ruth had been hidden from the public for years by sycophants who sought to push a baseball story rather than report on his whoring, gluttony, gambling, and excessive drinking: "All that has been written of him and his conduct off the ball fields is news—surprising, shocking—to the baseball multitudes. It is not news to the newspapermen. For several years they have known of Ruth's conduct; they have known of his habits, of his wanderings from the narrow lanes that confined a clean athlete; they have known Babe Ruth as he really was."[115] Reporters kept Ruth's secrets to themselves. But there was no betterment in his conduct, "He became a bit more swagger, a bit more daring in his athletic misdeeds, a bit more brazen—and then the lightning hit him"[116]

Babe's performance on the baseball diamond following the messy stories of 1925 regained his hold on the American sports fans. For the next six years he had a batting average of .354 and averaged 50 home runs, 147 runs, and 155 runs batted in. Ruth led the Yankee team of 1927, famously called Murderers Row, with 60 home runs despite missing four games. After leading New York to the 1932 World Championship, his output began to decline. He played sparingly for the Boston Braves in 1935 and showed up for a couple of sinecures in the front office. Retired from baseball the following year, he enjoyed his Sudbury farm, golfed, and made personal appearances as a source of income. He died of cancer on August 16, 1948, a shrunken shadow of his former self. Babe Ruth never did clean up his personal life, which precludes him being named the first baseball superstar.

COMPILING CHRISTY'S LIFE STORY

Following the death of Christy Mathewson on October 7, 1925, an outpouring of grief and reminiscences appeared in newspapers across the country. It seemed that every writer who had ever known Christy or had written a column about one of his ball games wanted to eulogize this fallen star. But it was impossible to catch the essence of Matty's life in a single newspaper column. Jane Mathewson, his widow, was determined to provide the reading public with a more intimate portrait of her husband.

Sportswriter Bozeman Bulger was the obvious choice to write this narrative. He had known Christy for twenty years, roomed with him on road trips, and watched him pitch more games than any other person on earth. Bulger was one of his closest friends and the pair had been virtually inseparable for two decades. A series of articles titled "The Life Story of Christy Mathewson" would appear across the country under agreements reached by the Bell Syndicate. Newspapers advertised these stories as full of pathos, humor, homely philosophy, and tragedy.

Bozeman was the perfect writer to present an insider's view of Christy's personal life. At the time, he was among a trio of the most prominent sportswriters in New York, the others being Grantland Rice and Damon Runyon. It was only natural that Jane would approach Bozeman to write what would be styled the official biography of her late spouse. It was not simply a Bulger production. Jane contributed three chapters of recollections, while others were written by Christy himself, apparently chapters for an autobiography that were discovered among his papers after his death. This editor has rearranged the chapters in a sort of chronological order and inserted several more of Bulger's earlier articles to fill in gaps to keep the story flowing. Italics show where there is a transition between authors. There have been minor stylistic modifications to standardize spelling, capitalization, and grammar. First names have been silently inserted for the convenience of readers unfamiliar with men from this era.

Christy Mathewson was known to every boy in America who ever played baseball in a vacant lot or on a crowded city street. His life and death presaged that of another famous ballplayer who would die too early. I am talking about the subject of my first baseball book, *Lou Gehrig: The Lost Memoir*. Both were college men who reached the pinnacle of their profession by constant discipline and attention to every detail of their careers. They also shared character traits such as having few close friends, being bashful in public settings, and regretting their ability to enjoy the company of others. Both men detested being called heroes in the nation's press. Each man loved to read, but there were also differences between the pair. Christy loved to hunt, golf, and indulge in cerebral contests like checkers, chess, and bridge. When not with his mother, Lou liked to go for long walks, ride rollercoasters, and spend time alone until his marriage to Eleanor. Each man died relatively young, Mathewson at age forty-five of tuberculosis and Gehrig at thirty-seven of amyotrophic lateral sclerosis (ALS). Upon Christy's death in 1925, the mantel of the ideal American ballplayer was passed to Lou, who had played his first full season with the Yankees that year.

Largely forgotten by the general public nearly a hundred years after his death, Christy Mathewson was an inspiration to all who watched his exploits on the diamond or followed his distinguished career in the sports pages. John McGraw said of him, "Mathewson's real greatness in the game was in the example he set for young fellows and the impression he left on the minds of the public. He gave our profession a dignity that it needed and was slow to acquire."[1] Sportswriter Bill

McGeehan noted that it was not just Christy's ability or his numerous records that appealed to fans, but "the character of the man."[2] He had it all—showmanship, color, and drawing power. Opposing clubs would schedule Ladies Days for games in which Christy would pitch and women would come in throngs, driving up gate receipts to see the blond god who also pitched. Fans from Miami to Spokane, from Boston to Los Angeles, could hardly wait to read the sports sections of their papers to find out how Mathewson had fared in his latest appearance.

Fig. 1. Sportswriters jotting down their columns at the Polo Grounds. Source: Library of Congress.

Fig. 2. OPPOSITE TOP: Newsboys ready to circulate the latest baseball news. Source: Alamy.

Fig. 3. OPPOSITE BOTTOM: Photographers adding illustrations to baseball stories. Source: Alamy.

Fig. 4. ABOVE: A blond god. Source: National Baseball Hall of Fame and Museum.

Fig. 5. An early pitching pose. Source: National Baseball Hall of Fame and Museum.

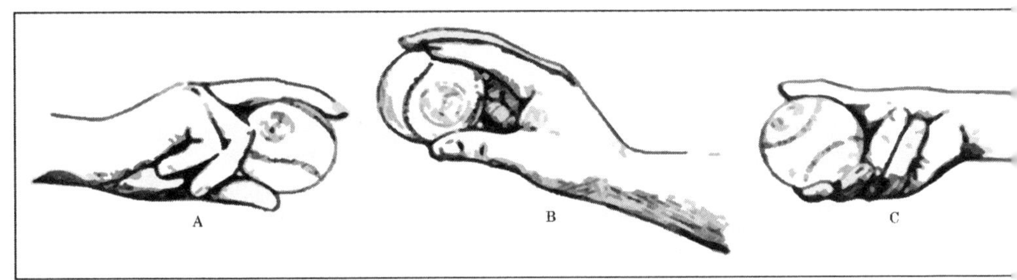

By Permission of the American Sports Publishing Co., New York.

MATHEWSON'S FADEWAY BALL

"A How the ball is grasped for the start of the 'fadeaway."

"B The ball is held lightly with the forefingers and thumb, And a slow twist is given to it. It sails up to the plate as dead as a brick, and, when mixed in with a speedy straight or in, often causes the batter to strike at it before it reaches him. It is a 'teaser' for the third strike."

"C The ball leaving the hand as it gets the final twist of the wrist for the 'fadeaway.'"

Fig. 6. ABOVE: His famous fadeaway pitch. Source: *St. Nicholas*, May 1912.

Fig. 7. LEFT: One of Mathewson's first baseball cards. Source: Library of Congress.

Fig. 8. ABOVE: Christy in 1905. Source: National Baseball Hall of Fame and Museum.

Fig. 9. OPPOSITE TOP: Christy Mathewson, John McGraw, and Joe McGinnity in 1905. Source: National Baseball Hall of Fame and Museum.

Fig. 10. OPPOSITE BOTTOM: A crowd of Mathewson's fans at the Polo Grounds. Source: Library of Congress.

NY

Fig. 11. OPPOSITE TOP: Teacher and student—McGraw and Mathewson. Source: National Baseball Hall of Fame and Museum.

Fig. 12. OPPOSITE BOTTOM: Warming up in 1911. Source: Library of Congress.

Fig. 13. ABOVE: Batting practice in 1911. Source: Alamy.

Fig. 14. ABOVE: The New York Giants in 1912. Source: Alamy.

Fig. 15. OPPOSITE TOP: Christy's glove. Source: National Baseball Hall of Fame and Museum.

Fig. 16. OPPOSITE BOTTOM: Christy with a young fan. Source: Alamy.

Fig. 17. Christy pitching the second game of the 1913 World Series. Source: Library of Congress.

Fig. 18. Teaching Christy Jr. to pitch. Source: National Baseball Hall of Fame and Museum.

Fig. 19. Manager of the Cincinnati Reds. Source: National Baseball Hall of Fame and Museum.

Fig. 20. An advertisement of Christy's last game.
Source: National Baseball Hall of Fame and Museum.

Fig. 21. Contributing to the Red Cross Fund in World War I. National Archives and Records Administration.

Fig. 22. Captain Christopher Mathewson, Army Chemical Corps.
Source: National Baseball Hall of Fame and Museum.

SARANAC LAKE.. June 22 '22

Jack in the Pulpit or Indian Turnip
Skunk Cabbage
Bellwort
Dogtooth Violet or Adder's Tongue
Clintonia
Wild Spikenard
Canada Mayflower or False Lily of the Vally
Purple Twisted-Stalk
Solomon's Seal
Indian Cucumber-root
Purple Trillium or Wake Robin
Painted Trillium
Larger Blue Flag; Blue Iris; Flanderswife
Blue-eyed Grass
Pink Lady's Slipper
Marsh Marigold
Common Buttercup; Crowfoot
Tall Meadow Rye
Wood Anemone; Windflower
Hepatica; Liverwort
Dutchman's Breeches
Crumblewort; Toothwort
Common (Black) Mustard
False Mitrewort; Foamflower
Wild Strawberry

Fig. 23. OPPOSITE: Christy's partial list of flowers identified on walks at Saranac Lake. Source: *Journal of the Outdoor Life*, February 1924.

Fig. 24. ABOVE LEFT: Ajeeb, the chess-playing automaton. Source: *The Sketch: A Journal of Art and Actuality*, March 11, 1908.

Fig. 25. ABOVE RIGHT: Not only a baseball legend, Christy was also an avid golfer. Source: *Golfing Magazine*, February 1915.

Fig. 26. Holding his *Big Six Indoor Baseball Game*.
Source: National Baseball Hall of Fame and Museum.

Fig. 27. As Christy looked at Saranac Lake. Source: National Baseball Hall of Fame and Museum.

Fig. 28. Christy and Jane Mathewson. Source:
National Baseball Hall of Fame and Museum.

THE LOST LIFE STORY OF CHRISTY MATHEWSON

Introduction

The newspaper series began with an introductory note announcing the Mathewson story and background on Bozeman Bulger. Bulger then began the first six chapters.

Publication of "The Life Story of Christy Mathewson" which starts tomorrow has aroused intense interest among sports followers through the Nation.

Partly because of Matty's unchallenged right to be known as one of the greatest pitchers of all time and partly because of the indelible imprint which Big Six's personality and character left on the national game, baseball fans everywhere have been looking forward to a biographical account of the great Mathewson that would do him justice.

It was quite an assignment, therefore, for Bozeman Bulger to be picked to prepare the memoirs of baseball's greatest. Yet a labor of love, for "Boze," as he is known throughout the newspaper and sporting world, was intimate with Matty over a stretch of 20 years, chummed with him, roomed with him, shared with him and loved him. That accounts for the charm of this simple story of one friend about another.

Of course, Mrs. Mathewson is a coauthor in the preparation of the memoirs and has prepared several chapters by herself.

Mr. Bulger is a New York baseball writer. He went to New York from Birmingham, Ala. about 20 years ago and was assigned as baseball writer to the New York Giants by the *Evening World*. Ever since then he has followed the fortunes of the National League club, always has accompanied it on its training and playing trips, and has probably seen it play more often than any living man.

Bulger always took his job seriously. While he was the idol of dozens of Giants players as one baseball generation followed another, he never allowed his personal sentiments to interfere with his candid and authoritative comments on games and players alike.

It was through his close association with Giant players that he became acquainted with the great pitcher, who later became president of the Boston Braves. The two were inseparable during the long journeys that took them around the Big League circuit. When "Big Six" became ill and was forced to go to the mountains, Bulger was in constant communication with him and none mourned more deeply over Matty's death.

As a major in the Army during the war, Bulger had charge of censorship of news dispatches of correspondents attached to the A. E. F. in France. He has written plays, Vaudeville sketches, innumerable magazine articles on baseball, and fiction short stories.

Bulger is so well known that it is not surprising for big baseball leaders to write to him in a personal vein, appreciating his new literary undertaking. Commissioner Kenesaw M. Landis wrote: "I am glad that the memories of Christy Mathewson are to be given to the public. Such was his career and influence upon American character that I feel a sense of personal gratitude for your undertaking."

John McGraw wrote to Bulger:

> "Dear Boze—Mrs. Mathewson, who has been visiting at our home, has told me of the official biography of Matty which is to be done by Mrs. Mathewson and you.

"It is hard for me yet to talk about Matty. We were so closely associated over a long period of years and were such intimate friends that thinking of him revives all the old memories and the consequent grief.

"I won't undertake to express my feelings about him here, but I do want to say that the annals of sport would not be complete without an official biography of Matty and I think every boy, young man, old man and a great many women will read it. I knew him intimately and realize that his life was one of the most interesting ever lived, in spite of the fact that he died when only forty-five years old.

"Yours sincerely, John J. McGraw."

Wilbert Robinson, president of the Brooklyn club, wrote to his friend Boze:

"I have just heard about the Mathewson biography. I wish you would send me a copy of it as soon as it is completed. A great many of my friends have asked me since Matty died where they could get a complete biography of this greatest of all pitchers and I was not able to tell them.

"Everybody is going to be anxious to read the first biography of Matty. I congratulate you on the undertaking and know that you are worthy of the subject, which is a big order in itself."

Cullen Cain also wrote to Boze:

"It pleased me very much to hear that you are to write the biography for Matty. It will be done in a fashion worthy of this outstanding character of baseball.

"As a member of the Matty Memorial Committee of the National League, I would wish to endorse your literary venture. It is to be doubted if any one outside of his immediate family knew Matty as well as yourself or appreciated his character so truly. You will present his as his more thoughtful admirers would wish him to be presented—real, faithfully, free from gush and from being overdone or stilted."

Chapter 1. In The Beginning

Christy Mathewson's start as a baseball pitcher is best told by himself in a little narrative that he prepared for small boys about fifteen years ago. The simplicity and directness with which he writes this is characteristic of Matty's mental attitude throughout his baseball career.

"When I was a boy about eight or nine years old, I lived in Factoryville, Pennsylvania, a little country town. I had a cousin older than myself who was always studying the theory of throwing. I used to throw flat stones with him and he would show me (what I suppose almost every boy knows) that if a flat stone is started with the flat surface parallel to the ground, it will always turn over before it lands. That is, after it loses its speed and the air cushion fails to support it, the stone will turn over and drop down. The harder it is thrown, the longer the air sustains it and the farther it will carry before it drops. If the stone started with the flat surface at an acute angle to the earth, instead of parallel to it, the stone, instead of dropping, would curve horizontally. I began to make all sorts of experiments with stones.

"I got to be a great stone thrower and this practice increased my throwing power and taught me something about curves. When I was nine years old, I could throw a stone farther than any of the boys who were my chums.

"From this I became interested in baseball games and before long I was allowed to stand behind the catcher when the Factoryville team was playing and "shag" foul balls or carry the bats or the water. For I was born with the baseball instinct and a mascot or bat-boy is the role in which many a ballplayer has made his start. So, at the age of ten, I became a known factor in the baseball circles of Factoryville and might be said to have started on my career.

"My next step was learning to throw a curve with a baseball and one of the pitchers of the town team undertook to show me how this was done. He taught me to hold the ball for an out-curve and then to snap my wrist to attain the desired result. After considerable practice, I managed to curve the ball, but I never knew where it was going. I used to get another youngster, up against a barn with a big glove and pitch to him for hours. At last, I attained fair control over this curve and then I began practicing what is known as the 'fastball,' but what most boys call the 'in-curve.'

"Every boy knows that if he grips a ball tightly and then throws it with all his speed, off the ends of his fingers, the ball will curve in toward a right-handed batter slightly. This curve is easy to accomplish, as it is merely a matter of speed and letting the ball slide straight off the ends of the fingers—the most natural way to throw. It does not require any snap of the wrist, but the bend of the curve is naturally slight and that is the reason most Big Leaguers call it a fastball and do not recognize it as a curve. At the age of twelve, having no designs on the Big League, I called it the 'in-curve' and reckoned, with some pride, that I could throw two curves—the 'out' and the 'in.' Big Leaguers only refer to two types, the fast one and the curve."

Matty always thought that he might have been a much better hitter and for that reason, might not have made a specialty of pitching, but for his hitting cross-hand. Standing as right-handed batters do, he would place his left hand forward on the bat—a most awkward and impossible style. He was a natural left-handed batter, he says, but did not know it. He hoed potatoes and chopped wood left-handed. In correcting this batting style, though, he put his right hand forward and became just an ordinary right-handed batter.

"When I was fourteen years old," Matty wrote, "the pitcher on the Factoryville team was taken ill one day, just before a game with a nine from a town a few miles away, and the contest was regarded as very important in both villages. Our second pitcher was away on a visit and so Factoryville was up against it for a twirler. You must remember that all the players on this team were grown men—several of them with whiskers on their faces and roly-poly bellies—but I had always looked up to them as idols.

"Someone told the captain, 'That Mathewson kid can pitch pretty well,' but the backers of the team were skeptical. So, they told me to come down on the main street in Factoryville the next morning, which was Saturday, the day of the game, and take a tryout.

"Most of the population of the town gathered to see me get my tryout and I pitched for two hours, while the critics stood around and watched me closely to discover what I could do. When, at last, I had fanned out the captain of the team, he came up, slapped me on the back, and said, 'You'll do. We want you to pitch this afternoon.'"

In recalling the big moments of his life, Matty always insisted that the one just mentioned stood out above them all. Incidentally, he was called "Husk" in those days, being unusually large for his age.

"The thrill that lasted me for twenty years," he used to say, "was when I climbed in the bus with the men and looked down at the other kids who stood around nudging each other and saying, 'Husk is going to play with the men!'

"I can remember the score of that game to this day," Matty said while on his last trip to Florida. "We won by 19 to 17. And another thing I won't forget—no other ballplayer would, either—I broke up the game. Batting cross-handed, I caught one in my groove and hit the ball over the left fielder's head with the bases full."

Matty went to Keystone Academy the next year and played on the ball team, but they wouldn't let him pitch. Being much younger than his teammates, he was made to play right field. If you older readers will remember, it was a theory in our youthful baseball days that anybody could play right field.

"But I got my rights the second year," declared Mathewson. "I was elected captain of the team and you know what that means. Most of you who have been on big ball clubs know that the captain always makes himself the pitcher. That is his prerogative. In fact, that's the only reason I knew for being captain."

When against a weak team, Matty laughingly explained that he would put somebody else in to pitch and he would play second base "to strengthen the infield," an idea he got from reading about John McGraw, a man he never expected to meet.

The main idea was that the other pitchers couldn't hit or play anywhere else and the captain was making himself a certain berth in every line-up.

Chapter 2. Youthful Pranks and a Sense of Humor

From the very start of his professional career, the name and deeds of Christy Mathewson appealed to the imagination of the small boys and to their elders in such a way that he was often placed on a higher pedestal than he desired. Often, he was used as the text for sermons. Schoolteachers directed the attention of the youngster to him as a man whose example they should emulate.

This created the impression that his thoughts and his conduct were different from those of his teammates, that he held himself aloof, was never boyish or mischievous. Perish the thought that Matty was a goody-goody boy or a molly-coddle or that his impulses were very different from those of any other healthy-minded and healthy-bodied young human being.

His mother smilingly tells of an afternoon that several small boys came to see Matty when he was five years old. They went out to practice throwing and selected the side on an old white horse in the barn lot for their target.

That is the one occasion of his life, Matty used to say, where control was neither a virtue nor an advantage.

"I can remember to this day," he laughed in recalling the incident of his babyhood, "that I plunked that old horse squarely in the side on every throw. Finally, Old Charley, the horse, started to run about the barn lot and then is when my uncle caught us and I got it good."

His mother says the lecture and the spanking that she gave Matty that day served him as a good lesson for life.

When he was fourteen, the boy, then a pretty good pitcher, would finish his chores at home and walk five miles to a neighboring village to pitch ball games at one dollar each. On these journeys, he had his little quarrels and scraps as did you and I.

Matty got his first real start as a pitcher when he went on a day's visit to Scranton, Pennsylvania, which, to him, was then a big city. While there, Matty, then seventeen, learned that the Scranton YMCA was to play a ball game that afternoon. He decided that he could not leave the city without seeing those big fellows play. So, he went to the ball park and was seated in the little grandstand eating peanuts when he noticed that the Scranton club was troubled about something. It developed that their pitcher was absent. One of the players who had seen him pitch at Factoryville noticed him in the grandstand.

"There's a kid up there who can pitch," he told the captain. "He's only seventeen, but he's nearly six feet tall and can throw like a bullet."

A few minutes later, the captain spied Matty and asked him if he wanted to pitch. That would be like asking a poor man if he wanted a million dollars.

"So eager was I to take the job," declared Matty in later years, "that I leaped over the railing and, in doing so, left a half a bag of peanuts uneaten, which was no compliment to my natural sense of thrift. That alone would indicate my excitement."

That afternoon established young Mathewson in Scranton as a pitcher. He struck out fifteen batters and won his game. His work for the YMCA was directly responsible for the later offers he received to join professional teams. The local players went crazy about the Factoryville boy's speed.

Throughout his baseball life, Matty liked a joke as well as anybody. Whenever the old Giants of 1905 meet nowadays, they recall a practical joke played on Luther Taylor, the deaf-mute pitcher, at Memphis, Tennessee during a spring training season. Matty was one of the chief conspirators.

On account of his deafness, "Dummy" Taylor was always obsessed with a fear of some stranger getting in his room at night. Incidentally, Taylor was a great practical joker himself.

Across the street from the baseball hotel, Matty and John McGraw had noticed a life-sized cigar store Indian, with a full head of black hair, standing in front of a store. Calling Roger Bresnahan into consultation, they went out and unbolted that wooden Indian from the sidewalk while Taylor was at the theater. With speed and secrecy, they dragged the wooden Indian into the hotel and up to Taylor's room where they put it in his bed and pulled the covers up around the neck. When the job was completed, they turned out the light and hid in a room across the hall to await developments.

Taylor came in after eleven o'clock. Turning on the light, he suddenly spied the figure in his bed. He reached the door in one leap and didn't stop until he had run to the desk downstairs and was busily writing on a card, trying to make the clerk call a policeman.

When Taylor finally got back to the room and the covers had been pulled back, disclosing the wooden Indian, he turned to see the grinning faces of Mathewson, McGraw, Bresnahan, and Mike Donlin, who stood in the doorway. He wanted to fight, but they ran out of danger.

Matty's first catcher in the Big League was "Broadway" Alex Smith, a player noted for his display of clothes. Smith also took great pride in being paged by bellboys at the hotel, as do most people inclined to be vain. Some hotel guests have been known to engage a boy and have themselves paged so as to draw attention to their prominence.

On one occasion when the Giants stopped in a fashionable hotel in Boston, Smith, Matty's battery mate, had donned a brand-new suit of clothes and, wearing a fancy necktie, was strutting about the lobby. This appealed to Matty's sense of mischief.

He called a bellboy and paid him fifty cents to go through the lobby for fifteen minutes, calling, "Mr. Smith, Mr. Alex Smith of the New York Giants!"

"After you've done this for some time," he instructed the boy, "wait until you see Mr. Smith talking to some ladies. Then go up to him and ask, "Have I paged you enough, Mr. Smith?"

The boy did as directed and, though the players in the plot had a great laugh at the embarrassed Broadway fashion plate, the lad had to run for his life.

Mathewson was an ardent game hunter, a good golf player, a good baritone in the quartette, and a fisherman. He did everything with thoroughness. In fact, he became such a good shot that, with Otie Crandall and Chief Bender, he toured the country as a professional trap shooter. Like most other young fellows, he had a try at everything. He was on the stage for fifteen weeks as a star in a comedy playlet. He also had a whirl at the movies.

Yes, Matty was more than merely an example for the boys. He was a very human, likable fellow. He often said that his one drawback was a natural diffidence that he could never quite overcome.

Chapter 3. His Fadeaway Pitch

Matty later said, "Later along in the summer of 1898 I went to Honesdale, Pennsylvania, where I was given twenty dollars a month and my board to pitch for the team. This seemed to be a princely salary then and I began to mention 'J. P. Morgan and me.'

"Honesdale was important to my career. There I learned the rudiments of the fadeaway curve and there also I stopped batting cross-handed."

The one thing to complete Mathewson's equipment and make him the master of all twirlers, instead of merely a great pitcher, was his discovery of the fadeaway or fall-away curve. He began working on that when but a lad and the fact of his taking six or seven years to master it is characteristic of his thoroughness.

No other pitcher was ever able to pitch the fadeaway and the chances are that no one will ever add it to his repertoire of deceptive throws. Dozens of pitchers knew the theory of it. Most any old-time player can explain it to this day, but none other has ever mastered it. They will not devote the time and practice to it.

Contrary to a general belief, Mathewson did not hold this fadeaway ball as a secret. He tried to teach it to many of his teammates. In fact, as early as 1910 he wrote an article on the mysterious curve with a complete explanation and elaborate drawings to show exactly how it was done.

The great mass of fans had an idea that Matty's familiar drop curve that he used so often and with such deadly effect was his fadeaway. It is doubtful if any of these fans seeing the fadeaway would recognize it. Matty rarely used it. It was his custom to save it for emergency only.

In the first place, the fadeaway, as will be shown later, was a terrific, unnatural strain on the muscles of the pitching arm. Continuous use of it would have ruined his arm for other curves and, Matty reasoned, would sap the zip out of his fastball. Besides that, frequent use of the odd curve would have given opposing batters an opportunity to familiarize themselves with it. Matty was always apprehensive that he might betray his intention to use the fadeaway by some mannerism he had in the way he held his arm and wrist.

"Once they discover when I am going to pitch it," he used to say, "they can get set for it. Its value is in its surprise and I want to keep it a surprise."

The fadeaway that, by the way, was named by George Davis, former manager of the Giants, was nothing more than a slow curve that broke in toward a right-handed hitter instead of away from him. All curves thrown by a right-handed pitcher, you know, curve away from a right-handed batter. This ball thrown by Mathewson was delivered with exactly the same motion he used for his fastball and for his regular curve. It seemed to slow up, however, as it reached the plate and then would fall in toward the right-handed batter's feet, spoiling the timing of the swing. Very few ever hit it at all. It was so surprising that at times they would miss the ball a full twelve inches.

Mathewson always gave credit for the discovery of the fadeaway to a left-handed pitcher named Dave Williams, who played on the Honesdale team when Matty was doing his first professional pitching. The left-hander's curve, as you perhaps know, curves in to a right-handed batter, the reverse of a right-hander's curve. This man Williams, though, could pitch a peculiar out-curve to a right-hander. He couldn't control it very well, but occasionally he exhibited it in practice simply as a freak curve.

It occurred to the practical-minded Mathewson that if a right-handed pitcher could master the principles of that freak ball, it would be a tremendous advantage in pitching. Williams showed him how he held the ball and gave all the help he could. The theory being firmly implanted in the Mathewson brain, the boy went to work on it with great diligence. He kept steadily at it for three years. At the end of that time, he could control the fadeaway as well as any other curve, though he dared not use it too much.

To realize the extent of his patience and determination, a more detailed explanation of the fadeaway is necessary. The ordinary curve ball is thrown by first gripping the ball with the thumb on top and the fingers beneath. The ball is allowed to slip off the end of the thumb with a spinning motion, given by a snap of the wrist, which causes the ball to bend away from the right-handed batter. The hand is held up.

"Now," Matty explained it, "I figured if the wrist were turned over and the hand held down—that is, thumb underneath and fingers on top—the ball would slip off the thumb with a twisting motion, but the wrist being reversed, the thumb would be toward the body instead of away from it. According to my calculations, that ought to change the rotary motion and produce an in-curve to the batter instead of an out-curve. That is exactly what happened. What we ordinarily call an in-curve when boys, is nothing more than a fastball. This was a real in-curve that went up slowly and curved in and downward.

"Remember this," he emphasized, "to pitch the fadeaway, the hand must be turned over until the palm is toward the ground instead of the sky. The ball is gripped exactly as one grips an ordinary out-curve."

Two things make this a very difficult ball to pitch and those two things likewise make it very hard to hit. First, the hand is turned in an unnatural position for control. If any of you will try to throw a ball this way—the palm of your hand to the ground—and then snap your wrist with the back of your hand to your body, it can easily be seen what difficulties Matty had to overcome. Second, the seemingly impossible trick is to snap the wrist away from the body instead of toward it. The perfection of the curve really lies in the precise development of that peculiar snap of the hand and wrist.

Matty tried to teach this to Red Ames of the Giants as a likely pupil. Ames got to where he could produce the curve occasionally, but he never knew where it was going. He did not have the unlimited patience of Mathewson. Nobody else did. Thus, the fadeaway curve passed out of baseball with Mathewson.

When Matty first came to the Giants as a boy of nineteen, he was taken out to the box to see "what he's got," as ballplayers express it.

George Davis hit the first curve he pitched over the outfielder's head.

"I've a sort of freak ball," Matty told Davis upon his demand for something better, "but I never use it in a game."

"Well, let's see it."

Matty threw his future manager the fadeaway with perfect control and Davis missed it by a foot. His eyes bulged in wonder.

"Boy," he said, "that's a wonderful ball. Never saw anything like it before. It's a slow in-curve to a right-handed batter. Boy, you've got a change of pace with a curve ball. It's a regular fadeaway—falls right away from where I hit!"

Right there the freak curve got its name. Davis agreed that Matty would do as a pitcher and instructed him to practice on the fadeaway ball all the time.

Often Matty would practice a full hour on that curve alone. He did that for years. It established him in the Big League.

Chapter 4. Bucknell University

Christy Mathewson had played professional ball before he entered Bucknell College. In fact, he played professional ball while he was still a student there. In those days—it was back in 1899—the athletic laws regarding the pure amateur and the professional were not so rigid as now. A college boy was considered very fortunate who could play professional baseball in the summer to help himself along through college in the winter.

Mathewson got the idea of the fadeaway curve while playing at Honesdale, Pennsylvania, at so much a game prior to entering college. His remarkable success as a pitcher at the age of seventeen had attracted the attention of professional club owners throughout the country. He was offered a job as pitcher for the Taunton, Massachusetts club in the New England League at ninety dollars a month. Matty used to relate with a wry face that he jumped at this offer.

"I pitched good ball, too," he said, "but I could never get the ninety dollars. The club was up against it all the time and paid me barely enough to settle my board bills."

On his way to Taunton, Mathewson had to stop over for a few hours in New York, where he changed trains. It was the first time in his life he had been in New York and he went to the Polo Grounds, which was to be the scene of his many triumphs. He bought a bleacher seat for twenty-five cents, the price in those days. He watched the game between the Giants and Louisville in which Honus Wagner took part. Matty was so impressed by Honus Wagner that after the game he waited outside the players' gate to see the big, bow-legged Dutchman make his exit. In telling about it afterward, he said rather shamefully: "I felt like a stage-door Johnny hanging around that gate, but I felt I must see the great Honus Wagner. Little did I think then that I would someday pitch against him." In after years, Matty had many fans waiting at the clubhouse gate to see him leave the grounds.

Returning from Taunton, Mathewson entered Bucknell in the fall, carrying with him a lot of knowledge about baseball and considerable skepticism about contracts. Back in his head was tucked away the principles of the fadeaway curve, though, and he saw a chance to work it out in college. Never did he even think of giving up that curve as a hopeless task.

"I discovered to my surprise, though," he often said, "that they were not so keen on baseball in the college. Football was the main game. So, I decided I might as well have a fling at that."

At that time, Matty was six feet tall in his stocking feet and weighed close to a hundred ninety pounds. It was almost impossible for the athletic directors to believe him only eighteen years old. He was spotted as a member of the football team before he had crossed the campus a dozen times.

In the meantime, the Mathewson boy had joined the basketball team and was as good at that as at football and baseball later. He also took the lead in his studies.

A striking characteristic of Mathewson was that he never tried to fool himself. He was keenly self-analytical. Even after he became the peer of all pitchers, he was fully aware of his weaknesses. If he developed a fault, he would calmly check himself, locate the trouble, and correct it.

"I could see in a little while that I was not so fast as those other boys in the football squad," he once told me, "and I began to figure how I could make the best use of myself. The thing that struck my fancy was the dropkick.

"If, I reasoned to myself, five points could be scored by kicking that ball through the goal posts, what is the use of using so much speed and strength in trying for a touchdown?"

In those days, the dropkick was not so common as in later years because there were not so many dropkickers. That is why a field goal counted five points instead of the three that are allowed today. A touchdown then counted for four points only, an extra point being allowed for kicking goal afterward. In other words, a dropkick from the field counted one point more than a touchdown.

It was characteristic of Matty that he sensed an advantage in perfecting the dropkick just as he did the possibilities of the fadeaway curve.

They will tell you at Bucknell that, in season and out of season, Matty could be seen most any day on Loomis Field with a single companion, booting the ball over the bar by the hour. He always had unlimited patience and determination. By incessant practice, Matty reached such perfection that Walter Camp declared him to be the best dropkicker he ever saw at any time.

Matty's first big chance to make use of his dropkicking skill came in the fall of 1899. Though against a superior team, Matty scored ten points for Bucknell by booting goals from the field. Penn scored twenty points and won, but Mathewson was the individual hero.

Mathewson's second chance at football fame came at West Point, when he played fullback for Bucknell against the Army. In a hard game with Bucknell frantic to score, Matty was given the ball on the Army's 48-yard line. It was a desperate chance, a deed of daring that the boy assumed without a change of expression in his face. Even then, he was noted for his coolness under fire. He dropped back calmly and, from a difficult angle with the Army ends running toward him, Matty sunk his toe into the ball and made a perfect dropkick of 48 yards, the ball whirling squarely between the goal posts. Older officers at West Point today refer to that as the most brilliant and difficult dropkick ever made in football. It was largely on that kick, following his work against Penn, that Walter Camp selected him as the All-American fullback. Camp always insisted that Mathewson was the best dropkicker the game ever knew.

It was the Pennsylvania game, however, that gave Matty his greatest thrill. It was responsible for the job that gave him his real start as a professional ballplayer.

Before the Penn game, John Smith, known in minor league baseball circles as "Phenom" Smith, hunted him out at the hotel. He had seen Matty pitch at Taunton.

"Mathewson," he said, "I'm going to manage Norfolk in the Virginia League next season and I'll give you a steady job at eighty dollars a month. I know your contract called for ninety dollars at Taunton, but you are going to GET this money."

Stepping over to a table, Matty signed the contract then and there and, followed by Phenom Smith, started for the football field. Smith was his most enthusiastic rooter during the game. That night, he followed the Bucknell team to the hotel and saw Matty again.

"Give me that contract, Mathewson," he directed. "I'm going to make that contract ninety dollars." So saying, he scratched out the first figures and wrote in 90. "I liked the way you kicked those goals," was the reason he gave.

Chapter 5. From Minors to the Giants

In two days after the end of the spring term of Matty's first year at Bucknell, he was on his way to Norfolk, Virginia, to fulfill his baseball contract with Phenom Smith, made just after he had kicked those two field goals against the University of Pennsylvania.

Manager Smith made good his promise to make the salary ninety dollars a month. Of greater importance to the businesslike young Mathewson, the salary was paid regularly and in full.

In the spring of 1908, the Giants went to Norfolk for an exhibition tour. "Say," Matty called to a group of us in the lobby of the Monticello Hotel after breakfast on the day of our arrival, "want to take a walk? Come on. I'll show you something."

His idea was to take us to the office of the Norfolk club and ask permission to see his original contract. That, however, was unnecessary. Arriving there, the first thing that greeted our eyes was Matty's contract in a frame, hanging on the wall. It was still hanging there three years ago. To this day, the baseball people of Norfolk reckon themselves the real discoverers of Christy Mathewson's greatness as a pitcher.

Under the likeable Phenom Smith, Matty improved rapidly. He practiced incessantly. The result was a record that I understand is still unbroken in any minor league. Mathewson pitched twenty-three games that season and won twenty-one of them.

"He had such tremendous speed and such a deceptive curve," Phenom Smith used to relate, "that toward the end of the season that boy could beat any ordinary club by simply tossing his glove in the pitching box. He not only had them bluffed, but could deliver the goods."

All this time, Matty was diligently working on the perfection and control of his fadeaway curve. He didn't use it often, but when he did cut it loose, the result, according to Phenom Smith, was laughable.

On one occasion, a hard-hitting fellow named Bascombe came to bat with three on bases. As but one batter was out, Matty found himself in a bad hole. If ever there was a time to use the fadeaway, this was it. Finally working Bascombe in the two-three hole (two strikes and three balls), young Mathewson cut loose his odd, slow curve that broke in toward a right-handed batter (the fadeaway). Bascombe, never having seen anything like that, swung so hard and in such an awkward direction that he missed the ball a full twelve inches. But that wasn't all. His descending bat hit himself on the ankle and put him out of the game for two weeks.

Phenom Smith was nobody's fool. He knew full well that he had a star on his hands and he knew also that some Big League owner would step in and rob him of his prize unless he "kept his head up," as he expressed it.

One day he called Mathewson into the office for a serious talk. "Boy," he said, "I've got a chance to sell you to New York or to Philadelphia. I know I'm going to lose you some way, so I'm going to let you have your choice. The Cincinnati club is beginning to dicker."

In this connection, I might say that during the early days of the war between the National and American Leagues, much was said about Mathewson having signed a contract with the Athletics while he was a recruit for the Giants. Connie Mack's explanation of this is the clearest we have heard. Very recently he said:

"When Mathewson had joined the Giants, the owner of the Norfolk club, a Mr. E. H. Cunningham, I believe, protested violently that he should have received $2,500 for Matty instead of $750. He insisted he would collect the money. Andrew Freedman was then owner of the Giants.

"To avoid any financial difficulty with Cunningham, I was told then, the New York club made arrangements to release Matty to the Cincinnati club. Matty did not want to go to Cincinnati. I then offered to take him on the Philadelphia club and offered him a contract which he signed. He did not accept any money on that contract, though. He came down to see me and explained to me what salary he was to get from the Giants. I made the mistake of not offering him more. The matter hung fire for a few days and then New York, in some way, cancelled its release to the Reds and Matty again became a member of that club. With that settled to his satisfaction, he considered the contract with me not in force.

"It always has been one of my regrets that I did not increase Matty's salary at that time. I did not consider Matty a contract breaker. It was simply one of those many mix-ups that came up. Incidentally, I have always regarded him as one of the outstanding characters in baseball. I admired him personally and as a master pitcher."

Anyhow, Matty listened to Phenom Smith and carefully considered his next move. His reasoning is characteristic of his orderly mind, even at that early date. "I'll let you know in a couple of days," he told Smith.

Matty's shrewd decision and his reasons for making it are best told by himself. I am quite sure that Matty never forgot a detail in his life. Here is what he told us in 1908 and what he afterward wrote in 1912:

> "I began to study the list of pitchers with each club—the Giants and the Athletics. The Giants, as you know, in those days were usually down at the bottom of the standing of the clubs at the end of the season. I could see that they were badly in need of pitchers. So, I

> decided that if I went to New York as a youngster, I would have a better chance to pitch regularly. The competition wouldn't be so keen. They wouldn't have much to lose in giving me a thorough trial and I would have more opportunities to work. Having reasoned it out that way, I went back to Smith. 'I'd like to go to New York,' I told him."

That is how this remarkable boy of nineteen became a Big League pitcher in the summer of 1900.

George Davis was manager of the Giants then. He received Matty by ordering him to put on a uniform and pitch to every batter on the club, including himself.

It was in that morning practice that the boy created a sensation among the Big League ballplayers by striking out his prospective manager with a fadeaway ball. He had pitched it in desperation because Davis had murdered his first ball and had then hit his roundhouse curve to the far corner of the field.

"Is that all you've got?" he asked the boy.

"I've got a freak ball, but I don't use it often."

"All right, let's have a look at it."

As has been told before, he was fortunate enough to pitch the fadeaway curve with perfect control. After the amazed Davis had struck out, he went back to the bench knowing that he had uncovered a really great pitcher.

Instead of working the boy regularly, Davis nursed him along, handling him as one might a great treasure. Davis was indeed a wise baseball man.

Chapter 6. In a Pinch

Matty came from the Norfolk team to the Giants at the age of nineteen, a big, blond, gangling youth so modest as to be actually bashful. He made no great impression on the ballplayers or the baseball writers. He had been hanging around two or three days before some of the writers took the trouble to inquire who he was.

"Some kid," said George Davis, then manager of the Giants, "who is supposed to be a pitcher. I don't think much of his motion, though.

It's too hard on his arm and won't stand the Big League racket long. He's awkward."

Matty lasted longer than did most pitchers who get into the big show, but he, himself, always knew and admitted that his motion was hard on his arm. He had a jerk to his swing that he could never iron out. That objectionable jerk, however, was largely responsible for the sharp deceptive breaks he could put on the ball. During his last several seasons, Matty pitched more with his head and his heart than with his arm.

John McGraw was watching Bugs Raymond warm up one day, admiringly. The Giants manager always maintained that Raymond had the easiest, smoothest pitching movement he ever saw.

"With that easy swing and Matty's brain," McGraw observed, "you would have a pitcher who would never be beaten. And," he sighed, "one who would last forever."

Mathewson's greatest asset was his control. In some ways, odd as it may sound, this worked against him.

"You could sit in a rocking chair and catch him," Chief Meyers, Matty's regular catcher, used to say, meaning that the ball always came where it was expected. The Chief frequently talked to Matty about this. I've heard him say:

"All those guys are up there crowding the plate because they know you won't bean them. Why don't you cut one loose for the old bean once in a while—dust them off? They'd back up then and would stand up with so much less confidence. Just watch them stick their foot in the water bucket when Rube Marquard is working."

"I just can't do it," Matty would answer. "You are probably right, but I'm afraid of hitting a batter and hurting him."

Ballplayers credit Mathewson with having the greatest memory of any pitcher in the history of the game. He knew the batting weakness of every batter who had been in fast company and knew how to pitch to that weakness.

One day a group of sportswriters tried to catch him unawares on this.

"Say, Matty," I asked him, "what was the first ball old George Van Haltren hit off you in batting practice when you joined the Giants back around 1900?"

"An old-fashioned roundhouse curve," he answered without the slightest hesitation or smile, "and he slapped it down to the clubhouse steps which at that time came down to the rope in deep right center."

Matty also had the knack of easing off when he was in front and saving something for the pinch. My, how he could put on pressure in those crises!

Saving something for the pinch is a good rule to follow in any line of endeavor. The idea of too much control might also be applied to other enterprises. Isn't it possible that the businessman with too much control and confidence gives his rivals unusual confidence because they know he won't blow up? Still, control that is too perfect is better than no control at all.

Speaking of what Matty could do in a pinch, I recall one of those great games—crucial, they were called—between the Giants and Frank Chance's old Cubs.

Jack Pfiester and Hooks Wiltse were in a southpaw duel. In the eighth inning it looked so safe for the Giants that McGraw told Matty he could wash up and call it a day, that he would not be needed for relief work. In the ninth, the Cubs turned on Wiltse and began to pound him just as Matty had got under the shower in the clubhouse. They had the bases full and were within one run of tying the score when McGraw sent the mascot on the run for Matty. The Giants, in the meantime, began to stall for time.

Pretty soon, the lumbering, half-dressed, knock-kneed figure of Big Six came loping through center field to the pitcher's box. His blond hair was wet, his shirt neck open, shoes unlaced, and he was trying to buckle his belt. The umpires were impatient. So, without taking time to tie his shoes, Matty stepped in the box cold and struck out the next two batters. Without a windup, he turned loose a curve that took a wicked hook. Del Howard swung at the ball so badly and missed it so far that the bat went all the way through and he hit himself on the ankle, striking out, and putting himself out of the game for three days. Then Matty went back and finished his shower. There was a pitcher!

Eddie Plank, of the Athletics and one of the smartest ballplayers contemporaneous with Matty, paid him this tribute:

"In my opinion, Matty was without a peer as a pitcher. His control was perfect and his ability to remember the batting weaknesses uncanny. He pitched against me in the 1905 World Series and discovered that I had a hell of a time hitting a ball in close, knee-high. Then he went for six years without working against me. In the 1911 World Series, the first ball he pitched me cut the inside corner knee-high and he kept them there through the Series. The rest of the boys told us he worked them, too."

A good joke on Matty and one that he always appreciated happened in that series. Though it was a boomerang to him, it throws a clear light on the true character of the man.

Rube Marquard lost a game, after having pitched masterfully, when Home Run Baker, in a late inning, pasted a long drive into the stands and broke up the game. Mathewson was writing a daily analytical article for the old *New York Herald*. In his review of that game, Matty said that Marquard had figured Baker wrong and had pitched to his strength—a serious mistake.

The next day Matty pitched. In a tense moment, Baker caught hold of one of Matty's offerings and hit a home run even farther than he had off Marquard and with disastrous results. For one of the few times in his career, the fans rode Big Six. All of his friends were giving him the laugh. With characteristic frankness, though, he wrote for the publication: "Yesterday I criticized Marquard for pitching the wrong ball to Baker. If Rube made a mistake, as did I, I am frank to say now that the only weakness Baker has is a base on balls."

Christy Mathewson did more for professional baseball than any other player. He found it a rough pastime, peopled by a rough cast of characters, young men often guilty of cutting the corners of sportsmanship. Matty brought into the game the spirit, the class it needed. He brought sportsmanship and a sense of fair play that fans promptly recognized.

Following Matty's lead, more college men took up baseball. Even those who were not college men saw the advantages of clean sportsmanship and serious application to their profession. The whole game is now on a higher plane. The roistering, drunken, bullying ballplayer has gone.

Chapter 7. Early Days with Jane

Jane Mathewson now contributes some recollections of Christy Mathewson's early days and how the wedded couple adapted to New York City following their marriage in 1903.

Even as a schoolboy Christy was always very studious and thoughtful. I first came to know him when he arrived at Lewisburg, Pennsylvania, to enter Bucknell University. I was a student at the Female Institute of the same university. Our home was very near the Bucknell campus and Christy often called there.

I have been asked to write something of our courtship days, of little incidents that happened and what we said and did, but, somehow, I had rather not do that—now.

Let me say, however, that the characteristic that attracted everybody to the man who later became my husband was his upstanding character and serious determination to overcome all obstacles. His way through college was not made easy. He worked his own way without any help from his family. That, I think, did much to implant in him a serious outlook on life and a deep sense of responsibility. It also gave him an early understanding of what business relations meant.

Christy earned a scholarship at Bucknell through his work at Keystone Academy. It was up to him, though, to pay his own expenses other than the tuition. To do that, he became the caterer for the student's eating club. He ran the entire business of buying supplies and of superintending the service and the collections. His success in this was so pronounced that he became very popular with the other students. He also attracted attention and respect by his advance in his classes and his athletic achievements. Christy was large and powerful for his age and was always an outstanding figure.

I have seen many references in the newspapers to the directness of his conversation and the careful way in which he used his words. Always he was that way. I remember quite distinctly this trait in him when we first got to know each other well. He rarely indulged in foolish conversation. In discussing any subject or in ordinary conversation it was noticeable that he always took pains to use the right word for expression. When he made a remark, there could never be any doubt as to exactly what he meant. Even in later life, he kept up this close study of the English language and made a point of choosing his words well. He was a member of the Euepia Literary Society and his junior year—his last—was president of his class.

Christy had a keen sense of humor and loved fun just as any other heathy-minded, strong-bodied boy does. I have read that he could use strong, untempered language when he felt like it, but I doubt that he did. In all my life, I never knew Christy to utter an oath or to use any expression that was at all unseemly. He had such a good command of English words that he could express himself forcibly without resorting to profanity or ugly slang.

Christy's greatest regret was that he was never able to sing a high tenor in a quartette or in the church choir. Unfortunately for his ambition, he had a clear and rather pretty baritone voice and always loved to sing. Never shall I forget him as he sang in the Presbyterian Church choir and our family sat in a pew facing him. Our family, the Stoughtons, always kept that pew. Christy sang in the choir regularly and I was always in that pew where we could see each other as he sang. Neither of us ever forgot those days. He was a member of the glee club and was on the Junior Prom committee. He also played a bass horn in the college band.

Christy used to call and talk over his plans with me. I remember quite well when, with an amusing drollness, he told me about his summer engagement as pitcher for the Taunton, Massachusetts, club in the New England League and of his having to return without having been paid his salary. He was not bitter about this, but took it philosophically, just as he did reverses later on in his pitching career.

Later came his joy in his success at Norfolk, Virginia, and in the Big League. He used to send me clippings from the New York newspapers with comments written on the margins that were very amusing. He was never taken off his balance by extravagant praise. On many of the clippings, which I still treasure, were such observations as: "This is fine, but just wait until I have a losing streak" and "See, they are trying to make a hero out of me" and "Isn't this nice of them."

After we were married in 1903, Christy was the same thoughtful boy that he always had been and a dear companion. He never talked much unless he really had something to say. Somehow, we used to feel a comfort at sitting together at nights without the feeling that it was necessary to talk.

Often, we would spend a whole evening in the sitting room without talking at all. He would be at a table working out some checker problem, wholly absorbed, while I sat and sewed. It was the delightful companionship of peace and calm. He never had to rush about in search of amusement. We found peace, contentment, and harmony right there at home.

Christy was always a good businessman and very carefully planned for the future. He invested his savings so that we would be provided for when his pitching days were over. It didn't cost so much to live then.

When we went to live in New York, we made an arrangement with our friends, Mr. and Mrs. John McGraw, and rented a seven-room apartment together. Mr. McGraw paid the rent, which was fifty dollars a month, and Christy paid fifty dollars into the family food fund to make it even. Then we divided the other living expenses. It was, indeed, a happy experience.

Later, after little Christy was born, we moved to Washington Heights where our apartment overlooked the Polo Grounds. From the front window I could see the scoreboard at the Polo Grounds and, with the aid of a field glass, could read the figures. You can imagine how closely I watched when Christy was pitching. If he were losing, I often prepared for his dinner some special dish that he liked, so as to revive his spirits. He felt a loss very much.

Christy liked desserts and his favorite was pie à la mode. I would have the pie ready and, if the score indicated that he would need a little extra comforting, I would send out and get the ice cream to put on the pie by the time he reached home. He would never say much about the game, but I knew instinctively how he felt.

Chapter 8. His Character

Bozeman Bulger now continues the narrative.

The sense of responsibility was so ground into Christy Mathewson during his early youth that his nature was never of the buoyant type. At times, he found great difficulty in being affable. Never could he force himself to engage in small talk or meaningless chatter. In everything he saw room for thought and he applied that thought relentlessly.

The reticence in his disposition gave many the impression that Matty was conceited and arrogant. Nothing could be further from the truth. As a matter of fact, Mathewson was unusually modest. His diffidence reached a point of actual timidity.

Though Mathewson died in his forty-fifth year, it should be borne in mind that twenty-five years of that life were punctuated with weekly crises, any one of which would have been an outstanding event in the lives of most men. When he was but twenty-four, his importance to sport quite rivaled that of mature men in other walks of life. He inspired more actual publicity than an admiral of the navy, a general of the army, or the executive head of our greatest industry.

Mature newspapermen who gravely sought the views of Matty on different subjects and analyzed or criticized these statements in a sober vein, did not realize, perhaps, that they were picking apart a flaxen-haired boy. Men of affairs who gathered in clubs and other places to speculate on what "Old Matty would do against the Pirates tomorrow" never reflected, possibly, that they were placing a civic responsibility on a boy of twenty-four—a lad as immature as their own office boy.

Hundreds of boys, coming into a major baseball league, are confronted with such a condition and the wonder is that even a few of them survive it. Without a solid foundation, a commonsense training in their tender youth, they would not be able to do so. For that reason, Mathewson himself always insisted that ballplayers who lose their balance in this early glare of prominence and publicity, should be judged with generosity, kindness, and charity.

Fortunately, this marvelous young Mathewson, this college boy who suddenly lifted his club from a tail-end position to one of prominence, was brought up in a thoughtful atmosphere. Christy Mathewson came from prominent pioneer stock. His forebears settled in the section of Pennsylvania in which he was born. In Factoryville they will still show you the spot where Matty's grandfather erected the first home and will tell you that a bearskin decorated the front door.

Though well-educated and polished in manner, there were no frills about young Mathewson. He was never misled by undue praise. His mother had implanted in him a sense of honesty and directness. Before taking any step, important or unimportant, he considered the whys and wherefores of it. To everything he figured there was a reckoning.

"You know," he said to the writer one day, "my mother had intended that I be a preacher. Rather, that was her ambition. She never insisted that I change my profession. At that," he added seriously, "I guess I can do some good in this game—baseball."

Shortly after that, the manufacturer of a safety razor [Durham Duplex] inquired of the writer if it were possible to get Matty to sign a recommendation for his razor for advertising purposes. If this could be done, he would pay me a hundred dollars and give Matty two hundred dollars.

I approached Matty on the proposition. He was interested immediately, being at all times a good businessman.

"We certainly can't afford to let that money get away from us," he remarked. "But, say," he suddenly demanded to know, "is it a really good razor?"

"I use one myself," I told him. "Anyway, what difference does it make? The other players make money boosting products."

"Yes, that's true, but, you know, the reason they are willing to pay me two hundred dollars to recommend that razor is because, when they put the ad in the paper, people will take my word for it. Isn't that right?"

He was assured that such was the general idea.

"Wait a minute—you say you use that razor?" He suggested, "Let me have it. We've got to get this money, but I want to be sure."

Without the least hurry, he walked to the bathroom, lathered his face, and then proceeded carefully to shave himself with the razor in question.

"Seems to work all right," he decided.

He then walked over and signed the testimonial which had been previously prepared by the company. We collected the money that afternoon.

"I'm not finicky and I don't want to be a sap," he explained, "but I just couldn't recommend that razor until I had tried it."

In the Mathewson home, Christy's mother, a devout Christian, always insisted on a quiet, restful Sunday. She would never permit the boys to play baseball on Sunday. It was an established family rule that Matty never forgot or violated.

"There may be some good arguments in favor of Sunday games in some places," his mother said, when asked about this, "but I should not like to see my boy playing on that day and he knows it. He will never do it."

The public generally believed that Matty's objection to playing on Sunday was due to some religious conviction of his own. As a matter of fact, he had no objections, personally, to playing ball on Sunday. No promise was exacted from him, either. He simply knew that it would displease the mother who had so carefully brought him up and never did he pitch a ball game on Sunday.

Another principle ground into Matty was not to be insincere or deceitful. This often caused him to be misjudged. If an enthusiastic fan rushed up to shake hands with him and remarked, "You remember me, don't you, Matty?"

"No, I do not," he would reply, if such were the case, "but I am glad to know you now."

Even the sporting writers, especially those who did not know Mathewson intimately, felt aggrieved at his lack of cordiality. This they attributed, mistakenly, to conceit, what we would describe nowadays as "putting on the high hat."

An incident that illustrates this occurred on a tour of the spring training camps by one of the best-known sporting editors in the country. He was familiar with the activities of the ballplayers, but his personal knowledge of them was indirect. For years he had been an ardent admirer of Mathewson.

Arriving at the camp where Matty was then acting as assistant to John McGraw, the sporting editor spied him in the hotel lobby.

"Why, how are you, Matty?" he exclaimed, holding out his hand. "I'm mighty glad to see you."

Mathewson did not recognize the man at all, though he knew his work and would have recognized the name had it been mentioned.

"How are you, sir," said Mathewson, shaking hands impersonally.

With that, his attention was attracted to some ballplayer in the lobby and Matty walked away.

"What's the matter with that fellow?" complained the writer, very much offended. "Why, he's all swelled up. Deliberately walked away from me."

The editor had felt that he had been snubbed.

It had never occurred to Matty to stop and force himself to be pleasant and pretend to recognize this visitor. A few weeks later, he was told about the incident and felt very badly. He apologized as best he could.

Those who knew Matty intimately would never have thought of this as a rebuff. It was his nature to be that way. I remember quite well going to a box at the ballpark to shake hands with him for the first time in three years on his return from Saranac Lake. Mind you, we had been close friends for twenty years.

"Hello, how are you?" was his greeting and in answer to my question about his health, added, "Lots better."

From then on, we watched the game without another word being spoken between us.

That gave no offense. In fact, it was pleasant to feel that he was the same old Matty. Often there was more of friendship and contentment in his long periods of silence than when he forced himself to talk.

Chapter 9. Magnificent in Defeat

In Matty's effects was found a clipping that he prized more highly than any of the unbroken records he left in the official archives of the league. It is an extract from an editorial in the *New York Herald.* It says:

"There have been pitchers almost as great as Mathewson; one or two, maybe, were more expert physically. But none approached the rare mixture of qualities that endeared him to the public and made him a genuinely good example for the youngsters. For him no sulking, no spiking, no quitting. In victory he was admirable, but in defeat he was magnificent. No sportsman, amateur or professional, ever took a beating with better grace."

The greatest game of ball ever pitched by Christy Mathewson—though others may show technical superiority in the records—was against the Boston Red Sox in the World Series of 1912. It also was last in the series of crucial diamond events that centered about him. He pitched after that, of course, but never again was the stage so perfectly set for baseball drama. Moreover, that was the day to which Mathewson looked back with the greatest personal pride and the keenest disappointment.

"If ever we prepare an autobiography," he once remarked while we were contemplating one, "we will talk about the ball games and not me."

For fear of making himself appear a hero, however, he persistently postponed the publication of his memoirs. He declined an offer of ten thousand dollars to do that during his long stay at Saranac.

"The greatest game of my life," he said, "wound up in defeat and you know the one I'm talking about. That was a tough break."

At the conclusion of that nerve-racking defeat that took with it the world's championship, Christy Mathewson was paid the greatest tribute of his career—the only public tribute in the knowledge of the writer ever offered by an opposing crowd to a loser in baseball.

In that historic Red Sox—Giants Series of 1912, a record was established when eight games were necessary to decide the winner. Mathewson pitched three of those games without winning one. Nevertheless, his work was practically faultless. Hard luck hovered over him throughout the Series, finally reaching a climax in the eighth game when Fred Snodgrass made his famous muff of an easy fly ball and Fred Merkle and Chief Meyers let a pop foul fall between them.

Though he could not win, Mathewson was not taken out of the box in any of the games. In fact, no situation arose where there was even a question of relieving him.

Rube Marquard had pitched successfully and, being younger, the first plan was to send him in for the final game. After some deliberation, however, John McGraw decided that this important task should be given to Matty, then regarded as the greatest money pitcher in the world. A money player who is at his best when the stakes are highest. Marquard declared that he would rather risk his share of the prize money on Mathewson than on himself.

"Matty can pitch for my money," the players declared in chorus when McGraw announced his plans in the clubhouse.

"I hope I can do it," declared Matty, "but I know I can take no chances on letting up."

Three of the New York players had bought homes during the summer and were counting on the winning end of the World Series to pay off their mortgages. They were insistent that Matty make or break them, as they put it.

With all this on his shoulders, Big Six stepped in the box that afternoon and with deadly precision began mowing down the Red Sox batters. He was pitching shut-out ball throughout the game, but the ill luck started bearing down on him early. Larry Doyle hit what would have been a home run but for a remarkable catch by Harry Hooper, who fell over the low fence as he stopped the ball with one hand. It was much the same as that catch made by Sam Rice in the 1925 Series at Washington. That break of luck cost the Giants at least two runs.

Even so, Matty, calm and unruffled, kept up his fire, not a Boston runner scoring until the seventh inning. The Giants had scored in the third and the game went to the tenth a tie. For a moment, it looked as if the hard luck had been shaken off. The Giants in their half scored a run. Then came the downpour of hard luck.

Three disconcerting incidents ruined for Mathewson that perfectly pitched game. Snodgrass's historic muff of a fly ball and the failure of Meyers and Merkle to catch a pop foul that fell between them in the tenth inning put a climax on the tragedy, but neither of them quite so disastrous and downright unlucky as the pinch hit of Olaf Henriksen, a youngster, when he went to bat for pitcher Hugh Bedient in the seventh inning and tied the score. Two were out at the time.

The extreme care with which Matty studied a batter is illustrated in the case of Henriksen.

"I had never seen Henriksen before," Matty explained afterward, "and I had no information at all as to his weakness. I simply did not know how to pitch to him. Jake Stahl was on second and if he scored the game would be tied up. If you will remember, Jack Murphy had been shifted to left field on account of the sun. He had the best throwing arm in the league. It was up to me, therefore, to make Henriksen hit toward left. If the ball got by the infield, there would be a chance of Murray making a good throw to the plate.

"With all this in mind, I pitched carefully and got two strikes on Henriksen. I then pitched him two bad balls, both of which he let go by. For a young batter, that boy showed wonderful nerve. In a crisis like that, most any batter, with two strikes on him, would have gone after a bad ball. But Henriksen took them. The only thing left was for me was to pitch so as to make him pull the ball toward third base or left field. Jack Murray knew what I was trying to do and set himself for a desperate throw. And Henriksen did hit exactly in the direction that I wanted him to. As luck would have it, though, the ball hit the sack at third base and bounded off at right angles, far into foul territory, good for two bases. The runner, of course, scored."

That to Matty was the heartbreaking turn of the game. But for it, the other incidents could not have happened. The Giants would have won in nine innings.

He never blamed Snodgrass as others did. When Snodgrass muffed that easy fly ball, the crowd turned on him. For the rest of the afternoon and for months afterward, for that matter, no man ever suffered such harsh criticism as did Snodgrass. Some wild-eyed fans even talked of mobbing him.

After the game, one of the baseball writers, overwrought and indignant, went to Mathewson in the hotel.

"What are you going to say about Snodgrass?" he wanted to know. "Honestly, you'd be justified in going right out and killing him. He's tossed away your reputation and at least $30,000 for his fellow players."

Instead of showing anger, Matty smiled.

"You are a little excited, I guess," he said. "I don't blame Snodgrass for that and I feel downright sorry for him. I'd much rather be in my place than his. I never blame a ballplayer for making a physical error," he went on. "He went after the ball, all right. He had his hands set, but when the ball came down, it happened to strike his hands in the wrong place and slipped from his grasp. That has happened to other players. Poor Snodgrass couldn't help it. Instead of criticizing him harshly, I think you fellows ought to join with us in sympathizing with him. The poor fellow is miserable."

On the train going home, Matty did everything in his power to console Snodgrass. He also got the other players to do so.

But to get back to that game. With all these bad breaks coming on top of each other, it seemed that the Fates had decreed defeat for Mathewson.

When the final blow was struck and a Red Sox runner had crossed the plate with the winning run, the great crowd of Boston fans sat dumbfounded. Their relaxation from the agonizing tenseness was silence.

Those who saw that game will not find it easy to forget the picture of Mathewson standing there in the box in a sort of daze. The supreme effort of his life had been wasted by those ghastly breaks. He hesitated, as if in doubt how to proceed. Hundreds of hard-boiled fans actually wept.

Suddenly the tension broke in a most surprising way. John McGraw jumped out of the dugout and started on a run to the box to console the great pitcher. As he did so, the dumbfounded Boston fans also came out of their trance and, in a scrambled mass, found themselves running across the diamond to acclaim Mathewson rather than the victorious Boston club. Such a thing had never been seen in baseball before. So impressive had been the work of Mathewson and so apparent had been the hard luck breaks against him, that he was escorted from the field by a horde of fans who had rooted against him. In defeat, he was a greater hero than if he had won.

McGraw put his arm around the big fellow's shoulder and made no attempt to restrain his tears.

"Don't feel badly about it, Matty," he said. "You did nobly. Nobody could do more than that."

The exact details of the finish of that historic game in 1912 have been confused and warped in the constant retelling. Mathewson, however, was never vague or inaccurate when asked about it.

As an example of his thoroughness and keen regard for facts, here is a record of the tenth inning and the box score taken from a little file, that he kept for reference, that was furnished by Mrs. Mathewson:

"In the tenth inning, Clyde Engle was called to bat in place of Joe Wood. He sent a fly to left center which Snodgrass muffed, Engle taking second on the error. Hooper sent another fly to Snodgrass, but this time the New York center fielder made no mistake and Hooper was out. Mathewson walked Steve Yerkes. Tris Speaker, coming up amidst an ovation from the frenzied spectators, swung hard at the first ball pitched, but a groan went up when it was seen that he had raised a puny foul near the coacher's box at first. Merkle and Meyers both started for it, became mixed up, and let the ball drop between them. Then Speaker singled to right, scoring Engle with the run that again tied up the game. Yerkes took third and Speaker second on Devore's throw to catch Engle at the plate. Duffy Lewis was purposely passed, the Giants planning on a double play with the bases filled. But Larry Gardner sent a long fly to right. Devore caught it and threw to the plate, but not in time to catch Yerkes, who came across with the winning run."

Chapter 10. Archenemy Joe Tinker

For several years before his death, Matty had discussed the preparation of his autobiography. He always feared, though, that it would make him appear as a self-made hero and the work was never completed. In his effects were found several subjects that he had outlined and partly completed. This is the first of seven chapters in his own words.

If you were to ask any ten baseball fans to name the toughest batter that Christy Mathewson ever faced—the man who always had his number—at least nine of them and possibly all ten would immediately answer, "Joe Tinker."

That is not exactly true, but it comes pretty close. I know that when I get into a conversation about great hitters, the question almost invariably asked me is, "Why is it that Joe Tinker is always able to hit you?"

The story of Tinker being my nemesis has been repeated so often that it has come to be a sort of tradition. On account of this, very few fans remember that during his first two years in the Big League, Joe was a very weak hitter against my pitching. During that time, we never regarded him as dangerous. In fact, he often has told me that his failure to get a hit off me was one of his greatest worries.

At that time, Joe was what we call a chop hitter. That is, he choked his bat up close and punched at the ball. Most of the pitchers were quick to find his weak spot. I discovered that his weak groove against me was a slow curve on the outside corner of the plate away from him. With a choked bat, he could not reach it. For two years I fed him nothing else but that.

All this time Tinker has been studying me as closely as I had studied him. Suddenly, his style changed completely. I heard about it afterward—his decision to make a change.

In an important game between the Giants and the Cubs, Joe had struck out three times against me. That caused him to do something desperate. He knew quite well that I had been feeding him that slow curve ball on the outside and he had wondered at his inability to hit it. Instead of getting disgusted, he decided to look for the antidote.

After that game, Tinker went to the clubhouse with his head down. He was not quitting, but thinking. Sitting on the dressing room bench near Johnny Evers, he suddenly stopped in the act of pulling off his stockings.

"Say, Johnny," he spoke up, just as if they had been talking about what he was thinking, "I've got it. Nothing to it. I've got the answer."

"The answer to what?" asked the surprised Evers. "What's troubling you?"

"I've found out the way to hit that Mathewson. He made me look like a sucker today, but I've got him now. Just watch and see."

"I wish you'd have thought of it sooner."

"Well, just wait 'til he pitches again. I'll show you."

I'll never forget the next time I pitched to Tinker. It was during that four-game series in Chicago. Having won the first game—the one in which I struck out Tinker three times—John McGraw decided that I should pitch the last one. I was going pretty good, too, until Tinker came to bat with two out and two men on the bases.

As usual, the outfielders moved in a little closer, Joe being known as a short hitter. I noticed something unusual in Tinker's style, but for a minute I couldn't decide what it was. Then I saw that he was standing far back in the box and had a long bat. Instead of choking the bat, he had his hands gripped right over the small end of the handle, much like Joe Schultz held a bat. Still, I saw no reason to change my pitching prescription.

I nodded my head when Roger Bresnahan, who was catching, gave me the regular sign for a slow curve ball outside. I felt absolutely confident when I turned the ball loose and it went exactly where I had aimed it. I mean it started there.

Tinker must have been expecting the ball just where I placed it. With that long bat, he took a full swing, catching the ball squarely on the nose. It whistled over George Browne's head for two bases. The two runs scored and that pair of runs eventually won the game.

"Hey, Matty," he yelled at me from second base, "I've got your number now."

He didn't know how true that remark was going to be in the future. He had solved the problem with exactness. That long bat had enabled him to reach the ball on the outside and the big swing had given it a real ride.

The reader will say immediately, I imagine, "Well, why didn't you shift on him as soon as you found that out?"

The fact is, it took me a long time to find out all the things that I have put down here so quickly. It took me as long to solve Joe's new style as it had taken him to solve my old prescription. The fan may also ask, "Why didn't Tinker discover that earlier?" I don't know, but the fact is he didn't.

That was the beginning of my tilts with Tinker. He didn't always get the best of them, as many believe, but he did often enough to keep me worried every time I faced him. Instead of a short chop hitter, Tinker became a long hitter. It took time for the outfielders to realize this and to play him accordingly. Those things are not done in a minute.

The main thing, though, is that long hit by Tinker gave him confidence against my pitching. That meant everything. After he had made two or three long hits off me, he felt absolutely sure of being able to do it any time. He became aggressive instead of defensive. Often Joe has told me that he felt sure of getting a hit off me. He could take his time and wait, he said, because he knew I wasn't going to hit him. He thought I had too much control.

For several years, Joe kept me studying. He is a mighty hard man to beat in a battle of wits. When I would shift, he would shift. He seemed able to call the turn. The old slow curve became his favorite. He broke the heart of many pitchers by poling it for long hits.

I found by degrees that the only thing to do was to keep the ball in close to him and put a lot of speed on it—in other words, try to outguess him. Outguessing Tinker was never an easy job.

Though Tinker had that uncanny, dangerous knack of hitting me in the pinches, there were other batters even more dangerous.

Chapter 11. More Formidable Batters

I have said there were other hitters more difficult to pitch to than Joe Tinker. Among these I list Fred Clarke, Hans Wagner, Claude Ritchey, and Frank Baker. Sherwood Magee was also a dangerous man with whom to take liberties.

Clarke was one of the few batters I ever have seen who could not be fooled by a change of pace. By that, I mean a slowly thrown ball following one of great speed without giving any indication of it in the swing.

Clarke was unique as a batter. Though a left-handed hitter, he was what we call a natural left-field hitter. The left-handed batter, you know, ordinarily hits to right field. Clarke's tendency to hit in the opposite direction was due to his hitting late at the ball. It was more habit than design. Naturally, his favorite ball to hit was a curve on the outside—away from him.

When a pitcher finds that a change of pace is not effective, his only resort is the free use of curves. But if a pitcher threw a slow ball of any kind close in to Clarke, he would rap it with terrific force into right field. So, he had us going and coming.

It is an accepted rule in the game that when a left-handed batter hits late at a ball, it is suicidal to change the pace on him because he will pull it all the harder in the other direction. My only defense against Clarke was to use curves, varying them as to height and keeping them in close. No matter what the pitchers did, though, Clarke was always dangerous.

I regard Hans Wagner as the really best hitter that I ever faced. To me, he was always a threat, but in that respect, I was no different from other pitchers. If that big, gangly Dutchman had a definite weakness, no pitcher was ever able to prove it. Often the rumor went around that somebody had discovered a weak spot in Wagner's armor, only to lead a pitcher into trouble. Hans was fundamentally a free swinger. And let me say here, in all baseball there were never more than ten or twelve successful free swingers. To be a successful free swinger, a man must possess that natural gift of a great eye and the ability to take a full swing without losing his sense of sight or balance.

Sherwood Magee was a free swinger. So was Cap Anson, Dan Brouthers, Ed Delahanty, and so is Babe Ruth. These fellows could take a big, heavy bat and swing it as freely as a toothpick. But they also had the eye.

Wagner was different from the others in that he held his hands far apart on the bat, just as Ty Cobb does. They were the only two great batters who could hold a bat that way and still swing freely.

Wagner stood in a far corner of the box and would walk into the ball, poling it to the far corners. I have tried every device within my knowledge or ingenuity and it was rare that I ever found anything that would fool him twice. On one occasion, I tried to pitch out—waste a ball—on Wagner so as to give the catcher a free throw to catch a base stealer. I got the ball a half inch too close and Wagner, reaching far out, caught the ball on the end of his bat for a two-base hit.

Only one pitcher—Bugs Raymond—ever had Wagner's number. In some way that the other pitchers never could understand, he had a way of kidding Wagner that seemed to get his goat. By those tactics, Raymond could make Hans swing at bad balls, especially the spitball, a thing no other pitcher was ever able to do. Of course, Hans swung at a bad one when he wanted to and would often kill it, but that was no credit to the pitcher.

The only thing we could do with Wagner was try to mix him up by using curves, fastballs and slow balls and trust to luck. He was an instinctive ballplayer, seeming to foresee just what was in the minds of his opponents. The game never turned out a greater ballplayer than Hans Wagner.

Though Claude Ritchey was not regarded as one of the greatest batters of the game, he always gave me trouble. Somehow, I simply could not outguess him. Like Fred Clarke, he was one of those left-handers who swung late at the ball and hit into left field as a rule. If I shifted on him, though, and kept the ball inside, he would whack a vicious drive down the right foul line. I always feared him in a pinch.

To digress, I recall a game in Pittsburgh at the old Allegheny Grounds when we were winning our pennant in 1905. The Pirates had two runners on the bases and Ritchey was coming up. In the stands that day was Mrs. Charles Wilson, famous as a Giant rooter, a nice, loveable woman past middle age, who often traveled with the New York club. She would go right into the grandstand of a hostile town and gather the New Yorkers about her. Leading them as a cheering section, she would dare anybody to stop her.

As Ritchey came up this day, I feared the worst. I didn't dare give him anything like a good ball to hit, so I purposely walked him.

Mrs. Wilson, thinking I had lost control and was weakening, left the stand in nervous fear and waited outside for the Pittsburgh cheers which never came. She didn't know that I had disposed of the next two batters and had run the game into extra innings. She stayed out there until the fourteenth inning had arrived and, from the groan of the Pittsburgh crowd, she finally knew that we had won. We found her completely exhausted.

Frank Baker was one of the hardest, cleanest hitters I ever saw. We were not warned to look out for him in that 1911 Series, either. Our warning was to concentrate on Eddie Collins and rightly so. He is one of the smartest ballplayers that ever lived. But Baker came as a complete surprise.

Fans still remember, I imagine, how Baker hit that home run off Rube Marquard in one game and came right back to do the same thing off me the next day. I simply got a curve ball too close to him and he killed it. Baker could hit equally well in any field, which made it impossible for the outfielders to place themselves for him with any degree of certainty. The nearest to a weakness in him was a slow curve ball well away from him.

Chapter 12. Sign Stealing and a Perfect Shove

Perhaps the most interesting game that I ever pitched, that is the most interesting to me, was the opening game of the World's Series in 1911 between the Giants and the Athletics. It called on me for more mental and physical effort and there were more unusual plays than in any other game that comes to my mind.

As you will remember, we won that game 2 to 1 and the break came our way in the "lucky seventh."

All the way through I had against me Chief Bender, whom I regarded as the greatest pitcher in the American League at that time. There was never a moment of mental or physical relaxation for either of us until the last man was out in the ninth inning.

Ty Cobb, who covered the game as an expert, wrote in the papers and also has told me often that it was easily the best game that I ever had pitched. He says that I didn't pitch a ball incorrectly or didn't pitch a useless one for the first four innings. I think Ty a little too generous in saying that, but I do know that I pitched my hardest and with the most satisfaction during those innings.

To begin with, I had to do a great deal of experimenting. Only a pitcher can understand what a strain that is on the nerves. I had pitched against the Athletics in 1905 and had shut them out three times. This, however, was a comparatively new team. The only men I ever had faced were Bris Lord, Chief Bender, Danny Murphy, and Harry Davis. I had some tips on the other batters, of course, but most of the time I had to guess at their weakness and take a chance. You see, a batter who may be weak against another pitcher's curve might not be weak against mine. The information given to me, however, helped a lot as the game went along.

When it came to outguessing each other, it was about an even break between the two teams. We had been fully warned that the Athletics were apt to steal our battery signals and I had to be on guard constantly against that. They did get our signals after a few innings, but I was lucky enough to discover it in time.

To tell the truth, it was through their stealing of our signals that we were able to beat them. For fear that I may create a wrong impression, let me explain that sign stealing is perfectly legitimate and is in no way regarded as unsportsmanlike. On the contrary, a team that can solve the signal system of an opponent is justly credited with being unusually clever. It is much the same as a football captain being smart enough to decipher the enemy signals and anticipate the play. The base runners and coaches on first and third catch them.

The Athletics were noted for their cleverness at sign stealing—we call them signs in baseball, not signals. Danny Murphy was probably the best in the world at that. Being forewarned, we were forearmed.

In an early inning, Harry Davis came to bat and, with utmost confidence, waded right into a curve ball and hit it solidly for a single. In a flash, I knew that they had found the key to our catcher's signs. I walked straight to Chief Meyers.

"He knew where that ball was coming," I told him.

Just then, the Chief looked toward the Giants bench and John McGraw was waving to him. He also had discovered that our signs were being read by Murphy and relayed to the batter.

"The boss says to shift," whispered Meyers. "Hereafter watch my feet."

From then on, the Chief gave the pitching signals with his feet, at the same time going through the other signs with his fingers.

In a tight place, Frank Baker came to bat with Rube Oldring on second base. Oldring, who could see Meyers's hands, tipped to Baker to expect a curve ball on the outside. Baker stepped in so close that he came near being hit in the head. He had been completely crossed. With his fingers, the Chief had called for a curve ball outside, but with his feet—the real sign—he had called for a high, fast one in close. Baker had a narrow escape from being hurt. He was so upset and bewildered that he struck out on three pitched balls.

The Athletics knew then that we had shifted our signs and for the rest of the game they could not decipher the code. From then on it was one of the prettiest fights I ever saw. The only advantage I had on Bender was the one run brought in on a hit by Josh Devore, but I kept the advantage.

The most remarkable play I ever saw in baseball occurred in that game and, though I figured in it, I will have to relate it. Never before had I been called on to use football tactics in baseball.

In the fifth inning with one out and the score tied, Chief Bender had singled and was forced out at second by Lord. A long two-bagger by Oldring put Lord on third. Here I had runners on second and third with two out and Eddie Collins at the bat. It was a dangerous situation. A hit would have won the game.

Collins hit a slow roller directly toward first base. Fred Merkle advanced to field the ball and I ran over to cover the bag. Merkle, in the act of fielding the ball, was directly in my path to the bag. Collins saw this in a flash. He is one of the quickest thinkers in all of baseball. Eddie knew he would have no chance if he bumped into two heavier men. He decided in that flash of thought to make a slide and go around us to the bag, while we were colliding.

In the same flash, I caught his purpose. I saw that Merkle could not get back to the bag if he took time to field the ball. Neither could I.

Mind you, the remarkable feature of this odd play was the rapidity with which the three of us thought out the problem. It was no more than a second of time.

Thinking and acting simultaneously, I deliberately bumped into Merkle and shoved him with all my might toward the bag. It was fully ten feet, but he fell sprawling across the bag with the ball in his hand and Collins was out by a foot. I have never seen another such play as that. The football shove prevented two runs and saved us the game.

A funny feature to that play was that in the New York papers the next day, Collins was accused of deliberately running into Merkle. In the Philadelphia papers, Merkle was charged with roughing up Collins so as to block him.

Chapter 13. Born Hitters, Pitchers Excluded

It is my opinion that the great majority of ballplayers—more than 95 percent, I should say—are born and not made. For that reason, I do not intend to make a ballplayer out of my son. There is not enough money in the game unless you are a top-notcher and there is only about one chance in a hundred fifty of a man making good in the Big Leagues, so the dopesters have figured out. I would rather see my boy go into some other business or profession. Still, if he is a born ballplayer, I suppose he will be one and I couldn't help it.

In all my days on the diamond, I have never seen but one manufactured ballplayer, and that was Harry McCormick, or Moose as he was called, who used to play for the Giants.

McCormick was a fellow student of mine in Bucknell College, but he never played baseball until his sophomore year. Oddly enough, this future Big League star was not on the varsity team. He was a basketball and football player. In the spring, he used to come out to exercise with the ball team, but that was all. Harry could hit the ball all right, but he couldn't judge a fly ball to save his life.

The college team made the usual Easter trip in McCormick's sophomore year and, as one of the players was sick, we had to send for him. In the very first game he won for us by his terrific hitting. One of his line drives knocked a board off the fence. But when a fly ball went out to his field, all that we could do was to watch it and breathe a prayer that he would get somewhere near it. If he judged half the flies correctly, he thought himself doing well. But we made him practice until he could judge the long flies. He was absolutely a manufactured ballplayer.

At that, McCormick may have been a born hitter. In fact, I am sure he was, even if he was not a natural ballplayer. He could hit the ball just as well the first time he ever tried as he could later on. In my opinion, he was the greatest pinch hitter the game ever knew.

I have gone down the list carefully and McCormick stands out as the only successful player I ever knew who was not born to the art. I don't mean to say that ballplayers can't be improved. Still, the latent talent must be there.

Take players like Ed Delahanty, Hans Wagner, Nap Lajoie, Frank Baker, Dan Brouthers, Eddie Collins, John McGraw, Willie Keeler, and Hugh Jennings. Those men were born ballplayers. It was in their blood. They learned their profession and forced themselves forward under all kinds of difficulties. Nowadays the clubs are seeking men like that. In their day, they were seeking the clubs. Though I may be mistaken and am willing to be corrected, I don't believe that all those famous stars, put together in their Big League beginning, cost as much as a single promising recruit does in this day and time.

Did you ever notice when the first call comes for baseball candidates in a high school, how easy it is to pick out the natural ballplayers in two or three days? There is a certain movement about the natural ballplayer that cannot be mistaken. Boys who never tried to make a team before will step out and field grounders with that easy, born-to-the-manor motion. Others may try all their lives only to appear awkward. They rarely get any better.

In many respects, a pitcher is not a ballplayer, though I think he should be. He is purely a specialist. If he has a good arm, he can learn curves and can also study batters. He can hold his job whether he can field or hit or run or not. Besides that, the pitcher doesn't play every day. He is much like the kicking experts that are called in for one particular play in a football game. They are not real football players.

The question is often asked, "Why is it that pitchers cannot hit?"

In the first place, that is not exactly true. Many pitchers are exceptionally good hitters—men like Babe Ruth, Jack Bentley, Carl Mays, Dutch Ruether, Doc White, and Doc Crandall, for instance. I was a fairly good hitter myself.

There should be no mystery about the weakness of pitchers as hitters, the rule I mean. The answer is that pitchers are not required to hit. I mean to say that when a pitcher is signed for a Big League team, the question of his hitting is never brought up. It is not considered a requisite. Through playing irregularly, they don't get the practice to improve.

An outfielder or an infielder will not be brought to the Big League unless he has shown some record or promise of being a good hitter. That is one of the first things considered by a scout in making his report. You might just as well say that it is odd that pitchers, as a rule, are not good outfielders. The answer is that they are not required to be good outfielders to hold a job. They are supposed to pitch and that is all.

That is why I say pitchers, as a class, are not really ballplayers, but specialists.

At the same time, the pitcher who expects to make a big success must acquire the knack of fielding, even if he can't hit. If he can learn to hit, so much the better.

The pitcher does not have as much chance at hitting as the regular member of the team. He does not have his regular turn in daily batting practice. On account of his being in and out, the pitcher is not considered a factor in working out any team batting plays. He is purely an outsider and he is made to feel that his efforts at being a hitter are not to be taken seriously.

Some pitchers, however, are all-round ballplayers. If they are born hitters, they will insist on getting their crack at the ball in practice. There is something irresistible in the feel of hitting a baseball. Many pitchers get discouraged and don't try to hit. They realize their weakness and admit it.

One day Leon Ames, after striking out four times, came back to the dugout and tossed his bat in the pile, disgustedly.

"You know," he said, "I wouldn't take the trouble to carry a bat up to that plate if the rules didn't call for it."

Chapter 14. My Worst Game

In many respects, the worst game I ever pitched, after I became a full-fledged Big Leaguer, was the playoff game in 1908 when the Cubs beat us out of the championship. I think that was the only game I ever pitched all the way through suffering from a bad arm. As a rule, my arm was in good shape.

None of us were in the right frame of mind nor were we physically fit for that momentous ball game. We felt that it should not have been played or, rather, that we should have been awarded the pennant without having to play it. Most certainly we had won the pennant. Many of our players were crippled and we were at a decided disadvantage.

It was, as you older fans remember, the result of the Fred Merkle incident and the subsequent action of the league directors in requiring the game to be played over.

John McGraw had told us that we could do as we pleased about it—play it or not. He was just as indignant as we were. John T. Brush, the owner, who was sick in bed at the time, however, gave us the impression that, if we did not play, someone might question our gameness. I was on the committee that called on him in his sick room. One look at his face and we decided to play.

I had some misgivings at the beginning of the game. In fact, I found that my curve ball was not working while warming up with Roger Bresnahan.

"What's the matter with it, Roger?" I asked him. "I can't make it break."

"It will come around all right as you get warmed up," he said.

I mentioned it to other players, but they wanted me to pitch. To tell the truth, I wanted to pitch, myself, but I didn't like the way my curve was acting.

Though I did not realize it, I had overworked my arm in the strain of those last few weeks which decided the pennant. I pitched two games a week and sometimes three.

When we finally decided to go through with the playoff game and it also had been decided that I should pitch, I rested up for several days to prepare for the game of my life. That is where I made a serious mistake.

Notwithstanding Bresnahan's constant encouragement and the prophecy that I would be going great in a few innings, the arm did not loosen up at all. Fortunately, or unfortunately as it may have been, the Giants got a lead right away off Jack Pfiester and I kept on pitching, hoping for the best. I had fairly good control, but I couldn't rely on my curve at all.

Many of my friends have been good enough to say that I pitched a great ball game and would have won but for Cy Seymour misjudging Joe Tinker's long fly to center field. That idea, which persisted for years, was more kind than accurate. I simply lost the game because I had nothing on the ball. Seymour's misjudging of that fly would not have changed the result.

During the game, I had noticed John Montgomery Ward, formerly a great pitcher as well as infielder and a manager, sitting in one of the boxes. I could see that he was watching me closely, more interested in what I was trying to pitch than in the game itself. Later I went over and spoke to him.

"I could see that something was the matter with your arm, Matty," he told me. "You couldn't get it loosened up."

"I took a pretty good rest before working," I reminded him.

"Too much rest," he said. "I've seen that happen before. When a pitcher has been under a long strain as you were the past month and as it frequently happened in the old days, it is best to keep right on working. A rest to do you any good would require ten days or two weeks. Charley Radbourn, in pitching those twenty-seven successive games, found that he had to keep right on going so as not to stiffen up. But he was never able to pitch afterward."

Ward had sized up the situation exactly. I would like some of the coming pitchers to keep that in mind.

When the fatal third inning of that game started and Joe Tinker hit his memorable three-bagger, I looked toward the bench, then walked halfway to the plate.

"Rog," I said to Bresnahan, "I haven't got a thing today."

"Keep at it," he said. "We'll get them yet."

From the bench, McGraw signaled me to keep on pitching.

Then Johnny Kling singled and Tinker scored. We got Three-Fingered Brown and Jimmy Sheckard out all right, but in trying to pitch too cautiously to Johnny Evers I lost him and he walked. The score was only tied and we still had a chance, but Frank Schulte hit a hard double to right and scored Kling. We fought on and I put every ounce of strength I had into every pitch, but the smoothness was gone.

I pitched in close to Frank Chance, whose face I can see to this day. He did the most remarkable bit of batting I ever saw. Though the ball hit close to the handle of his bat, he shoved it over Fred Tenney's head for a two-base hit, scoring both Evers and Schulte. That was the break of the game. We knew it, too.

Fred Merkle, who had blamed himself for all the trouble, was a doleful sight as he sat on a corner of the bench as if he felt himself an outcast. He had lost twenty pounds through worry over his mistake in the September game. His eyes were sunk, his whole face haggard.

"It was all my fault, fellows," he half-moaned.

Nobody answered him. Brown was pitching for the Cubs now and got better as he went. The cowbells had ceased to jingle and the rooters seemed to feel as we did—lost.

Our one ray of hope was in the seventh, the only time during the game that Merkle smiled.

Art Devlin started it with a single and Moose McCormick hit safely to right field. Brown passed Al Bridwell purposely and filled the bases. McGraw sent Larry Doyle, still limping from a broken ankle, to bat in my place. But Larry's eye had been dimmed by his long absence and he fouled out to the catcher. Fred Tenney hit a long line drive squarely into Schulte's hands, on which Devlin scored, but Buck Herzog went out on a grounder to Joe Tinker and our goose was cooked. We had lost the pennant.

In the clubhouse that night, Merkle went to McGraw, imploring him, "Fire me, Mac, before I can do any more harm."

Instead of firing him, McGraw told Merkle, in the presence of us all, that he was one of the gamest ballplayers he ever saw and the kind that he wanted.

Chapter 15. Pitchers and Psychology

A man can overthink himself sometimes in trying to dope out the psychology of pitching. Still, there is something in it. The only trouble about this study of psychology by amateur thinkers is that they arrive at a conclusion and then try to apply it to different minds in the same way. I have found that it can't be done that way. It must be applied individually.

For example, many a young pitcher is ruined by having been started too soon and by remembering the hard "ride" he got from the opposing players. That same ride or razzing will bring out the fighting qualities in another youngster and set him in right at the start. There are a lot of pitchers who get annoyed at razzing after they have been in the game for years and allow it to throw them completely off their balance.

In my early days, one of the worst naggers to get after me and keep at it continually was Clark Griffith. Oddly enough, it was some of his nagging that made me pitch my very best baseball. He has told me that he found that out when he was managing Cincinnati and decided to lay off.

One day, I remember, we were playing against the Reds and, as the game was close, Griff kept after me from the coaching lines every minute. It was maddening.

"Come on, fellows," he would yell, "we'll get this big blond bluff now. He's yellow! Look, he's yellow!"

At first, I paid no attention, but after a few innings I began to get annoyed and redoubled my efforts. I was pitching like a prize fighter starts to hit after he has been stung.

In a late inning there were two moderately good batters ahead of Mike Mitchell, who was a real slugger and always to be feared.

"Come on, now, fellows," Griff began again. "We'll get the big blond stiff now. Just wait 'til old Mike gets up there. Give him a chance! The big poser is yellow!"

I don't know what possessed me to do such a thing because I seldom show anger. Anyway, I accepted the challenge and took a long chance.

"All right," I called out to Griffith, "I'll bring Mike up and we'll see what he can do."

Deliberately I passed the two batters and took on the hard-hitting Mitchell out of pure bravado. Luckily, I got away with it. I was so steamed up over Griffith's cutting comments that I put everything I had on the ball and struck Mitchell out.

I never did such a thing again because I know it is foolish, but the point I make is that instead of rattling me into wildness, Griff's nagging made me all the more determined. It often works that way.

The coachers tried that same thing on Grover Alexander when he first came up, but he also was one of the type to be let alone. He actually pitched better when they were giving him a ride. Soon the word went around to lay off Aleck.

On other pitchers—good ones, too—the psychology works differently. You may have noticed that veteran managers like John McGraw will keep a new pitcher on the bench for a long time before starting him. They know better than anybody that a youngster, if upset in his first appearance, is likely to be ruined for years. It takes a long time to find the right spot in which to start him. Rube Marquard was set back fully two seasons by having been started at the wrong time. McGraw didn't want to start him, but so much had been written about the big price paid for this $11,000 beauty that the owners were eager to see him in action. McGraw finally heeded their requests even though it was against his better judgment. Marquard was sent in against the Reds during a double-header.

"Honestly, Matty," Rube told me afterward, "I didn't know where I was. All I could think of was that eleven thousand dollars they had paid for me and whether that big crowd would think that McGraw had been stung. When those players started to ride me, I went straight up in the air."

John Kane, a little fellow, was the first man up and Marquard hit him. He promptly stole second while Rube was worrying about that. Then up came Hans Lobert, the man who broke Marquard's heart.

"Now," Lobert said to Rube, as he walked up to the plate, "we'll see whether you are an eleven-thousand-dollar beauty or a busher."

Marquard, unable to think of a comeback, laid the ball squarely over the middle and Lobert smacked it for a long triple. As he scrambled to his feet at third base, the tantalizing Lobert looked at Marquard with a mocking grin.

"I thought so," he said, "an eleven-thousand-dollar lemon. That's you—you big busher."

Right then, some fan yelled "Take him out!" and Marquard's death knell had sounded, followed with another triple and a regular fusillade got under way.

That ruined Marquard for that year and the next. He had to be used for finishing out games. All he needed was one victory to give him confidence, but McGraw did not find the spot until after a disastrous series with the Phillies the next July. Marquard begged for a chance and got it. To reinstate himself fully, he struck out Lobert who by that time was on the Philadelphia club.

After that, Marquard was almost unbeatable. He was, indeed, a great pitcher.

"You can't hit what you don't see," is the way Joe Tinker spoke of the Rube's pitching. "He pitched me one so fast that I didn't know where the ball was until I heard it hit the catcher's mitt."

It took us a year to find the weak spot in Harry Coveleski's armor. You probably remember he beat us out of a pennant by pitching out of turn against us while with Philadelphia. That is not easy for a ballplayer to forget, especially as he went out of his way to do it.

The next winter, Eddie Ashenbach, a scout and a famous comedian, told McGraw that the only way to get Coveleski's goat was to ride him by imitating the sound of a drum with the bats or by the voice—rat-a-tat-tat.

We took it up in the spring. Coveleski heard nothing else. Every way he turned, he heard that rat-a-tat-tat or saw some Giants player imitating the beating of a snare drum.

"You think you are smart, don't you?" he said the first time, passing our bench.

When he talked back, we knew we had him. The rat-a-tat-tat never ceased.

In the very first game against us, Coveleski blew up and he didn't beat us a game all season.

Then Ashenbach gave us the answer. It seems that a girl would not become engaged to Coveleski unless he played in the village band out in his little mining town.

Having no musical talent, he selected the snare drum and began to practice. They were to have a big band concert and the girl wanted to be proud of Coveleski.

During the concert, the lovesick drummer became so nervous that he started in on his snare drum during a solo and almost broke up the show. He was the laughing stock of the village. So much so that the girl broke the engagement.

"We knew that the old drum stuff would get him in the minors," explained Ashenbach to McGraw, "but I forgot to tell you about it last year."

"Yes, and it cost us a pennant," declared McGraw.

Chapter 16. Tribute to John McGraw

It would be natural for me to consider John McGraw the greatest of all baseball managers, but after I left the Giants and returned as a coach, I had much opportunity to observe others and my opinion has not changed.

In addition to great executive ability, John McGraw has unusual vision that enables him to foresee events for weeks and months ahead. He is always prepared. The spark of genius in him, however, is his uncanny sense of perception. He has the faculty of seeing apparently insignificant little things on the ball field that escape the eyes of others.

Much of his success has been due to his taking advantage of those slight signs.

In the last few years, McGraw has remained on the bench and does not even put on a uniform. The older fans will probably recall that, when he did go on the coaching lines, he always went back to the bench when things were breaking against the team. Some attributed that to a feeling of discouragement, but that was far from the truth. It was from the bench that he made his hardest fight. He went there so that he could observe the whole field without anything escaping him. That is why he decided to stay there in the last few years.

To give you an idea: We were in a tight game with Pittsburgh one summer and Babe Adams, then a youngster, was pitching against Hooks Wiltse. With the score against us, we went to bat in the seventh inning.

"This fellow Adams is a youngster," McGraw cautioned our players, "and is liable to be nervous and wild. Wait him out."

The batters, following instructions, waited with the patience of Job. Each batter let the first two balls go by and made Adams pitch himself to the limit. It finally got on Adams's nerves. In the ninth inning, he passed a couple of men and a hit tied the score. Fred Clarke, being short of pitchers, could not take Adams out. The game went on to the thirteenth inning with Wiltse pitching like a machine. McGraw had not moved from his seat on the bench for a half hour, his eyes glued on the pitcher's box.

The waiting tactics kept right on. At last, in the thirteenth, the keen eye of McGraw saw Adams suddenly drop his pitching arm, as if weary. Not one of us saw it, nor did the Pittsburgh players or the fans.

"Now, hit it, boys!" McGraw sharply ordered. "Get him!"

Our tactics suddenly changed and the batters began slashing at the first ball. McGraw had called the turn to a nicety. The weary Adams had nothing on the ball. There was a quick cluster of hits and we won the game.

But for McGraw seeing that slight move, we might have lost.

That is what I mean by observing small details. All the successful managers are good at this, but none ever showed as much keenness as McGraw.

As a rule, there is little noise on the Giants bench. When the score is close, McGraw sits there, his eyes drawn to narrow slits, his entire attention concentrated on the field. He rarely as much as turns his head. The players talk in a low tone, as if in church. When he discovers a flaw in the opposition or a mistake by one of his own men, his sharp voice begins to crackle. Like an eagle, he watches for an opportunity and then swoops on it.

McGraw is always studying pitchers, especially new ones to the league. I remember one time there was a big, tall pitcher on the St. Louis club named Grover Lowdermilk. He had tremendous speed and gave us a tough fight and would have won, but for an error by one of his teammates. The papers called him a second Rube Waddell. McGraw read this and laughed.

"All we want," he told us in the clubhouse, "is just one more crack at that big Buttermilk. I learned a lot about him yesterday. He can't control his curve and all you fellows have to do is wait for his fast one. He came near winning yesterday because he had you fellows swinging at bad balls."

A few weeks later, Lowdermilk appeared against us again. McGraw gave orders to wait and Lowdermilk made his disappearance in the fourth inning. By waiting for his fast one, we got enough bases on balls and base hits to make five runs and send him to the shower.

Some managers give their players more leeway as to judgment and that probably makes for individual brilliance, but, according to McGraw's theory, it does not win pennants. If he has a team of young players, McGraw directs every move. He will not stand for argument.

"Do what I tell you," he will say, "and if it goes wrong, I'll take the blame."

After his team has won a pennant, McGraw usually allows the players more leeway, but toward the end of the season he has to jack them up invariably.

We had that experience in 1906. The team got to running wild on the bases and eventually lost the pennant.

In my opinion, a manager can be more successful from the bench than on the field. I have seen Frank Chance lose ball games through failure to see little things on account of being occupied at first base. Fred Clarke often lost games for the same reason.

"If I could only be in three places at once," was McGraw's constant lament. He meant that he would like to be at third base coaching, at first base, and on the bench.

One day while centering his attention on the opposing pitcher, he put Cy Seymour on the third-base coaching line. A runner could easily have scored on a long triple, but as he rounded third Seymour tackled him and threw him back to third. Even then, the runner, Moose McCormick, got up and scored.

"What was the matter with you, Cy?" McGraw demanded to know.

"The sun got in my eyes and I couldn't see the runner," Seymour explained.

"Then I guess you will have to wear sunglasses with the sun to your back," retorted McGraw. Seymour, realizing that he had been looking due east when the sun was sinking in the west, gave up his alibi and sat down, crestfallen.

"What did he pitch when McCormick hit that ball?" McGraw asked one of the players.

"I don't know. I was watching the play at third."

"If we are going to win this pennant," declared McGraw with biting sarcasm, "looks as if I would have to figure out a scheme to be in all three spots at once."

Fred Clarke, while playing left field and managing at the same time, used to start tying his shoe at the first sign of his pitcher weakening. That was his way of stalling until a fresh man could be warmed up. McGraw knew this and it was always his orders for us to jump on the pitcher before Clarke could get him out. Many of the battles with umpires occurred over Clarke's shoe-tying trick. He has been known to wear out a pair of laces tying and untying them during a single game.

Yes, the bench manager has a big advantage.

Chapter 17. A Seasick Sailor

Bozeman Bulger continues his story.

Though Matty was fearless and courageous in baseball and football, it is not exactly correct to say that he was entirely without fear. In the face of seasickness, he abjectly surrendered. The thought of a ghost was no more frightful to the superstitious man than was the thought of seasickness to Christy Mathewson. He also suffered from stage fright, but that was nothing to his dread of an ocean voyage.

The world tour of the Giants and White Sox before the world war suffered financially through Matty's pointblank refusal to go on the trip. Nothing could budge his determination not to put foot on the deck of a steamer.

In sailing for France as an army officer, it took a great deal more nerve on Matty's part than to have gone over the top in the face of heavy fire.

On McGraw's account, Mathewson was extremely anxious that the world's tour would be a success financially and artistically. To the promoters of that trip, Matty was the one big attraction they had counted on, his fame having reached to all corners of the world.

"I won't go on that ship," he told McGraw, "and that's final, but I will pitch on the tour cross country from New York to San Francisco, if that will help."

It was Matty's drawing ability on that preliminary tour that made the sea trip financially possible. Everywhere Big Six was a sensation. He worked hard and would appear as often as the manager wished and the gate receipts grew. When the two teams finally reached California, however, and boarded the S.S. *Empress of Japan*, Matty balked. The mere sight and smell of the ship made him sick. He would go no further. No amount of persuasion could budge him.

This failure of Matty to make the tour was a great disappointment to fans in other countries, as well as to McGraw and Charles Comiskey. In Japan, the players say the question most frequently asked was "Where is Mr. Masson?"

"Mr. Masson" spent the winter in California with Mrs. Mathewson and little Christy while his teammates were being honored everywhere.

This fear of seasickness obsessed Matty early in his career as a ballplayer. In the spring of 1905, the Giants trained in Savannah, Georgia, and went to the training grounds on a steamer, a voyage that proved disastrous to Matty.

The steamer ran into a severe storm off Cape Hatteras and, on account of the rough seas, had to leave its course, going far out to sea. The club was delayed three days in reaching Savannah, three days of intense suffering for those susceptible to seasickness. Arriving at Savannah, Mathewson was a physical wreck. It was two or three weeks before he struck the stride that gave him his most successful year.

In later years, the Giants trained in Texas, many of the players making the steamer trip to New Orleans. But not Mathewson. He went on the train.

Mathewson did not give up his fight with seasickness without a struggle. After the Savannah experience, he studied the causes of the malady carefully. He loved travel and his dread of the sea was to him a keen humiliation.

At that time, we were neighbors on Washington Heights in New York. Often, we planned hunting and fishing trips. Matty had never tried deep sea fishing. One day I called him up to say that we had been invited to go on a sea fishing trip out to Sheepshead Bay. His mind immediately thought of that as an opportunity to try out his theories as to how to avoid seasickness.

"I'll go," he telephoned the next night. "Will be ready to start at daylight."

All his life, Matty tried to escape being looked upon as a hero. He dreaded being held up as an object of curiosity for the public. For that reason, it had been agreed by our fishing hosts, Arthur Middleton and Mr. Kennedy, that Matty wouldn't have to meet any strangers, but would be regarded as an ordinary fisherman.

With all this understood, we sailed from Sheepshead Bay in a big motorboat and went straight out to sea. Arriving on the fishing banks, a sea anchor was thrown out to hold us and the fishing began with lines running from a hundred to five hundred feet.

In the excitement of catching several large sea bass, the movement of our boat was unnoticed for the moment. Presently, though, we began to feel the heavy roll. The sea got so high that it was necessary to pull up the anchor. Being strong and always willing, Matty took hold of the rope and began to pull. Suddenly, he stopped and sat down on the floor of the boat in utter helplessness and misery. His face had turned actually green, not merely pale.

His face was drawn in an agonizing expression. In a moment, he was vomiting at the side of the little vessel. He fell back completely exhausted. I have never seen a more distressing instance of a big, strong man suffering. It was not funny, but really pathetic. His condition actually alarmed Mr. Middleton, himself a real sailor.

"We'd better go in," he remarked to Mr. Kennedy. "Too much of that will kill a man. We'll take no chances."

So, we headed back to the land. By this time, Matty's face was chalky white. He could hardly lift his head.

On the way back he recovered somewhat, but when we finally reached the landing, Matty was a sorrowful sight. His eyes seemed to have sunk in his head; his whole bearing was one of abject misery.

Imagine, if you will, his feeling when a big delegation of Tammany politicians and other sportsmen appeared at the landing and helped us ashore. They were putting on a sort of carnival. Evidently these men, kind at heart, had not observed Matty's physical condition. Against his protest, they walked him along the pier and, arriving at the end, one man stepped forward.

"Gentlemen," he announced with real pride and feeling, "I have a surprise for you. I want to present one of our great heroes and celebrities, Christy Mathewson."

Though wobbly in the knees, Matty bowed, but could not speak.

"I could have died right there," he said as we caught the train. "Listen, I'm through with deep sea fishing or anything else that has to do with the sea for life!"

Never again could he be persuaded to put foot on the deck of a saltwater boat.

Chapter 18. First Years with the Giants

Christy Mathewson believed firmly in a sort of destiny or fate for every individual. Often, after he had grown old enough to be reminiscent, he declared that he never knew how he came to be a ballplayer. Certainly no one ever encouraged him that way or pointed out baseball as a worthy career.

"I remember, though, when I was eight or nine years old," he said, "that when men would ask me what I intended to make out of myself, I would say 'a Big League pitcher.'"

To emphasize his idea that a certain destiny governs the action of men, he used to tell of his first glimpse of the Polo Grounds at a time when he never had an idea of playing on the New York club and of what wonderful things came to pass within a year.

"I was probably the biggest hick that ever landed in New York," he narrated. "I had been offered a pitching job at Taunton, Massachusetts, in the summer of 1899. I had to go through New York and landed at Chambers Street, having come in on the Erie Railroad. I had two of those big telescope bags—you know the kind—that stretch like an accordion."

Seeing by the papers that the Giants were playing that day, this big country boy started for the Polo Grounds with his two telescopes when someone told him that he could check them.

Young Mathewson went to the Polo Grounds and got a seat in the bleachers where, in silence, he allowed himself two hours of genuine hero worship. Jouett Meekin was pitching that day and the young pitcher from Factoryville thought he was the greatest man in the world. In his most imaginative flights, the boy never dreamed that someday he would be standing where Meekin stood.

After the game, young Mathewson followed a crowd of boys and stood outside the entrance to the clubhouse, waiting to see the players come out. He waited until he saw Jouett Meekin at close range and then, after following him a block down the street, felt contented. He went back, got his traveling bags, and proceeded to Taunton.

"And to show you why I believe so firmly in fate, destiny or what you may call it," Matty said afterward, "a little more than a year from that day I was on the Polo Grounds in a Giant uniform and ready to go out and pitch as Meekin did."

Matty became a Giant on July 17, 1900. His start had nothing of the storybook flavor. There was no climax like the green country boy going in and saving the day. No, indeed. The young fellow was told that he wouldn't have much chance to pitch, but that he must keep working on his delivery in practice.

A chance finally came to Matty, just as it does to other young benchwarmers. Toward the end of the season, Win Mercer, pitching against the champion Brooklyns, had been knocked out of the box.

"Now, kid," said George Davis, the manager, "you can go in there and try yourself out."

Matty thought the Brooklyn batters the biggest men he ever saw in his life. Among them were Duke Farrell and Joe Kelley. And as they kept coming to the bat, he often related, each one seemed to be bigger than the other. At that time, the reader is reminded the Brooklyn outfit was considered the greatest ball club in the world.

Young Mathewson was both nervous and wild. He knew there was no chance of winning, but he was disappointed at not making a better showing. He was surprised, though, when neither the manager nor the players said anything about his performance one way or the other. Though he did not know it, his work had really made quite an impression on manager Davis. He saw that Matty had a lot of stuff. Davis was trying to get the rough edges knocked off in games that didn't count.

Toward the very end of the season, when the Giants had no chance at all and a victory or defeat meant nothing to them, young Mathewson was sent in to pitch a full game. As luck would have it, he drew for an opponent Clark Griffith, the "foxiest" pitcher of that day. Though he did not win, Matty always maintained that he learned a lot from watching Griffith. Griffith won his game by a score of 5–3.

"That's quite a young pitcher you've got there, George," Griffith said to Davis as they left the grounds. In reply, Davis told Griffith that in Mathewson he had a world beater for the future. Never did Davis have a doubt as to Matty's success. That in itself is proof of his baseball astuteness. One of the first things John McGraw did when he became manager of the Giants was to bring Davis back to the club as a player.

George Davis was one of the many managers and players who did not get along with the erratic owner, Mr. Andrew Freedman. According to Mathewson, the Giants used to have a manager every other day or so in those days. As a result of a run-in with Freedman, manager Davis, among others, took advantage of the chance to go with the American League.

When, during the winter, McGraw induced Davis to come back, he met with strenuous objection from Freedman.

"I wouldn't have that man on my team at any price," declared Freedman.

"But I am hiring him for the team, not you," retorted McGraw. "Don't forget that you gave me authority to run this club according to my own idea."

With that, McGraw showed Freedman his written contract and agreement.

That incident marked the beginning of McGraw's absolute authority over the Giants. His later success was due to his freedom from interference. Shortly thereafter, Freedman sold the New York club to John T. Brush.

Matty came into baseball during a very exciting and trying period. During the fall, winter, and spring, following his first appearance, many of the veteran Giants, especially pitchers, jumped to the American League. Andrew Freedman, the unpopular owner, was hard put for players. That in a way, though, worked to Matty's advantage.

Funds being short and interest at a low ebb, the Giants, in the spring of 1901, trained on old Manhattan Field, the vacant field adjoining the present Polo Grounds. They worked out in the snow, Freedman being firmly convinced that there was nothing in the idea of training in the South.

The reader can well join young Mathewson in his surprise and elation when, at the beginning of the 1901 season, Davis notified him that he was to pitch the opening game. Moreover, he was to pitch against the Brooklyn champions.

"I went home," Matty often said, "and went to bed early to be ready for the big day. But it rained. So, being conscientious, I went to bed early again. This kept up for four days! I never had so much steady sleep in my life. Finally, it cleared off and the game was on. My opponent was Wild Bill Donovan, one of the best pitchers that ever lived."

Having pitched against Brooklyn in a previous game, the studious boy had listed the batters carefully and, to the great delight of Davis, pitched to their weaknesses. Matty won the game against the great Donovan, 5–3.

That seemed to give him courage and confidence. Following that, he pitched in eight or ten games and won them all. His first defeat was on Memorial Day, when Jack Powell beat him, 1–0.

Chapter 19. Origin of His Nicknames

It may have been noticed in these recollections of Christy Mathewson that rarely is he referred to as "Big Six." That is more natural than studied. He was never called Big Six by his teammates or immediate associates. The sobriquet Big Six was more a newspaper usage than a personal one.

Among his friends, the great pitcher was always known as "Matty." More familiarly, he was known to the members of the old Giants of 1905 as "Gumboots." That nickname was even shortened to "Gummy" by players like Cy Seymour, Larry Doyle, and other old-timers. In all the twenty years that I knew Matty, I have never known a person to address him as Big Six. Probably he would not have turned his head had he heard it behind him. The name had no personal relation and he was not accustomed to hearing it. Big Six simply got into the newspaper headlines, as other terms do, and stuck.

The players used it only when they wanted to kid or josh Matty. If some batter hit a home run off Mathewson, for example, his teammates would say, "So, you are Big Six, eh?" It was not known as a term of affection. Its inference of greatness embarrassed the big fellow, naturally modest.

To his dying day, Matty never got over a misprint of the words "Big Six" in the headlines of a Cincinnati paper. It added to his personal distaste for the use of the nickname. The players had been good-naturedly riding Matty on a trip west because he had beaten them steadily in a card game on the train. Imagine their joy and laughter when a typographical error made the big headline read "BIG SIS IN THE BOX TODAY." He never heard the last of it by those who joked and skylarked with him.

There have been many explanations advanced as to how Matty got the sobriquet. All seem to believe that it came from some feat he performed in a ball game. If that be true, the writer was never able to put his finger on the particular game. I came to know Matty in 1904, the year he created a sensation by winning thirty-five games and losing only eight. He was called Big Six then in the newspapers, as he was in later years.

Matty, himself, never knew exactly where he got the nickname. He had an idea he was called Big Six when he played football, but wasn't sure. Old friends still insist that he did get the name in football.

A theory has been advanced that the name was given him when he came to New York because of the prominence of the local typographical union, still known all over the country as Big Six. The typographical union had won a great labor victory, so that story goes, and, when young Mathewson pitched a great game, some writer, formerly a printer, remarked that he handled himself with all the cleverness of Big Six.

That explanation was printed in a Western paper recently. It does not ring true to me—sounds a little farfetched. I know I never heard of it until recent years.

Another story, and the one Mathewson himself was inclined to believe, associated the nickname with the automobile industry, then in its infancy. Henry Ford turned out a six-cylinder car, a huge, ramshackly affair with terrific speed and power for that day. From his very first days in the box, Matty was noted for his speed.

"He shoots that ball through with the speed of a Big Six," a baseball writer wrote in a New York paper.

Whether that was the real origin or not, Matty was known as Big Six from that time on. Barney Oldfield, a great admirer of Matty, who was coming into prominence as a racing driver then, insists that Matty's name came from Ford's big car.

In the South, we once had a big African American fighter in Birmingham, Alabama, who was known as Big Six. In fact, he had no other name, so far as I know. After his day, we always called any big man of prominence Big Six. It was a name for any unusually large and powerful man, especially in sports and for the giants who handled cotton bales. When Matty first came to Alabama to train in the spring of 1904, the darky rooters immediately called him Big Six, the expression meaning to them an unusually powerful and effective man. It seemed perfectly natural for others to use the nickname. The files of the Birmingham newspapers show that he was repeatedly called Big Six Mathewson. Until these later theories were advanced, the writer was under the impression that the name started there.

Inasmuch as he was six feet tall and of imposing weight, it seemed to be as good an expression as any to surmise that the nickname came from his size.

Though Mathewson was known in the newspapers as Big Six, he was more affectionately referred to by his fellow players as Gumboots. Cy Seymour hung that name on him, it being his custom to nickname every player on the club. It was Seymour who named Arthur Shafer "Tillie."

One day Matty was walking across the field in that odd, shuffling gait of his when Seymour looked up from the bench and observed, "Say, look at the big fellow. He walks like he's got on gumboots. Hey, where you going, Gumboots?"

From that day on, Matty was affectionately known to his intimate associates as Old Gumboots. He was always fond of Seymour, eccentric as Cy was, and Matty always liked the nickname Gumboots better than Big Six.

Baseball writers never used that nickname in the papers, but to his last days the old-timers referred to their friend personally as Old Gumboots. It always made him smile.

Chapter 20. McGraw Instills Discipline

There was an incident in Christy Mathewson's career dealing with discipline away back in the spring of 1905 that had an important bearing on his whole baseball life. Trivial as it may seem, Matty often referred to it in later years as a milestone in his experience.

Mathewson, as older fans, perhaps, will recall, felt his first touch of greatness in 1904. That year the Giants won their first pennant under John McGraw, but declined to meet the Boston Red Sox in a series to decide the world's championship. John T. Brush steadfastly refused to recognize the American League until the National Agreement was signed the following season. The younger league, having violated what were considered the traditions of baseball by stepping in and starting a major league without the consent of the National League, was looked on as an interloper. The raids of the American League on players had left many unhealed wounds.

Notwithstanding McGraw's belief that with young Mathewson and Joe McGinnity as leading pitchers, he could beat the Boston club. Brush would not permit a meeting. This was a keen disappointment for fans who had been clamoring to see the great young pitcher in a big series. It was also a disappointment to the players.

Matty was then about twenty-two years old. It cannot be that success, or even partial success, had gone to his head. He was just as "oldish" and seriously deliberate then as he was ten years later.

That fall and winter, the National League partisans persistently proclaimed Mathewson the greatest of all pitchers, a statement stoutly denied by the American Leaguers. This never-ending discussion brought about so much publicity for Matty that he was one of the best-known men in the United States. That would have ruined most young fellows, but in the case of Mathewson it seemed to inspire him to deeper study and more practice. He wanted to live up to the reputation his admirers had given him. Always he worked out problems in his own way.

McGraw, realizing that he had discovered an unusual character in Mathewson, was inclined to give him more leeway in working out his ideas than he did the other players. And the players did not complain at this. Even they had recognized his mental superiority—the soundness of his calculations.

This had been proved many times in the card games and other games of chance played in the clubrooms and on railroad trains. Moreover, he had made a close study of the stock market and helped the older players in making their investments.

Professor E. E. Witford, Matty's mathematics teacher in college, declared Mathewson one of the few men whom he had ever known to possess that rare quality known as the perfect mathematical mind. All problems of figures were simple to him.

Realizing his own superiority of brain and having the utmost confidence in himself, it was but natural that Mathewson should feel that he had the right to figure out his own way of preparing himself to pitch. He was too young, however, to realize that individual ambition must work in harmony with team discipline. In fact, he had not taken into his calculations the tremendous power of discipline—the absolute necessity of it.

McGraw's alert mind was quick to see this and very promptly he decided to provide the remedy at the first opportunity.

John McGraw always had been the strictest of disciplinarians. Whether a player be a star or a recruit, McGraw made a point of seeing that he observed the rules and carried out orders to the minutest detail. The more prominent a player became, the more he must be careful of observing discipline.

"Matty was the easiest man I ever had to handle," McGraw said just a few days ago, "because he had so much common sense. I don't remember ever having to enforce discipline upon him, but once—you remember the incident at Memphis?"

Oddly, Matty had mentioned the same incident last spring in Florida.

While training at Memphis, it was a rule when the practice was over in the afternoon to have all the extra players, such as pitchers and catchers, run twice around the park before climbing into the bus to go back to the hotel.

On the afternoon referred to by Matty and McGraw, Matty had been working on a curve and he had not loafed. Evidently, he thought that enough workout for one afternoon. Probably it was, but McGraw could not permit him to avoid the run around the park and, at the same time, keep other players in line.

"Go ahead, Matty," the manager directed. "Take the run with those fellows and we'll go home."

"I've worked enough," Matty replied, looking across the field.

"Just the same you've got to go," insisted McGraw.

Matty did not move or even look around. The bats were packed up and the other players went for the waiting bus. Still, Matty sat there. The driver was about to start his horses.

"We don't move a foot," declared McGraw, "until Matty runs around the park."

In the meantime, the big fellow sat there, silently stubborn. We waited and waited, but Mathewson would not move. McGraw was just as determined.

"Come on, Matty," urged one or two of his teammates, "we'll run around with you. Be a good fellow."

"No, you won't," said McGraw. "He's got to run around the park just the same as the others did. He'll run alone or we won't move from this spot."

We waited a full half hour, the players silently and nervously expectant. We could see that somebody would have to give in and it seemed certain that it would not be McGraw.

All this time, Matty, sitting on the distant bench, had not said a word. At the end of a half an hour he got up. For a moment, he stood at first base, evidently trying to overcome his stubbornness. Then he set himself and ran around the park twice in a deliberate trot, looking neither to the right nor to the left. When his task was finished, he climbed silently into the bus and rode to the hotel.

"That was the most important lesson in discipline I ever had," he said afterward. "I realized that McGraw was right while I sat there alone. I had to win a fight over myself and I did it. I'll never forget that. It was worth a lot to me."

In all his years after that, McGraw says that he never even had to call Matty's attention to a club rule.

Chapter 21. Investments and the World War

The most lasting impression the writer has of Christy Mathewson was his thoroughness and utter apparent lack of enthusiasm or emotion. He was just as soberly thoughtful at the age of twenty-three as when he became the president of the Boston Braves in 1923. Though I was two years older, he always regarded me as a sort of happy-go-lucky boy that he should look after and advise. The advice was always sound, too, even though unneeded at times.

This middle-aged man of twenty-three very carefully explained to me one day that if I would save up and invest $1,000 a year in a gilt-edge bond, paying around 6 percent, and then reinvest the earnings, in fifteen years I would be worth $25,000. He pointed out that my local banker would give me the best advice as to what bonds to buy.

"I've made a bust of trying to explain that to some of the gang, so I'm going to straighten you out if I can."

His financial talk was just as sound and logical as we read nowadays in the articles written by investment experts, but, somehow, I was just as much a bust as the players. But Matty was not.

When he was getting $5,000 a year, he declared one day that he had estimated his living expenses at $50 a week. He had been married two years then.

"Now," he said, "I figure to last in baseball about ten years. In that time, I must save and invest enough money so that when I am through, I will have an income of at least $50 a week without working for it. If a man has to change his manner of living because he has lost his job, then he loses his self-respect. He mustn't ever let his family feel the difference."

Having made up his mind and outlined his financial program with exactness, Matty stuck right to it until he was sure of that $50 a week income from his investments. Just before his death, his income, independent of salary, was, he told me, between $7,000 and $8,000 a year.

Incidentally, there persists a misunderstanding about the testimonial given to Matty at the Polo Grounds on September 30, 1921, from which was raised more than $40,000. There was a general belief that this testimonial was a benefit to the great pitcher because he was without funds. It was, in fact, never called benefit and was not intended as an act of charity. It was merely a token of good fellowship.

At that time, Matty was ill at Saranac Lake and had been there for several months. He was earning no salary at all. His sickness was costly. He had quite a sum of money invested in securities, mostly railroad stocks and bonds. From these there was not sufficient income to defray his expenses at Saranac Lake and to realize more on them he would have to sell at a big loss as war control had brought confusion to the whole railroad situation. His friends did not want him to thus sacrifice his holdings. The testimonial was given as evidence of the esteem in which Matty was held. It was a wonderful tribute.

When business affairs of the country straightened out two or three years after the war, Matty's securities regained most of their prewar value and he was all right again financially.

And before going into a few of the high points of his career, this seems a good place to make clear the circumstances of his contracting the dread tuberculosis that finally took him away. The statement has been widely circulated that Matty was gassed in France, from which tuberculosis developed. That is probably true, but not in the manner the published story would make it appear.

Matty, himself, at times believed that his illness was due to exposure to the dampness and chill of a fall and winter in the Vosges region of France. At other times, he was convinced that his lungs had been affected by the poison gasses of the chemical laboratory in which he worked as a student officer and as an instructor. He was a captain in the Chemical Warfare Service.

In that work, Matty was just as thorough as in everything else he attempted. Colonel Orland Sweeney, under whom he served for two or three months, told me that Mathewson was one of the best teachers he ever knew, because of the immediate confidence he inspired in the men.

A big percentage of the early gas instructors contracted lung diseases from the occasional breathing of the gasses that they studied and demonstrated. As Matty did not reach France in time to get into actual battle, it is generally believed in the army that he was unconsciously gassed by degrees in trying to perfect his knowledge of these deadly fumes in the instruction camps of the United States as well as in France. He was keenly interested in his work as a gas officer as he was in all his undertakings.

The first time I saw him in uniform, he told me in most minute detail of a new gas that they had developed and how it would have been used. He also outlined the plans of a gas defense.

As an instructor, Matty had the knack of making the soldiers instruct themselves. One day, so Colonel Sweeney relates, Matty was lecturing to a big class of soldiers, many of whom had served at the front and were resting. He was pointing out theoretically what should be done for protection during a gas attack when suddenly he noted a corporal who wore a wound stripe.

"Corporal," he said, "you were probably in a gas attack at the front. You've been against the real thing and that is what counts. How do these theories I am advancing gibe with your actual experience? What did you find out? Put us right."

The soldier, having been thus put perfectly at ease, gave his views. Following him, others got up. Before the class hour was over, Colonel Sweeney says, that group of soldiers had worked out a most practical and intelligent plan of gas defense.

As a leader, Captain Mathewson had brought about perfect cooperation between theory and practice. The doughboys admired his quiet thoroughness and sincerity, just as young ballplayers did his masterly pitching. There was never an iota of sham or bluster in Matty and nobody recognizes that quality as quickly as a soldier.

Chapter 22. Record-Shattering 1905 World Series

The outstanding achievement in Christy Mathewson's career as a pitcher and the one in which he always felt the greatest pride was in the World Series of 1905, when he shut out the Athletics three times. He beat them the first game, 3–0; the second time, 9–0; and the third, 2–0.

The American League champions, in other words, failed to cross the plate on Matty in 27 innings. In those three games, the Athletics made 14 hits, an average of 4⅔ hits in a game.

"You've left out the most important feature of that," Matty remarked to the writer one day when this record of figures had been shown him.

"What is it that you are particularly fond of?" I asked him.

"Why, I only gave one base on balls in the three games. That was the real feature of the pitching. To tell the truth," he added, "I could have avoided that one free pass, but I wouldn't take a chance on putting over a good one. I had to work the batter."

John McGraw often has discussed that pitching feat in 1905.

"Matty was right," he said. "The main thing that won for him was perfect control. He had plenty of stuff, all right, but he had to have the control to make it useful."

In many ways that season of 1905 was Matty's banner year. It did not furnish his best pitching record, according to statistics, but, undoubtedly, he was then at the top of his form. In 1905 he won 31 games and lost 9. The year before, he had won 33 and lost 12, but he had not been aimed at such hard spots. For ten years after that, nearly every crucial game found him pitching for the Giants.

As was mentioned before, Matty always regretted his inability to try himself out in a 1904 Series. It was in that year the National League refused to play the American League for the championship.

A source of great satisfaction to the quiet, reserved Mathewson in 1905 was his convincing the American League that he was really a good pitcher. Going into that 1905 Series, Matty was much in the same position as Red Grange, the great football player, when he came to the East for the first time to play against Pennsylvania. The East had doubted the reports coming out of the West about Grange.

The feeling between the two major leagues in 1905 was intensely bitter.

"Mathewson may be pretty good in the old, moth-eaten National League," American League fans were saying, "but wait 'til he runs up against a real ball club."

In those days, a fan—even a baseball writer—was classified definitely as a National Leaguer or an American Leaguer. While traveling with a club in one league, it was considered almost treasonable to even discuss the good points of players in the other.

So, when a great crowd of New York fans escorted the Giants down to Philadelphia that fall, the intense rivalry frequently resulted in fistfights in the lobbies of the hotels. Harry M. Stevens, who has since become a millionaire, created a sensation by running about the lobby of the old Continental Hotel with bank notes between his fingers, offering to bet that Matty would win every game he pitched.

Most of the Athletic batters were pretty well known to McGraw, who had previously managed the Baltimore club in the American League. McGraw, incidentally, gave the Athletics their name of White Elephants. He had remarked that the Philadelphia club would be a white elephant on the league. They still resent that.

When McGraw arrived with the Giants, he was faced with White Elephant banners on every side. All this time, though, he was going over the batters with Mathewson, who never forgot the weak and strong points in any one of them.

Mathewson had just brought his fadeaway ball to the highest form of perfection that year, but the one he used most against the Athletics was a big drop-curve. Contrary to the belief of fans, Matty used his fadeaway only on rare occasions.

For a week, Matty had centered his efforts on control. Before he had pitched two innings, the great crowd was willing to admit him a master. He proved his right to greatness just as Red Grange did in the same town twenty years later.

At no time did the Athletics have a real chance of winning against Mathewson. He worked easily, almost carelessly, when no runners were on the bases, but when danger threatened he unleashed his arm and came through like a whirlwind.

When it came to the point where the Giants needed but one game to become champions, having won their third game, the wives of several of the Athletics were seated in a box in tears near the press box where we could hear. Chief Bender and Harry Davis came up to speak to them.

"You'll get them yet, won't you?" one of the women asked.

"We'll try," Bender said, "but that Mathewson will pitch the last one. I don't know what it is, but he's got something we can't understand."

In the last game, which Matty won 2–0, the Athletics were still as mystified and baffled as ever. He had proved himself the greatest pitcher in the world.

"Don't forget, though," Mathewson always reminded me when this pitching feat was brought up, "that I didn't give but one base on balls. That was the trick."

Chapter 23. McGraw's Secrets in 1905

While it may seem a little past due, John McGraw said something about the 1905 World Series that may throw some new light on how Connie Mack met his Waterloo. He disclosed some secrets that are likely to make fandom sit up and think. "First and foremost, you've got to give it to Mathewson," he began. "He pitched the most remarkable ball ever seen on a major league diamond and did a few things which no man in the grandstand could well observe.

"Matty and myself conferred about very batter that came up. In this connection he did the most remarkable piece of work of his career. When we had decided what kind of a ball to pitch, Matty went to work on him and during that last game his throws did not vary two inches from where the ball was intended to go. Just think of it! Among men on the 'inside,' that will probably stand as the greatest feat ever accomplished on a ball field.

"Of course," said McGraw, as he began to let out some secrets, "I had some valuable information on the Athletic batters, and I did not overlook any bets. Friends of mine who had pitched against the Athletics tipped me off to the weaknesses of certain men. With this start I went out the first day and confirmed or corrected this list. By the third day I had every batter on that list spotted. This was communicated to Mathewson, and with the knowledge he had gained we felt sure of victory.

"I wish I could dope out the races as well as I did that Series," said the now-famous manager. And then people say that baseball doesn't sometimes run according to form!

"For instance," he continued, "we had big Socks Seybold buffaloed from the start. All during the Series he waited for a ball to be pitched on the outside corner of the plate. He might still be waiting. Matty and myself knew that Seybold could hit a ball on the outside, so Matty kept whizzing them close to his neck."

This possibly explains why McGraw was not seen on the coaching lines more frequently. The question was asked McGraw. "That's easily explained," he said, with a sly chuckle.

"In the last game I had started to the coaching line and Mathewson asked me to remain on the bench as he wanted to discuss the batters with me. The advantage of this was apparent and is another evidence of Matty's head work. While he was pitching to the batter, I was watching the effect of the ball, and when he came in we talked it over.

"By this method we were cinching the game more securely every inning, and toward the finish the Athletic batters were more at Mathewson's mercy than at the start.

"While we went at the Series with all the vim we possessed, I think it was one of the easiest problems to solve I ever tackled."

McGraw called attention to a statement made by him in the *Evening World* while the Giants were closing the season at Cincinnati. A comparison showed that every opinion he offered on the World Series was verified to the letter. That little fellow is a remarkable man. A study of the above shows that, while he gives all the credit to Mathewson, his counsel and advice helped largely to give the great pitcher his marvelous record of three shutouts against a championship team in one week. Mathewson and McGraw were a team in themselves.

How's a fellow going to tell how a fellow will play in a big game by his past record? The weakest guy is likely to bob up as the strongest. Billy Gilbert was figured the weakest man on the club. The wise guys showed how the rest of the club would have to carry him. As it turned out, Billy led the club in hitting and was the infield star of the whole outfit. The average ballplayer does not like to game or take any chances at all. When the Giants and Athletics played the Series in 1905, some of the players of the two clubs got together and paired off so as to divide the prize money equally and take no chance on getting a winner's or a loser's share.

Not all of them did this, however. John McGraw went into a rage when he heard of what he considered a lack of gameness and fighting confidence. He and Christy Mathewson and Roger Bresnahan refused to pair with anybody, preferring to let it go as it lay. They each got a full winner's share.

At the big settlement, some real fun started that was never made public. Two of the Giant players went back on their pairing agreements and refused to settle with their Athletic partners—and nothing could be done about it. Since that time, there has been no pairing.

Chapter 24. Fred Merkle's Mistake

The greatest disappointment Christy Mathewson ever suffered as a pitcher, next to his loss of the 1912 World Series in Boston, was his loss of that historic game in 1908, due to Fred Merkle's failure to touch second. That not only took one victory from his remarkable record that year, but it lost the pennant for the Giants, as it later developed.

Though Matty was a staunch supporter of umpires as a rule, he never felt that the decision in that much-talked-of game was entirely correct. He admitted that there may have been some technical grounds for making the decision on Merkle, but he always insisted that the game should have proceeded to a decision in any event.

On that memorable day in September, the Cubs, pushing the Giants hard for the lead, came to the Polo Grounds for a bitter fight that had been heralded all over the country. As usual, under such circumstances, Matty had been selected to pitch. All through the game he pitched airtight ball.

In the last inning, with the score tied, Moose McCormick was on first when Merkle, who went in as a pinch hitter, singled, sending him to third. Al Bridwell, one of the gamest players that ever lived, came to bat and lined a clean single, on which McCormick scored the winning run. Right then things started to happen. The crowd, thinking the game won, rushed on the field. Suddenly, Johnny Evers was seen calling for the ball to be thrown to second.

To complete the play and make the hit count, under the rules it was necessary for Merkle to go to second. In the past, runners had not been doing that, it being taken for granted that as long as a runner could take the bag if he wanted to, the actual touching of it was not necessary. It is the rule, however, that if the ball is fielded to second ahead of the runner, he is forced out and, naturally, the run would not count. The runner on third could not score on a third out, which was a force out.

Admitting that Merkle did not go all the way to second, the writer, who was scoring the game, is convinced to this day that the play engineered by Evers was never completed. In the milling of the crowd on the field and the rushing about of players, I doubt if the umpires were ever certain as to just what happened. Hank O'Day knew of the play because they had worked it on him two or three days before. He understood quite clearly what Evers had tried to do, but the writer doubts if it was ever done. Matty always insisted that the ball never got to second base. He and Joe McGinnity discussed it at length three years ago at a World Series.

The ball, according to McGinnity's testimony—and I agree with him—was thrown past second base and rolled to the third-base coaching lines where pitcher Rube Kroh, of the Cubs, and McGinnity, who had been coaching there, scrambled for it. Joe did not know what was up. He thought Kroh was merely trying to secure the ball against the time-honored custom of the winner taking the ball. In the mix-up, McGinnity insists that he threw the ball into the left-field bleachers to keep it away from Kroh. That is the way it looked from the press box.

In the meantime, O'Day had turned over the extra balls to the bat-boy and, after standing at the plate for a few seconds, started for the little door under the stand which led to the umpire's dressing room. It was a full half hour later before we could learn what the decision had been. Finally, O'Day declared that the run did not count because he had called Merkle out for not touching second.

It is hard now to portray the excitement and confusion of that afternoon and the next day. The papers had gone to press declaring the Giants had won long before the sensational decision was learned. Even the morning papers were in doubt.

"Suppose he did make that decision," declared Matty after the game, "the score was only tied. Why didn't he proceed with the game?"

I never saw Matty angry before or since, but he was mad as a hornet that night.

Following his suggestion, the writer went to the Ashland Hotel, where the umpires stopped, the next morning and hunted out O'Day.

"The newspapers want to know exactly what your decision was," I told Hank.

"Why, I called Merkle out for not touching second," he replied.

"Then," I asked, "why did you call the game with the score tied?"

As a matter of fact, none of us had seen or heard the game called. It simply ended in a lot of excitement, the crowd taking it for granted that New York had won.

Hank, great umpire that he is, seemed to hesitate in answering this last question. Evidently, he had not thought it out carefully or was over-cautious in talking to newspapermen.

"Why," he finally replied, "it was called on account of darkness."

The umpires were plainly confused. Their correct action would have been to clear the field and order the game to proceed. Later, they figured that would have been impossible. As a matter of baseball law, it was up to the Giants to have the field cleared under the umpire's order. In the event of their failure, the game could have been declared forfeited. But the umpires gave no such order.

The whole affair was so badly confused that the directors of the National League met and ordered the game to be played over. In the memorable playoff, with Matty again pitching, the Giants lost. The Cub victory gave Chicago the pennant.

Matty never got over the fact that, after having won a game, he had to pitch again and be charged with a defeat.

That playoff game was another disappointing tragedy to Mathewson.

Several years after that sensational affair, John Dovey, at one time part owner of the Boston Braves, told of an incident at the secret meeting of the board of directors which, to him, was the greatest compliment ever paid a ballplayer.

Thousands of affidavits had been submitted on the question of whether Merkle actually touched second or not that day. Hundreds of fans swore that Merkle did touch the bag.

"The first affidavit we picked up out of the big hamper," said Mr. Dovey, "was that of Christy Mathewson. In it he testified that Merkle did not touch the bag.

"All right," spoke up two or three of the board, "there is no use in examining the others. If Matty says that Merkle did not touch the bag, that settles it. His word is good enough for us. He ought to know and, besides, he had everything at stake."

Thereupon, Matty's affidavit was accepted as conclusive evidence and not one of the other affidavits was read before the directors took action.

"It was," said Mr. Dovey, "the most remarkable tribute I ever saw paid to any man's integrity and character."

Matty told me afterward, "I knew Merkle did not touch the base because he walked across the field to the clubhouse with me."

Chapter 25. Games of Chance

Among the first things a ballplayer learns or is most apt to learn when he gets in the Big League is to play cards and smoke cigarettes. Mathewson was no exception.

These habits, which as a rule are quite harmless, according to my observation, seem to be a natural part of the ballplayer's life. They are the result of hours of enforced idleness, such as long train rides and lounging about the hotels while away from home. The question of card playing or cigarette smoking being physically or mentally harmful is still widely discussed, but usually by persons not familiar with the atmosphere of a ball club.

It is a fact, nevertheless, that 98 percent of all players enjoy these habits. Overindulgence in either can bring about harmful results as was proved when John McGraw had to forbid the playing of poker and shooting craps by the old team of Giants one entire season. Members of the team had been playing for too-high stakes. Losses had so worried a few of them as to keep their minds off the game.

There is usually no training rule against cigarettes, but the excessive use of them is known to have affected the work of a few players—a very few. Leon Ames had to cut down on his excessive cigarette smoking, as did others, because it affected his mind.

Mathewson had no excesses. He did not drink liquor or beer at all, but found great comfort in cigarettes after a hard day and he never thought they did him any harm. Card playing, however, was his greatest pleasure. He was a wizard at any game of chance, especially those requiring accurate memory or mathematical calculation. The size of the stakes never concerned him in the least. He was more interested in the game itself than the amount of money involved. Matty's keen intellect and cool calculation was just as apparent in a ten-cent limit poker game as in the pitcher's box during a critical contest.

Many managers have encouraged the players to play poker for the mental exercise it gave. Frank Chance used to say that in the spring he could pick out the smart ballplayers by the way they handled their cards. If that really be a test, then it is easy to understand why Mathewson was the greatest of all pitchers.

All games of chance fascinated Matty. Though he loved the spirit of contest and the matching of wits, his interest was largely mathematical. If he saw a new game, he would study it intently for a half hour or more, then proceed to outline its various possibilities. He would advance theories and then test them.

Cy Seymour was an inveterate but a very poor card player and dice shooter. Try as he would, Matty could never make Cy understand that he must observe the law of chances. He was very fond of Seymour.

"In trying to make a three-card straight or flush, Cy," he said one day, "you are betting against a fifty-to-one chance or even worse. You can never win the way you shoot dice. You are always taking the worst of it in odds."

"What do you mean, law of chances?" Cy inquired.

"Why, there is a mathematical law against that fellow there making a nine with the dice and still you are betting he'll win on a nine. The odds are three to two against you."

"I just had a hunch, that's all," was Cy's defense.

"Betting on hunches will break you. Now, I'll show you."

Matty, who was not in the game that day on the train, gathered up a handful of pennies and, after arranging them in two stacks on the window sill of the smoking compartment in sight of the game being played on the floor, proceeded to bet one pile against the other, according to correct mathematical odds. He followed the game by stacking his pennies against each other on every play. Against making a nine, he would lay three to two, against a ten or four he would lay two to one, against a seven even money, and so on. Seymour would·look up from his kneeling position on the floor every few minutes to watch this curious procedure. Matty was following Seymour's play and playing the right odds while Cy was going on hunches.

"How much did you lose, Cy?" Matty asked when the game was over.

"I lost plenty," said Cy. "The dice wouldn't run right."

"All right, look at this pile. I made these pennies be right with you except that I followed the law of chances. From this pile you can see that, with judgment, you would have won or just about broken even."

It was a perfect demonstration.

"Say, Gumboots," Seymour finally said to Matty with a sort of quizzical look, "where can a guy get a set of them laws?"

When auction bridge came into vogue twenty years ago, Matty was an immediate devotee. The possibilities of the game delighted him. He played a few hands with some good players just to get the feel of it and then went off to study it. In two weeks, he was about the most expert player on the club. His remarkable memory proved a winning asset.

One evening at our hotel in Marlin, Texas, I dropped in on Matty to get some information for an article on pitching. All alone, bent over a writing table, he was so intent that he did not look up for two or three minutes.

"Excuse me," he said, "I was just playing myself a hand of bridge and I beat it, too."

He carried with him a book of bridge problems and one of checker problems. When alone, he would spend hours working these out. His thoroughness in anything he undertook was almost unbelievable. His thirst or knowledge was never satisfied.

"I'm having a busy time of it between auction bridge and the people of Java," he told me that night.

"Java? Java? Did you say? What's the connection?" I asked, wondering if Matty had overexerted his brain.

"Yes, Java," he laughed. "The other day, I read an article in the *Geographic Magazine* on Java. Since then, I've bought two other books on the subject to find out more about those people. Between that and three problems on bridge, I'm sort of tied up for lack of time."

Obviously, the article on pitching had to wait. The next day he told me apologetically that I had been out of the room an hour before he had noticed my departure.

Chapter 26. On Stage, but Just Once

Though Christy Mathewson faced many a nerve-racking test on the diamond during the many years in which he was the mainstay of the Giants, the most dramatic moment—I might say tragic—in his life, he always maintained was in Hammerstein's old Victoria Theater at Broadway and Forty-Second Street back in 1910. That night Matty appeared for the first time as an actor.

To make it all the harder on his nerves, Mathewson's debut was made right in the heart of Broadway before the so-called wisest audience in the world—without a preliminary tryout. He and Chief Meyers had to sink or swim right at Hammerstein's. There was no opportunity to try the playlet in which they appeared "on the dog." The contract called for a first—absolutely first—appearance at the Victoria or nothing. Mind you, neither Mathewson nor Meyers had ever been on the stage in their lives. Up to that time, Matty had even hesitated at making a few remarks at a public dinner. They were game, though, when the terms of the contract were made clear to them.

"In other words," said Matty grimly, "we have just one strike. We either hit or we are out."

"Oh, don't bother," urged the stage director. "The crowd will overlook any little mistakes you make."

"But I don't want to make any mistakes," said Matty. "All I'm afraid of is buck fever—stage fright."

"Yep," agreed the Chief, "we either flop cold or we don't. There'll be no halfway ground. If I get stage fright, I'll leave that stage and beat any man in the world to 125th Street."

"You'll have to go some, Chief," declared Matty. "I'm ready to run now."

May Tully, the well-known comedienne who died in 1924, appeared in the playlet with the two ballplayers and directed the show, including their rehearsals.

"You don't mean to tell me," she said to Mathewson, "that you can get out there in front of thirty thousand people, some against you and some for you, without feeling embarrassed and then you are afraid to face a crowd of a thousand people in a theater."

"It's different," he explained. "Out there we've got something to do and know how to do it."

"Well," she finally told them, "if you miss a line or feel yourself in trouble, just turn to me and say, 'What next, Miss Tully?' The crowd will probably laugh at that and put you at your ease."

I had the dubious honor of writing the playlet in which Matty and Meyers appeared and was present at all their rehearsals. Miss Tully always insisted that they were the most studious actors she ever handled. Matty's inordinate love for detail and his desire to know the reason for everything was a constant source of amusement. Before the rehearsals were over, they had changed nearly every line.

"Say, I don't like that line," he would call out from the stage. "It doesn't fit my mouth."

"How would you like to say it then?" the director would ask and, when Matty expressed the idea in his own words, would add, "All right, say it that way."

The most difficult thing was to teach them to "hold their laughs." They could never understand how the director could anticipate a laugh. Matty was taught to stand perfectly rigid when a laugh started so that there would be no movement to divert the audience and stop the applause or laughter. He did that so meticulously that his pose itself was often a laugh.

On that eventful night at Hammerstein's, Matty, never of ruddy complexion, grew naturally pale through nervousness. It was necessary to put makeup on his cheeks, an operation that came near causing a riot among the other performers backstage. Everybody had to take a hand in it, Matty all the while sitting there like a man about to be led to the scaffold.

Chief Meyers, being a Redskin, didn't require makeup. When he caught sight of Matty as a finished product in makeup, he let out a whoop that could easily be heard in the audience. The Chief, also very nervous, had taken a drink to bolster himself up while Matty was being led to the makeup slaughter. That one drink did a lot toward getting the show over.

When the curtain finally arose with Miss Tully in the middle of the stage and Matty and Meyers about to enter, they both turned to Bill McHarg and myself, who stood in the wings of the prompters and said, "Goodbye."

Matty's first line was "Good afternoon, Miss Tully," and he said it without a muscle of his face moving. He was downright scared.

"So, this is Chief Meyers," Miss Tully quickly remarked. "Are you a regular Indian?"

"Yes, pretty regular," cracked the Chief, and for the first time Matty smiled. The whole house laughed. From that moment they did not miss a line.

In the second part of the playlet, Matty had to appear as a cowboy, riding to the rescue of the Wild Rose, a paleface maiden who had been captured by the Indians under Chief Meyers. In this he was, as he said, at least mathematically correct. The show got by.

"I'm getting a thousand dollars a week for this," Matty said when the curtain came down, "but I wouldn't go through it again for ten thousand."

He fulfilled his contract, though, and got to be a rather finished actor before he was through. The season's theatrical work netted him fifteen thousand dollars.

Last spring in Florida, Matty had just made a speech at a dinner, a very good speech, too.

"Say, Matty," asked someone at the table around which were seated Judge Kenesaw Mountain Landis, George Ade, Judge Emil Fuchs, and others, "can you put your finger on the most dramatic spot of your life?"

"Sure," he replied, smiling. "Hammerstein's Theater, fall of 1910."

On the bill with the Mathewson and Meyers skit at the Chase Theater in Washington was a song and dance team called White and Kreamer. White has since made a big reputation, but both were then new to the East, having come from the Pacific Coast. Kreamer, whose general knowledge of affairs and people was extremely limited, was greatly impressed with the attention and publicity given Mathewson and Meyers.

"Al," he said to his partner after the opening performance, "who is this guy Mathewson that I see three-sheeted all over town and his name in the electric lights?"

"Why, you ignoramus," White explained, "that's Christy Mathewson, the greatest baseball pitcher in the world. Haven't you ever heard of him? He gets ten thousand dollars a year just for pitching."

"No, I ain't," declared Kreamer, "but he ought to get thirty cents for acting."

Later, though, Kreamer was much enlightened when Matty, having heard of this, walked on the stage in the White-Kreamer act and, joining hands with the two real performers, brought them a real ovation.

"He may be a ham actor," admitted Kreamer, "but he's a real guy."

Chapter 27. Checkers and Chess

Aside from his success as a pitcher, Christy Mathewson's greatest satisfaction was in his mastery of the game of checkers. He was not only a good checker player but ranked with the best-known experts in the United States. His greatest difficulty while traveling with the ball club was in finding suitable opponents. He could beat any of the ballplayers or all of them simultaneously while blindfolded.

To keep in practice, though, and study out problems, he would organize a set of games with the players. During the rest hours in the clubhouse after morning practice, he would arrange ten checker boards about the room. Each player would be required to pay five cents for the privilege of playing with him. If they won or even got a draw, he would pay them fifty cents. He would play them all at once.

It was an old saying among the Giants that Matty never had to pay out fifty cents but twice on two occasions his opponent, Al Demaree, I believe it was, got a draw. Not one ever beat him.

At Pittsburgh, he asked two or three of us one night to accompany him to the YMCA where he was to have a checker game.

Arriving there, we found that Matty had agreed to play any eight men the YMCA would select—play them simultaneously while he was blindfolded. Out of those eight men, only two got draws.

"That is not particularly remarkable," he explained. "Any real checker player could do that. It is just as easy to play eight men as one and I had just as soon play blindfolded as not. It is merely a matter of having in my mind a set of defense for three or four forms of attack. They rarely ever use more than two—the double-corner game and the single-corner game. It is easy to offset either of those. Of course, I know the squares on the board by number. The moment they call out the block to which they have moved, I know, by heart, the defensive move."

For several weeks, Matty went down to the Eden Musée to play against the mechanical game of checkers, the opponent, if you will remember, being the metallic figure of a great Turk called Ajeeb. This statue was supposed to make his moves mechanically. He always won. Hundreds of ordinary players used to stop then and pay ten cents to play a game with Ajeeb and always were beaten.

This interested Matty a whole lot. He would go down there day after day and try his hand. In time, he was able to win several games. Often, he fought the statue to a draw. Matty knew that there was a good checkers player hidden somewhere who made these moves. He had made a deep study of checkers and was familiar with standard forms of attack and defense. This so-called statue, he noticed, played exactly according to the best books and recognized styles.

Matty had been playing there for two months when one day he won two games straight. Suddenly, Ajeeb failed to make his next move. A man stepped out from a place of concealment inside the statue.

"I've been very much interested in your play," he said. "I can see that you have studied and are a real checkers player. I was just wondering if you wouldn't sit in for me occasionally and let me take a walk."

He showed Matty the mechanics of the checkers-playing statue and Big Six went in and played several games for him.

We saw Matty pretty well embarrassed once in his checker playing. He had asked another baseball writer and myself to go to the Cincinnati fire department with him. Matty often had played there, but the firemen, he told us, had dug up a member of the department from another station who wanted to give the ballplayer a game.

"You'll have some fun out of him," they told Matty. So, we all went along.

Probably the most un-thrilling thing in the world is a checker game to a spectator. Anyway, we went around and waited patiently for the fun.

Matty and the fireman, who was in uniform, sat down to play. Game after game resulted in a draw. Neither man apparently could get an advantage.

Finally, Matty stepped out in what he explained to us afterward was a daring game. It would be dangerous to try on an expert, but it was his one chance to score. Without hesitating, the fireman moved a perfect defense to every play that Matty made in his daring offensive. This seemed to puzzle the big fellow. His brows wrinkled and he began to perspire.

"Looks as if I couldn't put that over," said Matty. "You seem to know that particular game perfectly."

"Yes, Mr. Mathewson," replied the fireman, a little shamefacedly, "I wrote it."

"You are—"

"Yes, I am the author of the book you have been studying. Let me say that your memory is remarkable. You play a beautiful game of checkers."

It developed that the firemen, so long beaten by Mathewson, had got this man—I can't recall the name—to pose as a fireman and show Matty up. He had been champion of England and Ireland and also had won championships in America.

Even so, he and Matty each won a game before the night was over, the rest being draws. They became great friends.

Until he had quit playing baseball, the firemen of Cincinnati never forgot their joke on Matty. He never forgot it, either. In those days, we went to and from the ball grounds in carriages.

The route took us by the firehouse and the firefighters never lost an opportunity to yell to Matty and ask if he wanted to play a little checkers.

The game of checkers was Matty's greatest solace at Saranac. He even wrote anonymous letters, written in the Ring Lardner style, to a checker magazine, signing them "Ajeeb." For a long time, no one knew the author of these contributions that were not only amusingly written but scientifically remarkable.

When the Giants trained at Marlin, Texas, for five years, old checker players used to come from all over the state every spring to have a set of games with Mathewson. It was there they told the story and probably do yet of the old grocer who roped Matty into a game with the crack player of the town, an old farmer who always pretended that he couldn't play and would then turn around and beat the smart alecks with ease. For years they had used him as a frameup on unwary strangers.

This old gentleman had been sent for to teach Matty a lesson, being under the belief that the city youngster didn't know the game.

After they had played for an hour and Matty had won six games straight, one of the amazed and disappointed jokers turned to his friend, who sat on a pickle barrel, and remarked:

"Huh, old man John don't seem to be the man he used to be."

"Naw, by gum," retorted the other, "and he never was."

That yarn has been told on other checker players, but the Texans always hung it on Matty and Old Man John. They were telling it and enlarging it when we left Marlin ten years ago.

Chapter 28. Big League Trickery

Though brought up in an atmosphere of sincerity and later imbued with the spirit of real sportsmanship in college, Christy Mathewson had an early lesson in the baseball trickery of the Big Leagues. At that time, trickery was regarded an important feature of strategy. To Matty's surprise, it was not looked upon with a frown. In fact, he learned very quickly that it was the real spice of the game. He grew to enjoy it.

One of his first experiences was against the old Phillies when Big Ed Delahanty was the slugger of that team. Delahanty was one of the few batters who could keep his eye on the ball and still take a full swing like that of Babe Ruth.

Big League pitchers have a sort of Masonry of their own. If one of them discovers the weakness of a certain hard-hitting batter, the tip is quickly passed around to other opposing pitchers for the protection of other members of the craft.

"When you go against Delahanty," was the first tip young Mathewson got, "the thing to remember is never pitch him a high fast ball."

He was informed that the tip went for nearly all of the Philly batters.

So, in a game at Philadelphia, Matty faced Delahanty for the first time and, with what he thought great shrewdness, pitched him nothing but curves. Delahanty hit the first one out of the lot. On his next time up, Big Ed hit one so far that George Van Haltren, the outfielder, nearly ran his tongue out chasing it. One batter after another kept him running down long hits.

When Delahanty appeared again, Van Haltren held up the game while he came to confer with young Mathewson.

"For the Lord's sake, Matty," he panted, "give this fellow a base on balls so that I'll have a chance to catch my breath."

Matty knew there was something wrong with the tip he had received, so, in the face of all advice, he pitched directly to Delahanty's strength—a high fast one—and the big fellow struck out. Before the game was over, Matty struck him out twice.

"That high fast one really was Delahanty's favorite and not his weakness," Matty used to say, "but he was fooled at that time because he was expecting a curve. Everybody had been pitching to him that way for two or three months."

The origin of this tip on the Phillies was the discovery of a signal tipping device, which for a whole season had warned each Philly batter as to what to expect. It had been abandoned when Matty came into the game, but the effect of it still had the pitchers fooled.

It seems that Morgan Murphy had discovered that, sitting in the clubhouse with a pair of field glasses, he could see the catcher's hands and read his signals to the pitcher. He would then tip it off by pressing a button which caused a buzzer to sound near the coach's box at third base. The coach would relay the tip to the batter. So, whenever the batter knew that a high fast one was coming, he could wade into it with confidence. A high fast ball can be hit farther and with more ease than any other form of pitching, provided the batter is expecting it.

After several encounters with the Phillies, the pitchers passed the word never to give one of those fellows a high fast one, especially Delahanty. Matty fooled Delahanty because the signal tipping device had been discovered and was no longer working.

Another form of trickery that was a common practice in those days was for the local team to soap the ground around the pitcher's box. After the soapsuds had sunk in the ground, there was no surface indications of anything wrong. When the pitcher's hands began to perspire and he tried to dry them with the loose dirt, the soap would become active and cause the ball to slip out of his hand. Matty soon found that his only defense in certain parks was to carry his own dirt in his hip pocket.

This use of soap on the grounds, incidentally, is responsible for the carrying of the powdered rosin, so much discussed in Big League meetings recently.

One day in Pittsburgh, the Giants found that Fred Clarke and his crafty gang of champions had given the pitcher's box a thorough soap treatment. It was particularly aimed at Bugs Raymond, who rarely had any difficulty in beating the Pirates and who was expected to pitch.

Sure enough, Raymond started the game and was going strong. Soon his hands began to perspire. As Fred Clarke came to bat, Raymond pretended to be rubbing his pitching hand in the dirt. It was noticed, however, that before delivering the ball, he would put his hand in his hip pocket. Bugs slipped a clean strike over on Clarke and struck him out. As the game progressed, he seemed to get better.

"Say, Fred," Raymond said to the puzzled Clarke as he passed the Pirate bench in the last inning, "that's good soap out there, but you ought to buy your own pitchers a little of this."

He reached into his hip pocket and sprinkled a little of the powdered rosin in Clarke's hand. "It's great for control."

After that, Mathewson and all the rest of the pitchers carried rosin or powdered pumice in their hip pockets. The defense against the soapy pitcher's box worked so well that the old trick went out of use.

The first time Matty pitched on Brooklyn grounds away back in 1900, he couldn't understand what was wrong. He told George Davis, the manager, that Willie Keeler looked twice as small as usual.

"I feel like I am pitching out a cellar," he complained.

"You are," Davis told him. "They've doctored the box for us."

That Brooklyn gang of baseball tricksters (and there was none smarter) would have the pitcher's box lowered six inches if a tall man was to pitch and would raise it like a small mountain for a short pitcher. This gave the batters a tremendous advantage.

Another old trick was to wet the baselines to first and third and then cover them over with dry dust when a bunting game was feared. The slippery ground beneath the dust would check the speed 20 percent.

Chapter 29. Advice for Youngsters

Many years ago, when Christy Mathewson was at the height of his pitching career, I was sent to him with a request that he map out a training schedule for schoolboy ballplayers, including diet and general conduct.

He had a rather keen idea of newspaper values, typographical makeup, and so on. In fact, it had been his ambition to become a writer and, as in all things that interested him, he studied it closely.

"A thing like that would look good in print," he said, "but it's a lot of foolishness. There is no use of fooling boys with a lot of hokum.

I won't make out any schedule, but I'll tell them the truth, if you want that."

The suggestion was accepted.

"You tell those boys," he said, "that if they are interested in what they are doing and are proud of their progress as ballplayers, they won't need any rules or regulations. All they've got to do is be in earnest. That goes for Big Leaguers also. If a young fellow wants to be a good ballplayer and he discovers that too much eating interferes with his work, why, he'll stop it, that's all.

"I don't drink, for instance, because I know it would affect my work the next day. That's common sense, isn't it? If I find that eating lunch makes me logy and indifferent on the ball field in the afternoon, why, I quit eating lunch. That's all there is to it.

"Cigarette smoking is likely to be bad for youngsters because they may smoke to excess. It might affect their wind. They probably have noticed that I smoke cigarettes. It gives me a lot of comfort. So far as I know, smoking never did me any harm. That is why I do not stop. If I found it did affect me, I would stop immediately.

"Tell those boys just to apply common sense to everything they do. There are no tricks about keeping in condition. Anybody can keep in condition if he wants to. The trouble is that some of them do not want to. A man is kidding himself when he asks another fellow to tell him how to take care of himself. The main thing is to be ambitious and earnest. The rest will take care of itself."

The article was printed according to Matty's idea and the effect was better than if we had run the conventional box with a lot of set rules and complicated instructions.

Very few of his friends knew it, but Matty had a profound admiration for anyone who could write verse—real poetry or mere jingles. The mathematical rhythm, as he called it, always fascinated him. He longed to be a poet, a verse writer. He made many attempts, but would never let one of them appear in print.

Matty took a great fancy to Langdon Smith, author of the famous poem called "Evolution" or "The Tadpole and the Fish." Smith traveled with us then as a baseball writer.

"I know there is a trick to the verse writing," Matty told him, "and I want you to give me the key, if you will, the mathematics of it. I can see that the lines run in regular combinations of syllables, sometimes four to the line and sometimes five."

Smith outlined for him the different forms of verse and gave him a book on scanning. That amused Matty for weeks, but he would never try any of his efforts on the public. In time, though, he was an expert on the mechanics of poetry. He could point out instantly a fault in the scanning of newspaper verses.

But to get back to his ideas of training and diet, Matty never had any system at all. He didn't believe in it. He was a very light eater, notwithstanding his size. For breakfast he would have the usual eggs and bacon and fruit and so on. He made a point of eating breakfast late, so that he would not want any lunch.

"Lunch makes me feel heavy," he said. As a consequence, he never ate lunch.

For dinner his favorite food was steak and potatoes. Mrs. Mathewson always made a point of having an excellent porterhouse steak for him after he had pitched a ball game. Matty was not an epicure, except in his judgment of quality in plain foods. Fancy dishes did not appeal to him.

"Christy always liked desserts," said Mrs. Mathewson not long ago, "and his favorite sweet, outside of pie à la mode, was elderberry jam. Often, I had quite a time in getting that when we were not at home. His liking for the elderberry jam and jelly became known at Saranac Lake and up there we always managed to have it for him."

It was Matty's theory that a ballplayer, whether a professional or an amateur, should try to live naturally. He should eat what he wanted and should get his sleep in the hours that suited him best.

"Personally," he often said, "I prefer to sit up until nearly midnight and then sleep until nine o'clock. I get most of my recreation at night reading when everything is calm and comfortable.

"You see," he pointed out, "a ballplayer's job is a regular one. He has to do the same thing every day just as do the laborers who dig ditches and so on. Therefore, he should live in a natural way. I can understand why a prize fighter has to do special training for a big event or why a football team has to have a training table. They are aiming at a certain event. In baseball, however, we are working at a regular job. Any regular workman knows what is best for him and he lives accordingly. As I have said before, the main thing is to be sincerely interested in your profession. If you make mistakes in eating or in other excesses, you will discover them before anybody else does. In other words, all you've got to do is to be on the level with yourself."

Matty liked games other than baseball. He was very fond of golf. He didn't play golf, though, because it kept him in condition for baseball. He played because he liked it. At the training camps, he always played handball while the rest of the team was working out on the field. He did that because he thought handball helped his legs and brought muscles into play that baseball would not touch.

Matty never liked to do anything without an objective. For instance, he could not be persuaded to take a long walk unless he was going to a definite place and for a purpose. He would walk all day to get a shot at one quail or he would ramble for hours in search of a wildflower, but he wouldn't go a step just for the sake of being in motion.

Chapter 30. Dueling with His Nemesis, "Three-Fingered" Brown

Among baseball people, the older fans especially, it is generally believed that Christy Mathewson's greatest thrill was in the World Series of 1905 when he shut out the Athletics three times in succession. That feat, incidentally, has never been duplicated.

The thrill of that performance was not merely the winning of three games, nor was it the holding of the American League champions scoreless. To Matty, the big reaction was the feeling that he had proved himself a great pitcher.

For two years prior to that, the American League enthusiasts had scoffed at the idea of Bix Six being the peer of all pitchers. The rivalry was so intense as to be bitter and neither league would admit superiority of the other in any form whatsoever. American League fans had even gone so far as to declare that the Giants had declined to play the Red Sox in 1904 through a fear of having Mathewson shown up as a pitcher.

"There was not such a thrill in the games themselves in that 1905 Series," said Mathewson, "because I had the upper hand from the start to the finish. They never had me in a real tight place. The kick I got was in proving that I was able to hold my own against the American League."

The big thrill of Matty's life, though, the one he always recalled with genuine pleasure, came in a game that has been forgotten for many years because of its relative unimportance. It was against the Cubs in one of those exciting games of 1908.

The two games of that season that stand out so prominently in baseball history as to obscure all others were the tie game when Fred Merkle failed to touch second and the playoff game at the end of the season. The one that stuck in Matty's memory until his last days, however, was played earlier in the season.

It was one of those pitching battles between Matty and Three-Fingered Brown and was staked in Chicago.

Matty's arm was in particularly good shape that day and the Cubs had been helpless for eight innings. The Giants had a one-run lead going into the ninth. This would also indicate the wonderful effectiveness of Three-Fingered Brown.

"It looked as if I would get by without exerting myself," said Matty, "and I decided to take some liberties with Frank Chance, the first batter in the ninth. Just to see if he would take one, I laid a fastball right over the heart of the plate. I had an idea he might be looking for my curve. But he didn't wait. He cracked the ball for a clean single. A moment later, Harry Steinfeldt, picking up courage from the yelling of the crowd, whammed into a curve ball for three bases, sending Chance home with the run that tied the score. In a second, it seemed my whole ball game had been shot to pieces."

The writer was present at that game and will never forget the scene that followed. The Board of Trade Rooters, an organization of wild fans, had sent up an effigy of John McGraw on a kite string with a placard reading "Cheer up, Muggsy." They knew full well McGraw's lifelong resentment over the use of the word "Muggsy." When Chance crossed the plate, they cut the kite string. Then they sent up a hundred or more little balloons, each labelled "Yellow Giants." The whole place was actually in a riot of excitement. No other words could describe it.

The urge to this demonstration was that Solly Hofman and Joe Tinker were to follow Steinfeldt at bat and Tinker was Matty's main nemesis.

Matty stood there during the outbreak and, while order was being restored, he calmly thought over the situation. Here was a runner on third with none out and only one run needed to win the game. One run would be as good as a dozen, so he finally decided not to take a chance on either of these strong batters.

When he began to pitch outside—deliberately giving a base on balls—the fans thought they had his goat. The turmoil increased. Without a change of expression, however, the cool youngster walked both Hofman and Tinker and filled the bases with none out.

Right then, Matty cut loose with everything he had. The fans had not noticed that he lobbed up every ball to Hofman and Tinker, employing no strength whatever.

None of us ever saw Matty use more speed than he did in the next few minutes. He struck out Johnny Kling with three fastballs that Kling always declared he didn't even see. Then he went after Brown. In just as short a time, he had struck out the great pitcher.

By this time, the crowd had quieted down. All that stood between the Giants and a tied score was Johnny Evers. Matty did not try to strike him out. Instead, he pitched to make Evers lift the ball, fearing that he might get hold of a fast one and kill it.

Evers, a little over-cautious, went after a curve ball and lifted an easy fly to left field. The inning was over and the score was tied.

In the extra innings, Matty seemed to get better as he went. The Giants finally won out in the eleventh inning, making three runs. The final score was New York 4, Chicago 1.

"That was my greatest thrill in a ball game," Matty always declared. "It was a thrill because I was in the hole and worked myself out. The beauty of it to me was that, when I decided on a plan, everything worked out exactly according to specifications."

It was the strain of that game and the exciting ones that followed that hurt Matty's arm. At the end of the season, he suffered a sore arm for the first time in his career.

"I guess the Fates were against us that year, anyway," declared Matty years afterward. "The Merkle incident forced us to play an extra game to decide the pennant and in that playoff affair I pitched the worst game of my whole career, due to a sore arm which prevented my curve ball from working. I couldn't get anything on the ball."

Chapter 31. Praise from Opponents (and Umps)

To have a man's opponents write of his greatness is a tribute that is seldom paid a man. Christy Mathewson is entitled to a feeling of pride that he should carry to his grave.

The work of this great pitcher during 1913 attracted so much attention that telegrams were sent out to all the leading batters who have faced him, asking their opinions as to his ability and their reasons for such. To a man, they awarded him the honor of being the "King of All Pitchers" and their explanation is: "An unparalleled combination of brain and physical ability."

Jake Daubert, captain of the Brooklyn club: Mathewson's wonderful pitching so far this season has not been any surprise to me, for I have always regarded him as the greatest pitcher that ever stepped into a box and, after watching him pitch thirteen innings against our team at Ebbets Field recently, I feel convinced that Matty is still good for years to come. During the four years I have been playing with the Dodgers, I have had many occasions to bat against Mathewson and I can truthfully say that I think he is just as effective today as he was the first time that I faced him. He has everything that makes a successful twirler. He is cool-headed, whether in pinches or not; has wonderful control, speed, and curves; and he mixes his curves up so well that he can fool the star hitters as well as the lesser ones.

Bill Dahlen, manager of the Brooklyn club: I look upon Mathewson today as just as good a pitcher as he was years ago. In former years, he worked harder while he was in the box, but he knows more now and, of course, works much easier. After watching him pitch that thirteen-inning game for the Giants against my club a few days ago, I cannot help but say what I have always said about him, and that is that he is without any question of doubt the greatest baseball pitcher the I have ever seen in action.

Nap Rucker, star twirler of the Brooklyn club: When you hear people say and read in the papers about Mathewson being the greatest pitcher in the country, that is absolutely the truth and, furthermore, it is not exaggerating things a bit. Matty is certainly a wonderful twirler and I am sure that he will be just as good in years to come as he is at the present time. I wish him every success and I only hope that I will be able to go along and pitch as he has for as many years.

Miller Huggins, of the St. Louis club: With his wonderful control, Matty does not have to use speed. The reason Mathewson is pitching such wonderful ball today, is because he knows every minute what he is going to do with the ball. I never saw any pitcher who could put the ball where he wanted it like this big fellow.

Ed Konetchy, first baseman of the St. Louis club: Why, I never could hit him and expect to go along the same way. He is the most remarkable pitcher I ever batted against. Many times have I had three balls in my favor, but he would shoot the next three over and I stood flat-footed waiting for a walk. Some players have told me they could hit him, but I can't and that is all I have to say. Matty is as good today as he was ten years ago and ranks with the best in the game. His effectiveness is due to his great control and reserve power. Matty never pitches hard to a batter unless he is in a hole and then you can bank on it that you will never get two balls alike and they all have a lot of stuff on them, too.

Hans Wagner, shortstop and center fielder of the Pittsburgh club: Mathewson is the greatest pitcher ever seen on the diamond. Some may differ with me, but I have batted against him many times and, just when I thought I had him, he would shoot one over and I went to the bench. He has as much speed now as he ever had, but as he can win games without using it, he does not resort to trying to knock the catcher down. I remember one game he worked against us last summer in which he did not use a curve ball. He had such excellent control that day that he used nothing but a fast, straight one. You can say for me that I think Mathewson is just as good today as he ever was.

Heinie Zimmerman, infielder of Chicago club: I do not know anything about what Mathewson was ten years ago, but I do know that he is the best pitcher in the league at the present time and has been since I came in several years ago. His wonderful control makes it easy for him to fool the batters for he can stick the ball just where he wants to and when he wants to. He uses his head more than the ordinary run of pitchers and knows exactly what a batter can hit and what he cannot hit. I always like to face him because I know that I can feel safe and take chances on swinging on the ball. He still has a lot of speed, but does not have to use it often because he has such a grand assortment of curves.

Jake Stahl, manager of the Boston club: The first time I ever batted against Mathewson was in 1909. The next time was during the last World Series. He was much better the last time. I think Mathewson will be one of the world's greatest pitchers for many years to come. I have seen lots of pitching, but I never saw, or expect to see again, anything like the work of Mathewson in the last game at Boston that we won. No pitcher can ever hope to get any nearer perfection. He had much more stuff on the ball in 1912 than he did in 1909 and in a week had discovered the weaknesses of our batters that other pitchers had not noticed after working against them for several years. Matty has a wonderful brain and his brain is just as good as his head.

Fred Clarke, manager of the Pittsburgh club: What do I think of Matty as a pitcher? Well, that is a pretty hard matter to say. I always considered him to be a marvel. Why, I look upon the big fellow as the greatest pitcher we have ever had and, although I have not batted against many of the American League pitchers, I have no fear in saying that the Giant twirler is better than any of them. Some pitchers come into the league and for a couple of seasons set the world on fire, but they depart to the bushes. Not so with Matty, for ever since he started in 1900 he has been a star.

Red Dooin, manager of the Philadelphia club: No man who has shown the remarkable pitching skill of Christy Mathewson, year after year, can do so unless he takes the best care of himself both during and after the playing season. Besides, Mathewson is a student of the game. He is always studying the strong and weak points of the various batsmen. He knows what they can hit and what they cannot hit—and he feeds them what they cannot get their bats against. Then, too, Mathewson has wonderful control; no pitcher, in fact, has better. He knows just where he wants every ball to go and he usually gets it just where he desires. Each year Mathewson's experience aids him more and age, instead of hurting him, has been a help. He is one of the pitchers who depends as much on his head as he does on his arm.

Umpire Mal Eason: Mathewson is the greatest pitcher this or any other league ever possessed. I have seen some pretty nifty pitching in my time, but I never met a pitcher who could handle a ball like the New York twirler does. I have pitched against him and umpired before him and can truthfully say he is in a class by himself now and, in fact, ever since he started. His twelve years has if anything improved him for he is doing just as good twirling now as he ever did. Any pitcher who can win games like Matty did the other day in Brooklyn is a wonder.

William Brennan, Eason's umpire partner: Mathewson would have been a success in any business he had started in. Why, he is a student of the game and he would have been the same in any other business he had tackled. I have seen Mathewson many times talking to his infielders in order to steady them in a critical stage of the game. It is generally the infield that is talking to the pitcher. Mathewson would have become a master at chess if he had devoted as much time to that game as he has to baseball, for he is without doubt the greatest student of the game we have ever had.

Chapter 32. An Avid Golfer

Christy Mathewson never gave up hope of a return to the old form that made him the greatest pitcher in the world. Friends who had been with him frequently since the end of the 1915 baseball season firmly believed that 1916 would be a good one.

The "Old Master" went at the job of putting himself in shape in his usual businesslike way and he had adopted a rather unique method. He played golf daily and proposed to keep it up until barred by the snow.

Not only had Mathewson developed new muscles while the ailing ones were given a rest, but he developed into a corking good golfer. In a game at Van Cortlandt Park, he made the game in 86, by far the best he had ever done. Some men play golf all their lives and never get below 90.

"If Matty would only improve his short game," said Charley Atherton, a retired ballplayer and an old comrade of Matty's, "he'd be a star golfer. He drives as well as most anybody and drives straight, too."

Though Mathewson, to all extents and purposes, had completely dropped out of sight, we caught him in the act of smashing a long drive off the first tee up at the public course.

"I like golf," he said, "because it is the only mild exercise I know of that does not wear on the same muscles that are necessary in baseball. It's a funny thing," he added, "but I have not felt that pain in my shoulder since the baseball season ended, the pain that caused me all the trouble last summer. If I can keep on building up gradually without that muscle being affected, I believe it will put me in good shape for next season."

"Has anybody ever given you a satisfactory explanation as to the trouble with that shoulder muscle that affects your pitching?" I asked him.

"Well," he laughed, "Charley Atherton here has just been telling me that he had the same trouble in his shoulder and that it lasted ten years. He discovered that it was muscular rheumatism caused from wearing wet garments. Now, that's encouraging, isn't it?"

It was evident, though, that Matty did not believe he was to have such a long siege.

"Honestly, I haven't felt it for a month," he said, "and if I can only keep my eye on this golf ball and my mind on that next green, I've got a hunch that the muscle will forget the trouble and string along with me."

Incidentally, the Old Master has given the golf game considerable study, as he does everything he undertakes.

"The whole thing in this game, I believe," he explained, "is concentration. If you keep your eye on the ball and your mind on just exactly what should be done with it, I believe you—even you—could be a fairly good golfer.

"In the matter of concentration, golf is not so very different from baseball. Unless a pitcher concentrates his mind on the batter and watches his every move, he cannot get along. The moment he allows the crowd, the shouting of the other players, and the score to disturb him, he is just like a golf player who loses his poise and begins slicing the ball. It's all the game.

"The swing in golf, however, is entirely different from that in baseball, but a man who has been a ballplayer ought to have an advantage in golf. His muscles are trained to coordinate and he is accustomed to using them more than the average citizen. In other words, an athlete in any line is apt to be better in another athletic line than the person who has not followed athletic pursuits at all.

"The man of forty-five or fifty who swings stiffly does so because his muscles never were used for swinging or, rather, he waited too long before starting. As a proof of this, the other day I saw an old gentleman past sixty who swings a golf club just as freely as anybody. Upon inquiry, I learned that he had been playing golf since he was eighteen years old. The muscles had simply stuck to their early training."

As soon as it got too cold for golf and snow began to fall, Matty headed out on a hunting trip where he would have to do a lot of walking. If he doesn't have a good season in 1916, it can never be said that the Old Master didn't try.

Chapter 33. A Trapshooter, Too

A party of wayfarers from the sporting pages drifted to Travers Island, drawn thither by the sound of shot and shell. The holiday was being proclaimed by gunpowder.

From the throng of islanders gathered at the landing place we heard such strange, but familiar sounds as this:

"Come on, Matty. Bust this one!"

"Gee, but the Old Doc can smash 'em! That's a good one, Otie!"

"Don't let that one get away. Crack it, Chief!"

"There you go, Harry. Nail it!"

And so it went, the babble of shouts being punctured by the sharp, whip-like crack of twelve-gauge, smokeless shells.

"What's the idea of all the excitement?" we inquired of a young woman, apparently more interested than her husband.

"It's the professionals giving an exhibition match," she explained.

"What d'you mean professionals—professional ballplayers?"

"No, indeed," she laughed at our ignorance, "professional trapshooters. It's the big event of the year."

Still that suggestion of baseball in the names clung to us and made investigation imperative. And, sure enough, here is what we found.

Christy Mathewson, Otie Crandall, Chief Bender, and Harry Davis, former captain of the Athletics, disguised as professional trapshooters and getting paid for the same at professional rates. Moreover, they were earning their "dough."

The quartet of baseball stars paled a little when caught with the goods by men of their own set and quickly set forth a defense.

"It's better than acting, authoring, or barnstorming," said Matty. "And, besides that, I'm getting stuck on it. In the last three weeks we have made a tour of the country, shooting at the various gun clubs, and we've made more money than a whole team of ballplayers could have made barnstorming."

To encourage interest in the sport of trapshooting, he explained, he and Crandall, Davis, and Bender have been engaged to appear at the various clubs and shooting matches.

The party of wayfarers was just in time to see the match between the ballplayers and a picked team from the New York Athletic Club and it proved a corking exhibition. The ballplayers lost a pair of turkey gobblers and the match, but they opened the eyes of those who never dreamed they were such crack shots. The best in New York was stacked against them and out of five hundred birds a side—clay pigeons—they were beaten by a score of 445–403.

Though Chief Bender is considered the best shot of the quartet, he was beaten out by Crandall, and Matty, who has been shooting like a wizard until now finished fourth. It was his first bad day in weeks.

Chapter 34. Manager in Cincinnati

The progress of Christy Mathewson in 1916 spring training was watched with keenest interest by every player on the club from the rawest recruit to the sophisticated veteran. He took things easy and worked up to a stage of efficiency with great caution. It would be well in April before he felt he could put the "old soupbone," as he calls it, to a real test. In the practice games he went in the box merely for exercise and made no attempt to put anything on the ball.

Matty's physical trouble was a most peculiar one. He had been examined by eight different specialists and all of them had confessed that they did not know the cause of his ailment. For that reason, they have been unable to prescribe any treatment that would eradicate it. There have been so many warped explanations as to the trouble that a statement, based on the statement of a specialist and of Matty himself, might be interesting.

The trouble was not in his pitching arm. The seat of the peculiar ailment was on top of the left shoulder, just halfway between the base of the neck and the point of the shoulder. There was a small lump just at the outer edge of the collar bone. To touch this was very painful. In lifting his hands above his head to get a swing with the ball, the twinge of pain was so sharp that a free movement of the arms was impossible. He consequently could not control the ball as in the old days and without control Matty lost the one factor that had made him the master of them all.

There was no twisted or overlapping muscle to cause this trouble and the X-ray pictures, a number of which had been taken, showed nothing of an abnormal nature.

"The most plausible diagnosis that I had," said Matty, "was that of a specialist in New York who said the trouble was due to a lack of lubrication in the bones and muscles. The little muscle does its work with an effort and the dragging caused the pain. Just how they could restore the missing lubrication was a problem that no one had been able to solve."

"Have you felt it since coming down here to Texas?" I asked him.

"Yes," he admitted rather dolefully. "But I do not believe it as severe as during last season. I find my right arm is in nice shape and so far the ailment in the left shoulder has not interfered with my work, but I cannot speak for the future. If the trouble continues, I am done, that's all."

But Matty's shoulder problem continued to plague him and on July 20, 1916, he was traded to the Cincinnati Reds. Mathewson looked upon this new move as a relief to a condition which, for him, had been at times unpleasant—unsatisfactory at least. Early that spring he realized that he was no longer a pitching star. To receive a big salary for sitting on the bench and, as he expressed it, "holding back the club" was not in keeping with his sense of fair play. For a year he had felt he was taking advantage of the New York club. Sincerely, he welcomed the change.

"There's but one thing left for me to do," he remarked, as we talked it over in May, "and that is to be a manager. This thing of me going into some other business is all rot. I have been in baseball too long to give it up lightly."

Before agreeing to go to Cincinnati, however, Matty insisted that Mr. Garry Herrmann and the directors gave him absolute charge. He started in with a big salary because the Cincinnati club assumed his contract with the New York club, which called for something like $10,000 a year.

The fans of New York joined the baseball writers in wishing him all the luck in the world.

It is difficult to make the layman understand just how these writers felt toward the Old Master. In all his years, he never kicked on a story that had appeared in the prints, whether it was in his favor or registered against him. He was always ready to help out a young reporter, willing to put him "right" of a story instead of to "josh" him. For a long time Matty had ideas of becoming a writer himself and he succeeded fairly well despite the fact that he did not think so.

Chapter 35. Cleaning Out His Locker

It is quite the thing, at times, for some of the hard-boiled fans or writers who regard themselves as cynics, particularly the younger ones, to decry the lack of sentiment in baseball, to aver that commercialism is always uppermost in the mind of the professional player.

Whenever a player, in negotiating a new contract, remarks that he must have a certain amount of money or he won't sign, this is pounced upon as evidence of a lack of feeling or sentiment toward the sport which is so close to the hearts of Americans.

I think it was the picturesque Poll Perritt, pitcher for the Giants, who remarked in his quaint Louisiana drawl, "I'm telling you, fellows, feelins is feelins, no matter who has 'em."

To show how carefully Christy Mathewson figured out his financial affairs and also to bear out certain parts of this quotation, I might tell the following incident.

When Matty first went to Cincinnati, he told me he decided to buy a new car, selected a new car that cost about $2,500, and then studied the stock market with the idea of making the money to buy the car. He selected a stock that he thought would yield him sufficient profit to buy the car and in two weeks he had accomplished his object. This incident reflects Matty's financial gift.

But to continue. Poll's philosophy might have been brought home to the cynics could they have been present in the clubhouse of the Giants on that afternoon when Christy Mathewson came to clean out his locker and tell his teammates goodbye. He was going to manage the Cincinnati Reds.

A long, low-hung car pulled up at the clubhouse as the rain spattered down on a sign proclaiming "No Game Today." A big-shouldered, blue-eyed fellow climbed from under the wheel and slowly made his way up the steps to the intimate home of the Giants. Nobody stopped him, though he did not belong to the New York club.

In the corner of the clubhouse—the new clubhouse—there was a locker that had performed its duty for more than a decade. Clubhouses had changed several times, but not that locker. The iron grating was fastened exactly as it was fastened on that day when the Giants licked the Athletics and won the world championship back in 1905.

The big fellow, mopping his blond brow, fitted a key to the lock and began dragging forth things that had not been touched for many years. Idling around on the benches, several pink-skinned athletes watched the rifling of the locker in oppressive silence. Over in a corner, a plain pine table had been rigged up for vingt-et-un and the muscular fellows, clad in little more than a breechclout, sat down to have a try at the game. The big fellow turned from his demolition of the locker to watch them.

"Say, Matty," one of them yelled, "don't forget that checkerboard and, mind you, there's a tab there on the shelf, showing how much the gang has won or lost during the last two months."

The blue-eyed athlete located the sheet of paper and walked over to the table. He had been the club bookkeeper and mathematician since a lad.

"Come now, fellows," he said, "and kick in. I'm leaving and this thing's got to be straightened out."

One at a time, the debtors were cornered and settled.

"And, say, Matty," another yelled, "don't forget that Larry and Poll owe a dollar on that last checker game."

Another dollar or two was turned over to the big pitcher.

"I guess there isn't much more use for these towels," he said, spreading them out on the table. "I'll stake you to this one, Fred, and I guess Fletch will grab the other one."

"All right," yelled Larry. "Get that locker straightened out and sit in with us for a few minutes. We'd like to have you lose one time before you go."

In a few minutes the locker was stripped and the steel-grated door swung idly on its hinges with a key stuck in the lock.

The man who had used it for years stood there, scanning a slip of paper that evidently had been lost in the dust of time. On it he made out this memorandum: "Mertes, .25; Bowerman, .60; Tenney, .50; Wilson, .50; Wiltse, 1.25; Ames, .75."

"An old twenty-one score," he mumbled, and there came the trace of a tear in the big blue eyes.

Evidently, he regarded it settled, for he started to tear it up and then, on second thought, carefully brushed off the little slip and placed it in a card case.

"Are you in?" an impatient athlete shouted from the vingt-et-un table. "Come on and take a hand. There's no ball game today. Never mind about that new club of yours."

Just then, the blue-eyed fellow dug up from the bottom of the locker a kodak print of a party of old-timers. In the middle he stood, flanked by Arthur Devlin and Bill Dahlen. That he also tucked in the big card case.

"Are you coming or not?" the athlete demanded from the table. "We are starting the deal."

More teardrops trickled down the cheeks of the big athlete. He edged over to the vingt-et-un table.

"Larry," he said, in a half-broken voice, "I don't know whether I want to become the manager of another club or not. This is the only locker I ever had in my life. Deal me in the game!"

The cards were slowly dealt, not a sound smothering the "flip, flip" as the pasteboards fell on the table.

"Larry," said the big fellow, without studying his hand, "the only run-in we ever had was when you accused me of saying you had been drinking a bottle of beer. Remember, you cracked it at me in an exhibition game down at Norfolk? I'm sorry that you thought that."

"Forget it, old boy," counseled Larry and he slapped him on the back, "we are with you hook, line, and sinker."

The game broke up without a hand having been played and, as the big fellow bundled up his things and trundled over to the clubhouse of the visitors, there were tear-dimmed eyes. Even the clubhouse boy felt badly.

Matty's locker was empty.

It was empty for the first time in sixteen years!

Chapter 36. Return to the Polo Grounds

Matty came, saw, and conquered on July 26, 1916, but the New York fan took unto himself an even break. Like the "hard-boiled egg" who pitched pennies on the basis of "heads I win, tails you lose," there was a chance for a yell any way the coin flipped.

While Matty was winning, Slim Sallee, Buck Herzog, and the Giants were losing and the confused fan is still wondering just which way he rooted. There can be no doubt but that we sent Christy Mathewson, the Old Master, off to a good start and there can be equally no doubt but that our heroes got a terrible kick in the shins.

"No matter which way it breaks," said John McGraw as the immense crowd was warming up to the new leader of the Cincinnati Reds, "I lose. If Salle and Herzog fail to shine, I'm in bad, and if Matty fails to make good, I'm disappointed."

Very likely there was never before a ball game played in which the spirit of sportsmanship ruled absolutely. Having put aside their partisanship, the fans sat back and rooted for the good plays. The ultimate result made no difference whatever.

At the finish, the most inconsequential fan could trek through the exit, proclaiming, "Well, we put that one over," and be perfectly right.

As far as actual ball playing goes, all of the new stars got a bad start. Herzog was weak at the bat and erratic in the field. Slim Sallee had little of his former cunning and, when the big moment came, he caved in, Poll Perritt having to relieve him.

Matty was on the coaching lines but little. His only words of encouragement to his new teammates were, "Take it easy up there"—meaning at the bat—"You've got plenty of time." During the game he gave very few directions from the bench.

It was quite evident that Mathewson would follow, to a large extent, the system of John McGraw. Not once during the game did he order a sacrifice hit. The Reds hit the ball hard every time and played to win instead of to tie. Years ago, McGraw soured on the sacrifice hit as an aid to run-getting and Matty evidently thought that the correct system.

Another thing noticeable to the old-timers was that Matty instructed his batters to wait out the pitcher and not swing at the first ball. Knowing Sallee to be a wise pitcher, Matty knew that he would switch his tactics the moment they began walking up and taking a slam at the first one. First-ball hitting is all right against a pitcher who does not think, but it does not work well as a rule against old-timers. Batters often have tried it against Matty himself.

For a few minutes I was privileged to sit with him and, while talking with the old boy who started in major league baseball at the same time I did, I noticed that the Cincinnati players were sizing him up with the same amount of curiosity as myself.

Ballplayers all respect Matty, and the youngsters were particularly anxious to hear him speak. But he didn't. Occasionally he would nod to the batter, indicating that he should hit and not sacrifice. But between times he was silent—almost morbidly silent.

"I don't know whether I'll like this job or not," Matty candidly admitted. "It is all so new and my thoughts and memories are so confused that I am somewhat up in the air. I imagine I would have felt much easier if practically my first game had not been against the Giants and in the Polo Grounds. You can't realize how much I appreciate the fact that all these fans are rooting for me and, at the same time, you can realize what lack of genuine enthusiasm I go at the job of beating the people who have been my people for the last fifteen years. It's tough."

"Have you any choice," I asked him, "as to the nature of the testimonial that is to be presented to you by the fans through the *Evening World*'s fund?"

Bix Six looked at me and his face was unusually serious. It could be told from his voice that he was deeply affected.

"If they really want to give me a remembrance," he said, "I would much prefer that it would be of their own selection."

"But what would you like at home—something that would be permanent?"

"I don't know," he said, confusedly. "Would you mind waiting until I speak to Mrs. Mathewson?"

A few minutes after that I happened to meet Mrs. Mathewson in the runway leading to the upper grandstand. She also was confused.

"I'll tell you," she finally said. "The one thing that Christy cares for is a painting by a master. It is a question as to whether he would prefer paintings or a fine library, but if the contributors do not mind, we'll talk it over before deciding. It has come so sudden that I really don't know what to say.

"But," she added with a smile, regaining her composure, "anything will be all right as long as it is not a loving cup."

It was also discovered that the Mathewsons now have a magnificent silver set presented to them by the ballplayers.

Chapter 37. End of a Career

On July 12, 1920, Mathewson sadly announced in the press that he was ending his baseball career.

I guess I've hung up my uniform up for the last time. I am through with Big League baseball as an active participant. The game, which has been my life profession, will know me no more except as a spectator.

The going was a great blow to me. I had hoped to be the leader of a Big League club again. McGraw had hoped so, too, and told me that someday I would be at the helm of the Giants—but now my health has broken down and the doctors say I must stay away from the Big League circuit and rest.

Once I was the manager of the Cincinnati club and like every Big League leader I had championship aspirations, but the war found me in France, and on my return I discovered that my job had been moved out from under me. It was some satisfaction to me to see the Cincinnati Reds win the World's Championship the first year Pat Moran had charge.

By saying this I am not trying in any way to detract from Pat's great performance, but I must be given some credit for the construction of the team that came through for him, the same as Frank Selee was for the first championship Frank Chance won with the Cubs.

I leave baseball without a regret. It is a clean game and a good one. Perhaps the strain of it is hard on the health, but I don't blame my illness on that. A combination of bronchitis and failure to take proper care of myself was responsible. Finally, the doctor stepped in and told me I would have to stop, so here I am in the mountains resting.

I'll miss the fans and the crowds and the excitement. The followers of the game stuck to me. Even in the years since I have not been participating in the game actively and regularly, whenever we struck a crowd at hotels and railroad depots, I have heard the question: "Which one is Matty?" It was always music to me.

John McGraw has been my almost constant boss ever since I started in the Big Leagues. To him I owe much and he always treated me better than anyone could be asked to be treated. From now on, I will have to depend on the newspapers and the gossip I get occasionally in letters for my baseball news.

Chapter 38. A Move to Saranac Lake

Bulger resumes the narrative here.

Probably the most surprising announcement ever made in baseball was when John McGraw came to the press box at the Polo Grounds one day and told a group of the older writers that Christy Mathewson had gone to Saranac Lake to be cured of tuberculosis.

Matty was under treatment before any of his closest friends had any idea that he was a victim of the dread disease. For a while after his return from France and his new association with the Giants as coach, he had been, apparently, in good health. He suffered from a nagging cold, but gave it little concern for a few days. With his usual thoroughness, though, he underwent a thorough examination. His friends were profoundly shocked at the doctor's report, but Matty showed no signs of mental disturbance.

"Well," he remarked to his physician, "we'd better get at it and the quicker the better."

So, Matty was in his room at Saranac, going through the first stages of treatment before the public knew he was ill. That a great athlete like Matty could be the victim of tuberculosis seemed impossible.

It was discovered that not only one lung but both were affected. It was decided to collapse one lung and use the other until one could be made strong.

Matty understood the principles of this treatment thoroughly and expressed a willingness to go through with it. He talked about his fight with the disease as if it had been a ball game. Never did he seek sympathy nor was he morose. He merely set himself for a long fight and went through with it.

During his long stay in the lonely mountains away from all his baseball associations, Matty amassed a great pile of clippings. Nothing in the newspapers escaped him. In going through these clippings since his death, this notation has been found on a number of them: "Save this one."

Oddly enough, none of those so marked has to do with baseball games. One was about a movement to help the Keystone Academy where he got his start as boy pitcher. Several were about his efforts to raise a fund for the benefit of other sufferers from tuberculosis. Several were about checker problems. One was an article in Spanish from a Havana newspaper.

Matty apparently valued editorials more highly than any other form of writing. He had preserved hundreds of editorials that had appeared in large and small newspapers. The theme of most of them was "Matty as an example to boys."

The whimsical turn of his mind is found in the preservation of many clippings dealing with "boneheaded plays" and of his having been turned into a first baseman by Horace Fogel, manager of the Giants back in 1900.

There is one about Josh Devore, a player of whom Matty was particularly fond. "I like this," he wrote on the margin. "Keep it."

When Josh joined the Giants, he was not very well versed in affairs of life and knew little of the world about him. It was his innocence, his naïve frankness, that appealed to Matty.

Like all country boys, Josh wanted to acquire the habits of the players of more experience in travel. He was rooming with Rube Marquard, who carried a huge wardrobe trunk filled with many suits of clothes and all sorts of haberdashery finery. Devore felt that he would be looked down on unless he had a trunk like that. To his mind, its possession meant social standing as a Big League player. So, Josh bought a wardrobe trunk exactly like that of Marquard.

Unfortunately, Devore had nothing to put into the trunk other than a necktie, two shirts, and a fancy vest. Just the same, he lugged that trunk around with him. Finally, the practical jokers of the club broke open Josh's trunk and left it open so as to disclose its emptiness.

Matty was touched by Josh's embarrassment and his failure to acquire standing with his highly prized wardrobe trunk.

"That's all right, Josh," Matty said to him, "I've lost my old roommate, so you come and room with me on this trip."

"Do you mean that, Matty?"

Devore could not believe that he was to be so honored. Rooming with Matty meant a definite standing among the other players. Matty did mean it, however. Devore, after that, roomed with him for several seasons.

Matty coached him in things that he did not know and improved Josh wonderfully. He would have died for Old Gumboots.

At Saranac Lake, Matty's observant mind was quick to see an outlet for the few activities permitted him. He saw how difficult it was for the victims of tuberculosis to give up their work and be treated. He organized the Adirondack Fund for Tuberculosis and wrote many of his friends to give a helping hand. At his suggestion, many benefit performances were given and he spent his spare time in autographing baseballs that were to be sold as an aid in raising money.

Some months later, Mrs. Mathewson wrote to several of his newspaper friends:

"This movement is for the clerks, stenographers, and people of the working classes who come here for their health. The fund has proved a wonderful benefit after their resources are exhausted. Christy approves of it and wishes that you could give the matter some publicity. Could you do this without dragging him too much into the limelight?"

That last is very characteristic of Matty. Always he shunned the limelight.

To help this movement, Matty did everything in his power. He would appear at amateur ball games and pitch one ball. He would give a checker-playing exhibition. He would write anonymous articles to the newspapers. The raising of such a fund became a sort of life work with him. It was his one regret toward the finish that it had not been completed.

The doctor says that Matty never fumed or fretted. He understood perfectly what was being done or attempted and he obeyed orders implicitly. "Such a pity," says the doctor, "that such a patient could not see success crown his efforts."

Chapter 39. Life with Tuberculosis

Jane Mathewson's recollections of life with Christy Mathewson after his tuberculosis diagnosis.

Though I had known Christy as only a wife can know her husband for twenty years, I never quite realized his strength of character and his fortitude and his sweet consideration for others until he was stricken ill and we went to Saranac Lake.

During all of his long suffering there, he never once complained or became fretful. Often, he went through an entire night without being able to sleep. In the morning he would be completely exhausted. The pain had left lines in his face. Even this nerve-racking experience did not make him peevish or bring a tone of complaint to his voice.

He was more concerned about my welfare than his own. Instead of seeking sympathy, his attitude was one of worry over me.

"Now, never mind that, Jane," he would say after one of these long, sleepless and exhausting nights. "That's all over and we can't do anything about it. Let's forget it and start over. Today's experience will be a new game. Now you go and get some rest and, above all, don't worry. We may have another battle to fight and win tonight."

The wracking pains and the exhausting nights did not lessen Christy's interest in the things he had loved. Often, he would try to forget himself in working checker problems as he lay in bed. The life of inactivity in itself was tortuous to him.

When Christy was first allowed to go outside, he took an immediate interest in wildflowers or, rather, he renewed his old interest, that being one of his hobbies from boyhood. His favorite flower, by the way, was the blue gentian.

I don't know if the public knew of his fondness for flowers and of his knowledge about them, but it was an odd and touching circumstance that, when he died, one of the most beautiful floral tributes was a large bank of solid blue gentians sent by Mr. William F. Baker of the Philadelphia National League club.

At no time did Christy ever give up the fight during those years at Saranac Lake. In addition to his rambles in search of wildflowers, he indulged his fondness for shooting. He was not permitted to do much walking, but he devised a way to enjoy quail shooting without the usual physical exertion required. We would drive along the mountain roads in an automobile. We watched the sides of the road closely. If signs of a covey of quail or grouse were observed, the car would be stopped and Christy, with his shotgun, would step to the ground on the side of the car away from the quail. Then he would slowly walk toward the birds until the covey flushed. He never shot one except upon the wing. By this method, which I am told was rather ingenious, he often secured the bag limit.

Christy never lost his interest in baseball affairs. He had many opportunities to earn some money by preparing articles for the newspapers on the pennant prospects of the World Series, but he declined them. I have just seen again a note that he wrote to his friend John N. Wheeler in October 1921. It would give an idea as to how he felt about doing any writing work:

"Dear Jack:

I am feeling pretty good these days and would enjoy seeing you, but I cannot do any work, such as cooking up baseball stories, because effort of that sort gives me a rise in temperature, which 'tho temporary, is not good for T. B.

Nearly every day on my auto ride I see ruffed grouse and two deer trotted across the road last week. The season for this game opens two weeks from today—but not for me. My 'foot radius' is only 100 yards.

Very sincerely yours,

Christy Mathewson."

It was in that same fall that Christy was honored by the testimonial game played at the Polo Grounds. That impressed him deeply.

His gratitude was intense. His feelings are best expressed, perhaps, in an extract from another letter that he wrote Mr. Wheeler about the same time:

"I am much indebted to the hundreds of my friends who honored me at the Polo Grounds, but I am especially pleased that you were there. And, also, good old Ring (Lardner)!

"Wholly aside from the financial part, I think the New York baseball club paid me a great honor on 'Matty Day.' And, also, the sport writers! The latter were all very kind. When you see Runyon, Rice, Trumbull or any of the bunch, I wish you would tell each one how I appreciate what he did. Sometime I hope to thank them in person. John McGraw started the whole thing. The idea was all his, but his partners, Stoneham and McQuade, went with him strong, though they were not in baseball when I was a Giant pitcher.

"Confidentially, the local Chamber of Commerce is arranging a group of prominent citizens to be Pathe-graphed when the Big Game check is presented to me, so, for a minute, I may again crash into the movies."

Christy was very fond of reading. He read more as a student than one seeking mere amusement. One of his favorite authors was Charles Lamb. He read and reread Lamb's essays. Christy could never read or get interested in fiction. He was particularly fond of informative books of travel and of great men—prominent characters in history.

If he happened to read a book on some foreign country and became interested, he would not be satisfied until we had found for him all the books on that particular country that were available. Christy was never satisfied with a casual knowledge of any subject. His information had to be thorough and complete.

That explains why new acquaintances, upon engaging him in conversation, were struck by his profound knowledge of the subject under discussion. If the fancy struck him and he should start reading about Tibet, for example, he would never stop until he had exhausted all sources of information on the subject.

Often, I was occupied for several days in seeking books for him that many of the clerks in the stores and young librarians had not heard of.

Chapter 40. Thoughts on the Babe

Bozeman now continues with Mathewson's story.

Matty looked pretty good as he came down the corridor in New York City during December 1922. He was easily overweight—around two hundred pounds.

Stopping at a lounge in the hotel hall, he sat down. His one strange act was to adjust a pair of tortoise-shell spectacles and seriously regard what seemed like a pair of dice in the design of the carpet.

"Say," he said with a reminiscent laugh, "you know I haven't tried to make a third pass with the bones in six years. Brings back old times, doesn't it?"

Matty came out of the room to talk because Mrs. Mathewson was dressing for dinner.

"You think this new lively ball is upsetting the pitching?" I asked.

"Anything will upset the pitching," he said, "when they let the batter get hold of the ball. It makes no difference whether it's a lively ball or an old-fashioned one, they've got to get hold of it to smack it. Right?"

"Babe Ruth didn't get hold of one."

"Yes, but he will. That bird hit the longest long fly in the last Series that I ever saw in my life. You remember the one that Joe Tinker hit over Cy Seymour's head in that playoff game with the Cubs in 1908? Cy played away back and then missed it. Lemme tell you something. On this one hit by the Babe to Bill Cunningham—well, if Cy had been that far back, he would have had to run in fifty yards to have caught Tinker's smash—that's how far out it was."

"The fellows tell me," I reminded him, "that the pitchers are up against it with the lively ball because they're not allowed to rough the surface and it often slips out of their hands."

"Maybe," he said, "but that sounds like the old gag of the infielders about a pebble making the ball bound wrong. Sounds like an alibi, doesn't it?"

"But it does slip out of their hands."

"Course it does. But lemme tell you something—in the Series with the Athletics in 1905 they fouled off so many balls and the fans kept so many of them that I had to pitch a shiny ball every inning. Certainly. It's tough, but what of it?"

"Then you don't think the lively ball is tough on pitchers?"

"Sure. It's tough on 'em to see the old pill busted out of the lot. They can learn how to pitch it, though. You noticed they pitched it all right to Babe Ruth, didn't you?"

"By the way," he added, laughing, "if Babe will keep his head up next season, he can cross those fellows. It's a hundred to one that every pitcher in the league will try to slow ball the Babe to death after what happened in that Series. One time, I noticed, he choked his bat and whipped one of those slow ones into left field—didn't try to take his swing for a homer. Suppose he chokes up on 'em next year that way and tries to slap one into left—why, it's a cinch. Well, the first thing you know they will have to stop pitching slow ones. Then he can belt them into the stands. There was never such a hard hitter as that bird."

"You think he's wise enough to see that?"

"Certainly, he is. Babe's a natural hitter and a natural ballplayer. Remember how Monte Cross balled us up in the Series of 1905? Well, he hadn't left the National League long. We got a chart of his weakness. Everybody knew that he couldn't hit a high fast ball. Consequently, everybody pitched it to him. When we tackled the Athletics, the first ball he cracked was a high fast one. He had learned to hit that one so that it was his favorite. That was all he could hit. We had to shift right back again and pitch him curves. Babe can do that, too, if he wants to. All he's got to do is choke that bat and hit into left and they'll quit slow-balling him."

"How do you account for all the home run busting this year?"

"Why, the fellows are using long-handled bats and are trying to hit home runs because they are popular. In the old days, if a batter took a swing like that he'd be fined. That's it. Why, Rogers Hornsby, Cy Williams, Babe Ruth—all of them—are taking that long swing simply trying to hit home runs. That's it."

"Feel like you'd like to get in there again?"

"Sure, but I won't. I'm getting mighty good at that. You know," he added, exhibiting his two hundred pounds of weight, "I am a full-exercise man now. Know what that means? It means the doc has said that I can take as much exercise as I want. Up to a few weeks ago, I could take only twenty minutes a day. I haven't got a sign of TB anymore. Neither the stethoscope nor the X-ray shows any indication. I'm about well—but I'm running on one cylinder."

"What do you mean—one cylinder?"

"This particular treatment—why, you know they use the air system and pump up one of my pleural cavities. That makes that particular lung flatten and go out of business. That pleural cavity is just like an automobile tire. Pump it up and the air pressure puts the lung out of business. You see, both of my lungs were affected. Now, with one lung well, they can gradually let the air out of the other cavity. If that lung resumes its functions and is perfectly sound, well, then, I'll have two cylinders to work—be perfectly normal. But I'm afraid I'll be too heavy to pitch again."

"What do you do to amuse yourself?"

"Why, I entertained myself by staying in bed the last two winters. This time I expect to knock around quite a bit and see the skating championships as well as the ski jumping contests up at Saranac Lake. My wife says that ski business is the greatest thrill of all, but she always hides her eyes when they take the jump, then inquires of a nearby spectator if the man landed all right."

"How long will you be in town, Matty?"

"A week. We are working hard to put over this drive for the sale of the stamps to aid the anti-tuberculosis fight. You'd be surprised to know the number of people I meet at the department stores who were up in Saranac with me—seems like meeting members of a college fraternity.

"But, say," he added, as Mrs. Mathewson called, "just for old times' sake, tell Babe Ruth to choke a little and bust some of those slow ones into left field, will you?"

Chapter 41. In Search of Flowers

Just after sunrise one morning, I was walking with Christy Mathewson across a meadow that led to a wharf from which we had planned to start on a fishing expedition. Suddenly, he stopped and plucked a yellow flower with a black center from beside the path. For a full minute he looked curiously at the blossom, examining it in minute detail.

"What do you call this flower?" he asked, evidently not for information, but to test my knowledge.

"That's an ox-eye," I told him, "at least that's what we call it in this part of the country. Some sort of wild sunflower, I think."

"You got the name all right," he said, still examining the yellow flower, "but you are dead wrong about one thing—most people are. This is an ox-eye, but it does not belong to the true sunflower family. Botanists will tell you that it is a false sunflower. In fact, that is its real name—the false sunflower. First one I ever saw around here."

Having a fair layman's knowledge of ordinary or common wildflowers, I became interested enough to ask for more details.

"The Latin name for this flower," he explained, "is *Heliopsis*. The true sunflowers carry the Latin name *Helianthus*. Because this is a false sunflower, its Latin name is *Heliopsis Helianthoides*. The difference is that some of the flowers on the real sunflower bear seed, while all of them on this are bearers."

"Don't you think it a lot of foolishness to burden a common little wildflower with a big Latin name?" I asked, a little groggy at this burst of knowledge. "The plain name seems good enough. Anyway, that's what everybody calls them by."

"That is exactly why Latin names are necessary," declared this expert. "We've the reason right here. In different parts of the country, flowers are called by different names. If we didn't have the Latin name, we would have no guide and the various species would be in a hopeless tangle. It's the same way with wild ducks and different kinds of fish. Every section has its own name for wild ducks and we have to have a Latin name for the family. For example, in the East we call a certain duck the broadbill. You call it the bluebill. In New Orleans they call it the *dos gris* (pronounced do-gree and meaning grayback). That bird's real name is the Scaup.

Matty was only twenty-five years old then. This incident will give an insight into his marvelous memory and his mental capacity for detail. He studied things and remembered what he had studied. Mathewson was never casual, which explains his inability to take part in light, meaningless conversation. Finding a subject that interested him, he would run it right down to its source.

Matty had an inordinate love for flowers and a rather profound knowledge of them. In rambles through the woods and fields with him, while hunting, I never knew him to mis-call a flower or a tree. If he ran across a strange one, he would pursue his inquiries until he had correct knowledge of it.

He became so interested in trees about that time that he made an intensive scientific study of forestry, it being his ambition to make forestry a lifework when he was through with baseball.

Though Matty liked to play and have a good time as well as anybody else, he was never content mentally unless making a study of something.

Up at Saranac Lake, when he was allowed to go out for walks for the first time in many months, he found an unexpected way to keep his mind occupied. Matty had made the acquaintance of a man from Philadelphia, also a patient. During the long winter, they had played checkers and, in addition, had studied the Spanish language.

When spring came and the early wildflowers began to pop up from the more protected spots, Mathewson suggested to his Philadelphia friend that they take up another subject and make a sort of game or contest of it.

"They won't let either of us walk much," he suggested, "but suppose we use those walks for studying the wildflowers?"

This idea was accepted and adopted with much enthusiasm. In fact, Matty and his friend found so much in it that other patients took it up.

Leave it to Matty, however, to be methodical. According to his plan, he and his Philadelphia friend were to see who could discover the greater number of varieties. The flowers had to be plucked and then listed as to families and as to different species of the same family. Points were to be scored accordingly.

The Philadelphia man, being a little stronger than Mathewson, developed into a flower enthusiast. He searched the woods for every strange petal that might bob up overnight.

"At the end of the first two weeks," relates this friend, "I thought sure I had won. I had found and listed 157 different kinds of wildflowers. With the pride of a small boy, I went over to see Mathewson and make my report. You can imagine my amazement when I found that he had discovered and listed 199."

Though Matty won the flower game, he laughingly admitted to the new enthusiast that he was playing with an ace in the hole. He had the benefit of the knowledge acquired in twelve or fifteen years' interest in wildflowers.

On a visit to New York the next summer, Matty told with genuine delight about this game of wildflower hunting and how he had won.

Once in Marlin, Texas, Matty plucked a little pink flower from a fence corner near the Giant bench. He told a rookie, sitting near him, all about this particular flower, explaining its habits and giving the Latin name.

Anxious to look good in the eyes of Matty, the youngster tried to appear deeply interested. Finally, Matty went out for his turn in batting practice and Larry Doyle took the seat he had vacated.

"Say," the youngster—he was a pitcher—said to Larry, "if a guy has got to know all that stuff about flowers to get a job in this league, I'm through!"

Chapter 42. Advice to Youth and President of the Boston Braves

Not until a few hours before the end did Matty give up hope of being cured. It was that spirit of hopefulness and cheerfulness, even more pronounced than when he played ball, that kept him in the fight.

In 1922, Matty felt confident that, as he expressed it, "the bugs have been licked." "I am almost well," he added. "They seem to be all gone."

It was then that he went back to Factoryville, the town of his boyhood, in the firm belief that he had won another big game.

While at his home in Factoryville, which, by the way, has no factories, Cullen Cain, now head of the National League Service Bureau, called on him for a newspaper interview. In the course of this talk, he asked Matty to write out a message to the boys of the country. After much deliberation, he gave this to Cain:

"I cannot put in mere words the feelings I have in my heart for the boys, but this I would say.

"By all means, play ball. It brings you to rub elbows with the world. It will teach you much, if you will but learn. It will help you to play the life game better and the business game, too.

"The boy with natural mental attainments and a college education often has asked me if he should try for the Big Leagues. I say, yes, try, if you love the game. But if you cannot make the Big League, give it up. Do not stick through your best years in the minors. Try another game. That, I think, applies to most any walk of life. The major league player not only makes enough money to be able to lay aside a nice sum each year, but he has a chance to make worthwhile and helpful friends in every walk of life.

"And after all, the friends we make and hold make our best success and most enduring happiness.

"You young players who have gained sudden or seeming great success, do not let it turn your head. Conceit and over-confidence are the worst enemies a ballplayer has. Sooner or later, you must fall or go back. If you have been humble and appreciative and sensible and a regular fellow and have not taken yourself too seriously in your sudden burst of bloom, you can fail gracefully, you can look back happily, you can still feel the grip of the hands of many fine and kind and true friends.

"More promising young players have been ruined in the bud by conceit and over-confidence than by lack of control or batting eye.

"The college man has helped professional baseball and baseball of any kind has helped the college man.

"Above all, keep well informed. It is not easy to turn the head of an intelligent man. Then, let me repeat, be humble and gentle and kind."

That is, perhaps, the last writing Matty ever did for a newspaper. Some have the impression that Mathewson did not know how to write, a mistaken idea. It was his ambition from boyhood. In the first years with the Giants, he wrote for the newspapers. At times during his early illness, he contributed occasional articles to a syndicate.

In fact, Matty had contemplated attending the World Series in 1925 and, perhaps, doing some analytical baseball articles. In answer to an inquiry from John N. Wheeler, one of his close friends during his playing days, he sent this sadly prophetic answer:

"Dear Jack:

I guess I won't be able to see the World Series this year. I have been curing here since April and it looks as though I will have to stick at the job a little longer.

Sincerely yours,

Christy Mathewson."

It was after his long and helpful rest at Factoryville that Matty consented to accept the presidency of the Boston Braves. He was eager to resume his baseball associations and that sort of work appealed to him. His mind was naturally of a constructive turn and he figured that he could build up a team there. He fully realized, however, that he could not devote all his time to it. He knew quite well that Saranac would call him back sooner or later.

Matty went at his work of building up the Braves in the calm, thoughtful way that characterized his other endeavors. He was not fooled by the glowing prospects printed in the newspapers.

"It will take a long time," he said, "and we've got to be patient. We will have to start at the bottom and build a machine of our own. The other teams are not going to help us and I don't expect them to. In baseball, every team has to look out for itself."

Matty was elated over the acquisition of Dave Bancroft as manager and predicted that sooner or later Bancroft would turn out a pennant winner. Matty never believed in shifting players around just to give the fans and newspapers something to talk about, as some manager do when eager to attract attention.

"You know," he said down in Florida, during his last spring training, "they tried to make a first baseman out of me way back in 1900."

For the first time, he explained this much-discussed incident as it really happened. Horace Fogel was then manager of the Giants and, having little real baseball knowledge, attempted all kinds of experiments.

"That big fellow ought to be a first baseman," he told Jack Warner one night. "Matty," he said to the youngster, "that's your chance to make good. With your size, you might make a great first baseman."

The next day, Matty was installed as a first baseman. He was willing to do anything to stick on the team.

"And the funny part of it was," he said to Bancroft, "I won that game by hitting a two-bagger with the bases full. But I was a joke as a first baseman."

George Davis was the man who insisted that Matty was a coming great pitcher. "That was because I struck him out in morning practice," laughed Matty.

Chapter 43. An Honest, Reticent Man

The baseball associations and professional interests of Christy Mathewson and the writer began about the same time. Starting out with the same club, we were pretty much together for nearly twenty years. Often on spring training trips we roomed together. Even when we both left baseball temporarily, it happened that we were thrown together in France. Aside from John McGraw, it is likely that I came as near knowing Mathewson as well as any other man. Nobody knew him intimately. He never made intimate friendships. Though cold and calculating in the box, painfully precise in his every effort, Matty was staunch in loyalty and a lesson to anybody in dignity. He was extremely bashful. His one regret in life was an inability to be genial or affable. Matty was never a hail-fellow-well-met. It was a trait that he could never understand in others.

One day while we were rooming in Mobile, Alabama, Matty had come in from a workout and was stretching on the bed reading the essays of Charles Lamb, his favorite book for years. The telephone rang and I answered it. He would never answer a telephone if anybody else was there to do it for him. He dreaded the possibility of talking to a stranger.

The voice over the phone asked for Matty and, following usual procedure, I explained that Matty was asleep and that I did not wish to wake him up until he had rested after his workout. All the while he was making faces at me, indicating that I cut the caller off. The man on the wire proved to be an old college mate from Bucknell. He and his wife wanted Matty to join them for dinner.

"Oh, he'll be delighted," I lied mischievously over the phone. "Call him up at five. I'll tell him that I made an engagement with you and he'll be tickled to death."

"My Lord," Matty complained. "You've ruined me. Still," he added whimsically, "I'd give seventy thousand dollars to be able to talk that way over a telephone." Three hours after the dinner hour, I found him still at the table.

"Best evening I ever had in my life," he declared later, "but if you hadn't crossed me up on the phone I'd never had done it."

A few years later we wrote a vaudeville playlet in which Matty agreed to star for $1,000 a week. He went through with his contract painstakingly and was fairly successful as an actor. All that time, though, he was suffering tortures, a fact that came out the next winter when we offered him another contract for $1,200 a week.

"No," he said. "I wouldn't do it for any price. I know I couldn't deliver twelve hundred dollars' worth of acting. I went through that torture last fall just to make myself easy in talking to a crowd. Now that I have conquered embarrassment in public, I'm through with the stage."

Matty's nature made it impossible for him to do a dishonorable act or even an insincere one. Though he could go into the pitching box and mercilessly cut a ball club into ribbons, as the boxers term it, he couldn't do an act of deception after the game.

One spring he wrote a magazine article on inside baseball for which he was to get $250. In true sincerity he laboriously wrote it himself. When he was through, he decided that it lacked rounding off at the finish. He admitted unfamiliarity with the tricks of the trade and asked me to help him wind it up.

To do this we added about six hundred words, an assistance that I was glad to give him. The next day he brought me his personal check for $25.60.

"What's this for?" I asked. "If it's for that article I was doing, that was a personal favor."

"No, you won't do that," he declared. "Writing is your business. I added up the words and you wrote just a fraction over one-tenth of the story. It comes to $25.60.

Matty's whole life was one of exactness. He pitched that way. One day he won a big game from Pittsburgh and quietly told me that he had pitched but ninety-nine balls. The average good pitcher will make around a hundred forty pitches in a game. The fact of it being a record didn't interest him.

"By doing that," he explained, "I saved enough arm to pitch another game this week."

He perfected control as much to save his arm as to fool batters. Matty always carried an enormous suitcase, but nobody ever saw him carry it in his right arm. He used the left arm for carrying luggage so as to save the right for baseball.

It is known generally that Matty could pitch the spitball. He used to practice on it every morning and had perhaps the most deceptive spitter in the business, but he never used it more than two or three times during his career.

"I don't use it," he explained, "because I am saving it for the time when my arm is no good for anything else."

It was neuritis in the shoulder that finally stopped Matty—not his arm.

Christy Mathewson positively and persistently refused to be a hero. He didn't like that at all. In his extreme reticence and diffidence, he gave to casual acquaintances the impression of being swell-headed. In fact, he was anything but.

He used to arouse the ire of opposing clubs by waiting until everything was set for the start of a game. Then he would walk across the field to the plaudits of the crowd. The players would razz him about putting on the high hat, having a swell-head, and so on.

"I do that because the fans want me to do it," he said one day, "and I think it sort of gets those fellows' goat, at that."

Matty's only escape from bashfulness was in a singing quartet. He had a deep baritone voice and could sing well, but never alone. Any time, day or night, though, he would join any quartet that gathered and cut loose with everything he had. He dearly loved that.

Chapter 44. Those Last Days

Jane Mathewson's letter in which she touchingly recounts Christy's struggle with tuberculosis in his last days.

"Saranac Lake, N. Y., Oct. 29, 1925
Mr. John N Wheeler,
154 Nassau St.,
New York, N. Y.

Dear Mr. Wheeler:

His right lung, which was collapsed artificially in August 1920, was kept in that condition until this spring. The collapsing was done by the pressure of air inserted hypodermically into the cavity in which the lung rests. This operation was performed every four weeks during the four and a half years he was here. The doctors rarely collapse one lung unless the other is in perfect condition, as it throws all the work on the one lung, of course. But in Christy's case, it was necessary to take the chance as he was failing very rapidly in August 1920. His left lung was affected quite a bit at that time. However, with all the extra work it had to do, it had healed and was in good condition until this spring, when the break started anew there and, as it was the only lung left to use, it was hard uphill climb to try to get back. Dr. Packard tried to allow his right lung to re-expand in April and May, but Christy seemed to cough more and to run a higher temperature at once, so that he did not allow it to expand any further, but started the old every-four-weeks collapsing over again. He had a total collapse and the lung was as flat as one's hand. This was a good thing had not the left lung given way again. You understand about how this collapse is accomplished. It is just like squeezing a sponge tight in your hand, as long as you squeeze tight the sponge is compressed. So, in the case of the lung, as long as it was surrounded by pressure, it could expand or breathe.

We felt as if we were going to conquer this second break and were so encouraged. The last week in September Christy had a normal temperature, the first since April, and was starting to gain. He had gone to 163 and on September 30, he called me to see the scales and they were standing at 165, a gain of two pounds in ten days.

He said, then standing on the scales, 'I believe we will beat this again.' And we both felt as if we were on the upgrade. On October 1, we were talking over the World Series and I was planning on having the radio extended to the porch and was attending to some of the details in the village on October 1 when he had his first and last hemorrhage. He had attention at once. It was not a large hemorrhage and would probably been a good thing as they often clear up a bad spot, but it was from his good left lung, which, in consequence, became congested with some of the blood remaining there. Having no other breathing space to fall back on, his brave, gallant heart could not stand the terrific pounding any longer. It labored for six days, trying to pump life through the congested lung, but it was too unequal a struggle.

He had a sinking spell Tuesday night, October 6, and for two hours I expected the end every minute. Dr. Packard was with me and he knew how close Christy was to the borderland. At 4:30 a.m. Wednesday morning, he opened his eyes, looked at his wristwatch and said, 'Doctor, it is four-thirty and you have had quite a session.' It seemed a miracle. It was a miracle. All Tuesday night he fought death for he had some things he wanted to say to me, some things he wanted me to do. I knew he wanted me to do them, but I did not know the way he wanted them done. Some dear, unselfish things that must not cease being done because he was gone. On Wednesday, all day his brain was clearer than I ever knew it to be. A grasp of detail that was amazing. I did some business things for him in the village as well as I could and, when I told him all I had done, he said, 'That is fine, no one could have done better.'

In the evening, he picked up our little local paper and read some of the comments on the first game of the upcoming Series. At 10:10 Wednesday night, he turned over as if he wanted to take a little nap and I asked him if he was comfortable and he answered, 'I'm alright.' I reached to cover his shoulder and he had gone. Just like a child turning over for a little sleep.

Christy always planned on getting well. He never gave up. The last afternoon he was with me, he said, 'If worst comes to worst, take a drawing room to New York on the way to Lewisburg.'

I answered him by saying he must not talk that way for it was not fighting and we were both fighters.

'You will not stop fighting,' I said and he answered me, 'No, I have not stopped fighting.' He planned on a new car for next spring and many happy hours we spent trying to decide between an open or a closed car and what color we would have, etc. We finally decided on a closed, five-passenger sedan, gray, to be delivered in April. This is just a little thing to show that he never gave not getting well a thought."

Chapter 45. Passage of a Superstar

Bozeman concludes the life story of his closest friend.

At the finish of the first game of the 1925 World Series, the great crowd romped across the street to the Schenley Hotel, less than a block from Forbes Field in Pittsburgh. In that hotel were quartered the baseball officials and more than three hundred newspapermen.

Despite his disappointment at the loss of the game, owner Barney Dreyfuss entertained the writers with a buffet luncheon before they began their early evening work. The sound of merrymaking mingled with the snapping of a hundred typewriting machines and the droning click-click of the telegraph instruments. The grand ballroom had been turned into a huge newspaper workshop.

"Gentlemen!" came a sudden announcement from the head operator. "Gentlemen, one moment, please!"

There was an ominous tone in the voice that caused everyone to turn.

"Gentlemen, we have a flash from Lewisburg, Pennsylvania, that Matty is dead."

In a second, the operators had shorted their telegraph keys. Every typewriter was silent. Newspapermen, old and young, turned to look at each other, their faces paled by the shock. Not a sound was uttered for fully a minute.

It is hard to imagine any possible announcement that could have produced such an effect. It was drama in its highest form. For a moment, all seemed at a loss for the next move. Many of those who had been merrymaking openly wept.

Then: "Have you notified McGraw?" "Has Judge Landis been notified?" "Tell John Heydler." "Let Judge Fuchs and let the Boston crowd know at once."

The jollification party suddenly had turned to one of mourning.

Never before had such a thing happened at a World Series. In all the history of baseball, no one had ever witnessed such scenes as occurred during the next twenty-four hours. Baseball enthusiasm had come to a dead stop.

Not even the death of a president could have so completely ended discussion of the big Series and the chances of the two teams.

Judge Landis was nonplussed as to what he should do next. There was no precedent. The feeling was not that a great ballplayer had passed away, but that a national hero had gone. Inside all of us there was a sort of emptiness.

The commissioner called a memorial meeting for the next morning and, while the players were getting ready for practice and the crowd was beginning to storm the gates, this service was held. Those who paid tribute to Matty in short addresses to the joint league meeting could look out across the street and see the preparations for the game.

There being no precedent for ceremony or paying respect at the approaching game, Judge Landis called into conference a group of veteran baseball men and veteran writers. He got little help in the way of suggestions.

"They must all know," the Judge finally said, meaning the fans, "so an announcement would be little less than cruel. I will think it over, alone."

An hour later, the baseball commissioner had directed what was, perhaps, the prettiest and most delicate, also the most effective, act of sentiment that baseball has ever known.

There was no announcement, but when the band gathered at the flagpole to play the national anthem, there was a sudden spell of quiet—oppressive quiet. The crowd seemed to feel and understand. Just as the last notes of the anthem died out, the flag was hoisted to the top of the flagstaff and then slowly lowered to half-mast.

The throng of fans, to a man, stood with bared heads in a silent tribute to Christy Mathewson. Though no explanation had been made, even the smallest boy knew instinctively what was meant. Even the players caught the spirit of the silent act of mourning and left their dugouts to stand with bared heads.

The soul of Matty must have seen. He must have felt that a life of devotion, of courage, of determination, of fair play and of upright living had been rewarded.

The young ballplayers who looked on, surely, must have felt new inspiration.

Mathewson had left more than a great baseball record behind him.

The game went on and Pittsburgh won, but there was little of the usual talk and excitement until all who could be spared had gone to Lewisburg and stood at the graveside, while Matty was lowered to his final resting place.

The third game also was stopped at the hour of the funeral, while a bugler sounded Taps.

Thus passed a great man, a man whose name will live as long as baseball, a man who left an immortal heritage of which every ballplayer is an individual heir.

Committees are already at work preparing a memorial to Christy Mathewson. It is planned to have a national monument on the campus of Bucknell University. In New York, another of more local nature is planned for the Polo Grounds, the scene of Matty's many triumphs.

The passing of Christy Mathewson ended for the writer of these memoirs a friendship of twenty years, a personal friendship. The only tribute that comes to me as an offering to my friend is that, in all those years, beginning when we were practically boys, I have never known Matty to speak ill of a human being. I have never known him to criticize the personal habits of a teammate, even when that teammate was not playing the game with consideration for others. I have never known him to fail in loyalty, even when the test was severe and I have seen him sorely tried.

His enduring hope, up to the moment of his death, was that something be done for those who suffer from tuberculosis and have not the funds to get proper treatment. He did all that he could. A continuance of that work, I believe, would be the monument that he would have chosen for his own.

NOTES

Prelude

1. "The Giants Champions, The Score, 2–0," *New York Times*, 1.
2. "Giants Win Baseball Championship of the World from Athletics, *Brooklyn Daily Standard Union*, 6.
3. "Giants Win Baseball Championship."
4. "The Giants Champions," 7.
5. "Victory for the Giants," *New York Daily Tribune*, 9.

Newspapers Created the First Baseball Superstar

1. Charles E. Chapin, *Charles Chapin's Story* (New York: G. P. Putnam's Sons, 1920), 179.
2. Arthur "Bugs" Baer, "Worlds Gone By," *San Francisco Examiner*, January 6, 1955, 26.
3. O. O. McIntyre, "New York Day by Day," *Buffalo Evening News*, 27.
4. Delos Avery, "I Worked for the Cruelest City Editor on Earth," *Chicago Tribune*, December 15, 1946, Grafic, 6.
5. Avery, "Cruelest City Editor."
6. Avery, "Cruelest City Editor."
7. O. O. McIntyre, "New York Day by Day," *Buffalo Enquirer*, February 22, 1919, 8.
8. McIntyre, New York Day by Day."
9. Arthur "Bugs" Baer, "One World Led to Another," *San Francisco Examiner*, March 21, 1950, 21.
10. "John H. Tennant Dies at Age of 64," *Washington Evening Star*, June 2, 1933, C, 4.

11. "The Final (Pink) Edition," *New York Evening World*, April 20, 1905, 1.
12. "Edgren's Column," *New York Evening World*, March 1, 1905, 12.
13. "Edgren's Column."
14. "Says Damon Runyan," *Dayton Herald*, March 6, 1924, 21.
15. "Says Damon Runyan."
16. "Says Damon Runyan."
17. "How a Famous Third Baseman Just Fell Under a Spell of Jinx," *Harrisburg Telegraph*, October 27, 1911, 19.
18. "Spell of Jinx."
19. "Spell of Jinx."
20. "That's Treating Them Some," *Birmingham Age-Herald*, April 2, 1904, 4.
21. "New Yorkers Had Things Their Way," *Birmingham Age-Herald*, March 17, 1904, 10.
22. "Barons Hit Ball Almost at Will," *Birmingham Age-Herald*, March 24, 1904, 10.
23. "Notes and Comments," *Birmingham Age-Herald*, April 3, 1904, 16.
24. "Notes and Comments."
25. "Correspondents Entertained," *Montgomery Advertiser*, March 11, 1905, 3.
26. "New York Nationals Here for Spring Practice." *Birmingham News*, March 14, 1905, 11.
27. Allen Sangree, "Man Hunt Barred," *New York Evening World*, March 15, 1905, 10.
28. Sangree, "Man Hunt Barred."
29. Allen Sangree, "Sangree Tells How," *New York Evening World*, March 24, 1905, 14.
30. Allen Sangree, "As Sangree Saw It," *New York Evening World*, March 25, 1905, 6.
31. Sangree, "As Sangree Saw It."
32. Grantland Rice, "The Sportlight," *Buffalo Evening News*, May 24, 1932, 25.
33. "Bozeman Bulger Is Here," *Shreveport Times*, March 19, 1914, 9.
34. Fred Lieb, *Baseball as I Have Known It* (New York: G. P. Putnam's Sons, 1977), 218.
35. "Notes Gathered in All Directions," *Birmingham News*, April 13, 1905, 11.
36. "Courtesies to Ballplayers," *Birmingham News*, March 25, 1905, 11.
37. "McGraw at It Again," *Buffalo Enquirer*, April 27, 1905, 8.
38. Lawrence W. Murphy, *Sport Writing of Today* (Champaign IL: Service Press, 1925), 7.

39. Murphy, *Sport Writing.*
40. Murphy, *Sport Writing.*
41. Murphy, *Sport Writing.*
42. Frederic J. Haskin, "Baseball Writers," *Washington Post*, April 13, 1910, 5.
43. Haskin, Baseball Writers."
44. Whitney Martin, "Baseball Reporters Really Made Game," *Cincinnati Enquirer*, January 6, 1945, 9.
45. Elmo S. Watson, *The Coach and Journalism* (Ann Arbor, 1924), 16–17.
46. "Knock and Boost for Baseball," *Buffalo Commercial*, March 26, 1915, 6.
47. Thomas S. Rice, "Churlish Type of Manager Is Fast Getting the Hook," *Brooklyn Daily Eagle*, November 25, 1911, Sports, 1.
48. W. B. Hanna, "Baseball as It's Writ," *Buffalo Times*, July 28, 1918, Magazine, 7.
49. "Apropos of Baseball Slang," *Miami News*, April 17, 1911, 4.
50. "To Fellow-Fans," *The Outlook* (June 13, 1923), 163.
51. "Some Additions to the Sporting Dictionary," *Pittsburgh Press*, March 8, 1907, 18.
52. "Some Additions."
53. "Some Additions."
54. "Preaches Sermon in Baseball Slang," *Philadelphia Inquirer*, September 5, 1910, 2.
55. "Baseball in the Pulpit," *Tampa Bay Times*, January 12, 1915, 2.
56. "Father Thomas' Humor," *Baltimore Sun*, January 10, 1902, 7.
57. "Boy, 6, Is Spanked for Using Baseball Slang," *St. Louis Post-Dispatch*, October 2, 1925, 23.
58. "Boy, 6, Is Spanked."
59. "Man Who Glorified the 'Hot Dog,'" *Honolulu Advertiser*, June 24, 1932, 10.
60. "Man Who Glorified."
61. "Man Who Glorified."
62. "Matty as Journalist," *Wichita Beacon*, June 24, 1905, 16.
63. Bozeman Bulger, "Flowers for the Living," *Lansing State Journal*, December 24, 1924, 4.
64. Sid Mercer, "Sports Scribes" *Cincinnati Enquirer*, March 16, 1934, 14.
65. Pat Robinson, "Veterans Miss Fun in Sports Days of Yore," *Tampa Times*, May 24, 1948, 9.
66. Abe Yager, "War Correspondents I Have Met," *Brooklyn Daily Eagle*, March 1, 1925, D. 6.
67. Yager, "War Correspondents."

68. Harold Parrott, "Ask Jack,—He Knows!" *Brooklyn Daily Eagle*, January 13, 1935, Magazine, 5.
69. Abe Kemp, "On the Nose," *San Francisco Examiner*, April 17, 1958, II, 14.
70. Damon Runyan, "Runyan on Coffee Making," *San Francisco Examiner*, April 12, 1921, 22.
71. John Wheeler, "He Always Knew What Time It Was," *Boston Globe*, December 14, 1946, 8.
72. Lieb, *Baseball*, 211.
73. "They Cheered But It Wasn't for HEC," *Scranton Tribune-Republican*, October 24, 1910, 8.
74. "They Cheered."
75. Alfred H. Spink, *The National Game* (St. Louis: National Game Publishing, 1910), 350.
76. "Baseball Writers Are Organized," *Detroit Free Press*, October 15, 1908, 7.
77. Joe S. Jackson, "Crisis Game Today," *Washington Post*, October 15, 1912, 8.
78. William Peet, "What's Become of the Ban on Ball-Player 'Writers'?" *Tucson Daily Star*, March 6, 1913, 3.
79. John Lardner, "Christy Mathewson Most Prolific of All Athletes Turned Authors," *Richmond Times-Dispatch*, January 16, 1934, 16.
80. A. Crack, "Fat and Comment," *Boston Globe*, November 12, 1912, 15.
81. William Peet, "Critic Tells Who Really Wrote Pieces," *Arizona Daily Star*, March 6, 1913, 3.
82. "Exit Fake Baseball Stories," *Sioux City Journal*, September 26, 1913, 6,
83. Joe Williams, "Christy Walsh Is Interesting Character," *Pittsburgh Press*, August 1, 1927, 23.
84. Williams, "Christy Walsh."
85. Westbrook Pegler, "'Little Nap' Has a Freshman Ghost," *Detroit Free Press*, October 1, 1932, 11.
86. Leonard C. Lee Jr., "Base-Ball Photography," *Photo-era Magazine* (August 1921), 68.
87. Lee, "Base-Ball Photography," 68, 70.
88. Lee, 70.
89. Watson, *Coach and Journalism*, 48.
90. Clayton Hamilton, *Seen on the Stage* (New York: H. Holt, 1920), 17–18.
91. Edward S. Martin, *The Wayfarer in New York* (New York: Macmillan, 1909), 226.

92. Edwin Greenlaw and Dudley Miles, *Literature and Life*, vol. 4 (Chicago: Scott, Foresman, 1932), 689.
93. Greenlaw, *Literature and Life*, 690.
94. Greenlaw, 689.
95. Mrs. William B. Meloney, "My Boy," *The Delineator*, June 1914, 8, 45.
96. Greenlaw, *Literature and Life*, 688.
97. Greenlaw, 689.
98. Greenlaw, 692.
99. Robert Edgren, "Greatest of All Pitchers," *Boston Globe*, August 6, 1916, 25.
100. Damon Runyan, "McGraw Puts Ruth Sixth on All-Star List," *Tampa Tribune*, May 15, 1929, 13.
101. Runyan, "McGraw Puts Ruth Sixth."

Candidates for the First Baseball Superstar

1. Grantland Rice, *Song of the Open* (New York: Century, 1924), 115.
2. Grantland Rice, *The Tumult and the Shouting* (New York: Barnes, 1954), 17.
3. Grantland Rice, "Who Are the Greatest Athletes?" *Vanity Fair*, June, 1938, 64, 98.
4. Jimmy Powers, "The Powerhouse," *New York Daily News*, March 3, 1948, 3.
5. "Harding Autographs Ball for Mathewson Benefit," *Baltimore Sun*, September 22, 1921, 2.
6. "Matty," *Indianapolis Star*, December 18, 1910, Magazine, 7.
7. "It's In History," *Billings Gazette*, December 22, 1908, 15.
8. Cullen Cain, "'Fadeaway' Wizard," *Miami News*, October 17, 1948, Magazine, 12.
9. "The Way 'That Cute Matty' Pitched Made a 'Fan' of Kate Carew," *New York Tribune*, June 30, 1912, II, 1.
10. Harry Daniel, "Hans Wagner: Slugging Infield Star," *Chicago Inter-Ocean*, September 18, 1910, Magazine, 1.
11. Bozeman Bulger, "Rise of Honus Wagner," *Atlanta Journal*, June 23, 1924, 17.
12. Bulger, "Rise of Honus Wagner."
13. Bulger, "Hans Wagner," *New York Evening World*, March 22, 1909, 10.
14. Daniel, "Hans Wagner."
15. Hugh S. Fullerton, "Wagner," *The American Magazine*, January 1910, 378.
16. "Wagner Is the Magnet," *Baltimore Sun*, August 19, 1917, II, 12.
17. Daniel, "Hans Wagner."

18. Christy Mathewson, "Matty's Big League Gossip," *San Francisco Call*, November 12, 1913, 5.
19. Mathewson, "Big League Gossip."
20. Brick Owens, "An Umpire Talks," *Pittsburgh Press*, March 25, 1941, 27.
21. Owens, "An Umpire Talks."
22. Al Demaree, "Players Used to Blacken Balls Early," *Brooklyn Times Union*, March 26, 1926, II, 2.
23. Honus Wagner, "'Soft for Rookies Now!' Says Wagner," *Pittsburgh Press*, March 2, 1936, 26.
24. Marion Porter, "Honus Wagner Recalls Gay Louisville of the 90s," *Louisville Courier-Journal*, April 3, 1944, II, 1.
25. Bill Corum, "Hans Was Good to Friends," *Vancouver Sun*, February 20, 1929.
26. Porter, "Honus Wagner."
27. Vincent X. Flaherty, "They Use 'Baskets' Now," *Pittsburgh Sun-Telegraph*, July 16, 1950, Magazine, 16.
28. Whitney Martin, "Wagner Hale at 73," *Cincinnati Enquirer*, April 1, 1947, 14,
29. Honus Wagner, "My Friend, The Umpire," *Boston Globe*, February 6, 1916, 52.
30. Harry Keck, "Sports," *Pittsburgh Sun-Telegraph*, September 6, 1945, 20.
31. Honus Wagner, "Baseball Keeps Same Old Fight," *Macon Evening News*, March 5, 1936, 10.
32. Honus Wagner, "Scraps on the Ball Field," *Washington Post*, September 12, 1915, Miscellany, 3.
33. Wagner, "Scraps."
34. Arch Ward, "In the Wake of the News," *Chicago Tribune*, April 10, 1951, 3, 1.
35. Al Abrams, "Sidelights on Sports," *Pittsburgh Post-Gazette*, December 7, 1955, 38.
36. Bozeman Bulger, "'Ty' Tells Own Story of Ups and Downs," *New York Evening World*, August 12, 1911, 7.
37. Harry Daniel, "Tyrus Raymond Cobb," *Chicago Inter-Ocean*, August 14, 1910, Magazine, 2.
38. Jesse Outlar, "Cobb Had to Be First," *Atlanta Constitution*, July 18, 1961, 27,
39. Outlar, "Cobb."
40. Ken Smith, *Baseball's Hall of Fame* (New York: Barnes, 1947), 102.
41. Bulger, "'Ty' Tells Own Story.
42. Bulger, "'Ty' Tells Own Story."
43. Rice, *Tumult and Shouting*, 19.

44. H. G. Salsinger, "Ty Cobb's Life Story," *Atlanta Constitution*, December 4, 1924, 11.
45. Salsinger, "Cobb's Life Story."
46. Smith, *Baseball's Hall of Fame*, 104.
47. Daniel, "Tyrus Raymond Cobb."
48. Ty Cobb, "Ty Wires Constitution Full Signed Statement," *Atlanta Constitution*, May 19, 1912, 1.
49. Cobb, "Ty Wires."
50. Bill Mooney, "The Baseball Strike of 1912," *Detroit Free Press*, April 13, 1960, Detroit, 26.
51. "Navin Talks Plainly on Cobb Situation," *Brooklyn Daily Eagle*, April 16, 1913, Sporting, 2.
52. "Navin Talks Plainly."
53. Smith, *Baseball's Hall of Fame*, 104.
54. Dillon Graham, "Golf and Hunting Keep Ty Busy Now," *Washington Star*, February 26, 1931, D, 2.
55. Jim Murray, "The Next Show," *Miami News*, December 3, 1961, C, 2.
56. Murray, "The Next Show."
57. "Walter Johnson Never Knew Baseball Until He Was Fourteen," *Portland Press Herald*, October 1, 1924, 1, 8.
58. Billy Evans, "Walter Johnson Game's Best Pitcher," *Pittsburgh Press*, July 27, 1927, 28.
59. "And What a Best It's Been These 16 Years," *Humboldt Union*, October 18, 1923, 4.
60. Ernest Mehl, "Sporting Comment," *Kansas City Star*, August 11, 1957, B, 2.
61. Walter Johnson, "My Twenty Years on the Mound," *Brooklyn Daily Eagle*, January 11, 1925, D, 5.
62. Cy Kritzer, "Sport Comment," *Buffalo Evening News*, December 12, 1946, 8.
63. Billy Evans, "'Play Fair and Work Hard' Is Walter Johnson's Only Formula for Success," *Pittsburgh Press*, August 1, 1927, B, 1.
64. Walter Johnson, "My Twenty Years on the Mound," *Brooklyn Daily Eagle*, February 1, 1925, D, 6.
65. Smith, *Baseball's Hall of Fame*, 109.
66. Bill Lee, "With Malice Toward None," *Hartford Courant*, December 12, 1946, 17.
67. Smith, *Baseball's Hall of Fame*, 110.
68. Whitney Martin, "'Big Train' Greatest, Belief of Al Schacht," *Cincinnati Enquirer*, December 13, 1946, 18.
69. Grantland Rice, "Cy Young, 511-Game Winner Beat of All Time Says Rice," *Boston Globe*, December 21, 1946, 5.

70. Rice, *Tumult and Shouting*, 48.
71. Arthur (Bugs) Baer, "One Word Led to Another," *Pittsburgh Sun-Telegraph*, October 19, 1946, 7.
72. Baer, "One Word."
73. Guy Butler, "Topics of the Tropics," *Miami News*, December 11, 1946, B, 2.
74. Christy Mathewson, "Praise for Walter Johnson by the Great Mathewson," *Detroit Times*, December 27, 1910, 4.
75. Joe Wiliams, "Talking It Over," *Indianapolis Times*, February 7, 1928, 10.
76. Will Rogers, "Johnson Went to the Ball Park Instead of to the Capitol," *Philadelphia Inquirer*, October 4, 1925, Society, 12.
77. Dillon Graham, "Dairy Farming, Not Baseball, Is Walter Johnson's Ambition," *Washington Evening Star*, February 29, 1936, C, 6.
78. Graham, "Dairy Farming."
79. "Truman Leads Fans in Tribute to Johnson," *Boston Globe*, December 11, 1946, 21.
80. Smith, *Baseball's Hall of Fame*, 113.
81. Smith, 122.
82. "Framed Elfin Spirit," *Abilene Reporter-News*, August 19, 1948, 6.
83. Babe Ruth, *Playing the Game* (Mineola, NY: Dover, 2011), 1–2.
84. "Babe Ruth as Schoolboy Was Excellent Pitcher," *Fall River Evening News*, July 11, 1918, 10.
85. Michael Wilbon, "Still Viewed in Black or White," *Madison Capital Times*, May 12, 2006, B, 3.
86. "Mrs. Ruth Met Home Run King in Boston," *Boston Globe*, January 14, 1929, 6.
87. Peter Golenbock, *Fenway* (New York: G. P. Putnam's Sons, 1992), 45.
88. Golenbock, *Fenway*, 52.
89. Golenbock, 52.
90. Edward F. Martin, "Fame for Shore, Sox in Twin Win," *Boston Globe*, June 24, 1917, 1, 15.
91. "On the Road with the Red Sox," *Boston Globe*, March 29, 1917, 7.
92. "Babe Ruth Has His Own Training Diet," *Boston Globe*, June 5, 1924, 6.
93. "Highlights and Shadows in All Spheres of Sport," *New York Sun*, May 2, 1919, 17.
94. "Ruth's Suspension Lasted Only One Day," *Boston Globe*, May 1, 1919, 14.
95. James C. O'Leary, "Red Sox Sell Ruth for $100,000 Cash," *Boston Globe*, January 6, 1920, 1, 5.
96. O'Leary, "Red Sox Sell Ruth."

97. Abe Yager, "Superbas Beat Yanks Third Straight Time," *Brooklyn Daily Eagle*, March 21, 1920, Sports, 2.
98. Yager, "Superbas Beat Yanks."
99. "Motor Cop Thought Babe Was a Boxer," *Boston Globe*, January 3, 1924, 17.
100. "'Babe' Gets Back in the Game After 'One Day in Jail," *Boston Globe*, June 9, 1921, 1, 2.
101. Denman Thompson, "Babe Will Be Missing in Battle Here Today," *Washington Evening Star*, May 26, 1922, 27.
102. Earl Wilson, "New York Doings," *Charlotte News*, August 17, 1948, B, 8.
103. "Youth of Nation Not Told to Emulate the Babe Save in Swatting Out Homers," *Richmond Times-Dispatch*, September 13, 1925, 22.
104. "Babe Ruth Fined $5,000 and Put on Suspension," *Baltimore Sun*, August 30, 1925, 1.
105. "Babe Ruth Fined."
106. "Ruth Assails Huggins; Aims to See Landis," *Baltimore Sun*, August 31, 1925, 1.
107. "Ruth Here Today for Showdown," *New York Daily News*, September 1, 1925, 3.
108. "Ruth Had to Explain," *Oakland Tribune*, September 7, 1925, A, 8.
109. Frank Dolan, "Dentist Cleared in Death; Babe Faces Kin's Hate," *New York Daily News*, January 15, 1929, 3, 4.
110. Dolan, "Dentist Cleared."
111. "Babe 'Saves' Game After '19 Scandal," *Baltimore Sun*, August 17, 1948, 16.
112. "Youth of Nation."
113. Paul Gallico, "Yuh Made Muh What I Yam," *New York Daily News*, September 1, 1925, 26.
114. Gallico, "Yuh Made Muh."
115. Frank G. Menke, "Ty Cobb Hero; Babe Ruth Dub; There's Cause," *Chattanooga Times*, September 11, 1925, 9.
116. Menke, "Ty Cobb Hero."

Compiling Christy's Life Story

1. John J. McGraw, "Matty Was Ideal Idol of Game, McGraw Says," *Washington Evening Star*, October 11, 1925, IV, 2.
2. W. O. McGeehan, "Sport Will Never Find Another Like Christy Mathewson," *Vancouver Sun*, October 31, 1925, 10.

BIBLIOGRAPHY

Chapin, Charles E. *Charles Chapin's Story*. New York: G. P. Putnam's Sons, 1920.

Fullerton, Hugh S. "Wagner." *The American Magazine* 69, no. 3 (January 1910): 378–85.

Golenbock, Peter. *Fenway*. New York: G. P. Putnam's Sons, 1992.

Greenlaw, Edwin and Dudley Miles. *Literature and Life*, 4. Chicago: Scott, Foresman, 1932.

Hamilton, Clayton. *Seen on the Stage*. New York: H. Holt, 1920.

Lee, Leonard C., Jr., "Base-Ball Photography." *Photo-era Magazine* 47, no. 2 (August 1921): 68–74.

Lieb, Fred. *Baseball as I Have Known It*. New York: G. P. Putnam's Sons, 1977.

Martin, Edward S. *The Wayfarer in New York*. New York: Macmillan, 1909.

Meloney, Mrs. William B. "My Boy." *The Delineator* 84, no. 6 (June 1914): 8, 45.

Murphy, Lawrence W. *Sport Writing of Today*. Champaign IL: Service Press, 1925.

Rice, Grantland. *Song of the Open*. New York: Century, 1924.

———. *The Tumult and the Shouting*. New York: Barnes, 1954.

———. "Who Are the Greatest Athletes?" *Vanity Fair* 22, no. 4 (June 1924): 64, 98.

Ruth, Babe. *Playing the Game*. Mineola NY: Dover, 2011.

Smith, Ken. *Baseball's Hall of Fame*. New York: Barnes. 1947.

Spink, Alfred H. *The National Game*. St. Louis: National Game Publishing, 1910.

Watson, Elmo S. *Coach and Journalism*. Ann Arbor: Edwards Brothers, 1923.